FREEFALL

FREEFALL

The Needless Destruction of Eastern Air Lines and the Valiant Struggle to Save It

JACK E. ROBINSON

HarperBusiness
A Division of HarperCollins *Publishers*

HarperCollins books may be purchased for educational, business, or sales promotional use. For information, please call or write: Special Markets Department, HarperCollins Publishers, Inc., 10 East 53rd Street, New York, NY 10022. Telephone: (212) 207-7528; Fax: (212) 207-7222.

FIRST EDITION

Designed by Laura Hough

Library of Congress Cataloging-in-Publication Data

Robinson, Jack E.
Freefall : the needless destruction of Eastern Air Lines and the valiant struggle to save it / Jack E. Robinson. — 1st ed.
p. cm.
Includes index.
ISBN 0-88730-556-3
1. Eastern Air Lines, Inc. 2. Bankruptcy—United States. I. Title.
HE9803.E2R63 1992
387.7'06'573—dc20 91-58510

92 93 94 95 96 ❖/HC 10 9 8 7 6 5 4 3 2 1

Contents

Preface

As a second-year M.B.A. student at the Harvard Business School in 1986, I wrote an extensive research report entitled “Creating Sustainable Competitive Advantage in the U.S. Airline Industry.” At the time, I honestly thought (and hoped) that would be my last serious foray into the world of writing.

However, my exciting experiences in the airline industry over the past several years, including the time spent during Eastern Air Lines' final days, have again brought me back to reducing what I have learned and observed to writing.

Perhaps the driving force behind this book was the amount of misinformation surrounding the entire Eastern affair dating back to 1986 when Frank Lorenzo's Texas Air Corporation acquired the struggling carrier. To satisfy my own curiosity, I thought it important to delve into the true reasons underlying Eastern's problems and to analyze the effect of those factors on the ultimate, and unfortunate, outcome. This book seeks to do so with as much dispassionate objectivity as I could possibly bring to bear on the situation.

But equally as important is the fact that I was fortunate enough to be right in the middle of the action during Eastern's last months of existence. Soon after Martin R. Shugrue, Jr., was appointed trustee of Eastern in April 1990, I was brought in to assist his turnaround efforts. I had worked with Shugrue before as an airline industry consultant and I had also previously worked at Texas Air Corporation and Continental Airlines. As such, most of the information contained herein and attributed to key Eastern, Texas Air and Continental officials comes from firsthand accounts, actual experiences and direct discussions with many of those key players who were involved in the Eastern drama.

Most of the interviews for this book were conducted off the record to protect the privacy and confidentiality of the sources. If there is one regret that I have, it is being unable to interview Charles E. Bryan, the leader of Eastern's International Association of Machinists local. One of his lawyers from the Washington, D.C., law firm of Guerrieri, Edmond and James, refused to allow me to speak with Bryan. Nonetheless, because Bryan made it a point to make numerous public statements about his various positions on the Eastern case, there is no shortage of comments by him in the public domain.

In November 1990, Eastern's creditors made a bold, and very public, move to have the airline liquidated. Judge Burton R. Lifland, the bankruptcy judge overseeing the Eastern case, not only refused their requests for liquidation but, over vehement objection, granted Eastern $150 million of creditors' money to operate. This money lasted Eastern but eight weeks before the airline was forced to shut down, for lack of capital, in January 1991. Although Eastern was ultimately successful in obtaining those funds from Lifland, should it have been? Does the fact that the airline was successful in its arguable quest for operating capital shed light on a more serious problem with the bankruptcy process altogether?

These are but a few of the many intriguing questions surrounding the Eastern bankruptcy. I sincerely hope that this book will go a long way not only in identifying those key questions, but providing some reasonable answers to them as well.

Acknowledgments

There are many colleagues, clients and friends to thank for their help on this book. In particular, I would like to thank my literary agent, Philip G. Spitzer of New York, who worked tirelessly in support of this project. I also owe a tremendous amount of gratitude to Mark A. Greenberg, the former publisher of HarperBusiness, who saw the unique possibilities of this project early on. Many thanks also to Jim Childs, the former executive editor of HarperBusiness, who took over for Mark during this project and was largely responsible for its timely completion. I would also like to thank Dean John H. McArthur of the Harvard Business School, who, in 1986, took time out of his hectic schedule to convince me to pursue my goals in the airline industry.

Finally, I dedicate this book to my family and to my late grandmother, Ruth Byers, formerly of Sarasota, Florida, who always pushed me toward higher and better pursuits.

FREEFALL

Introduction

THE FATEFUL DAY

Saturday, January 19, 1991, was a fateful day in the history of American commercial aviation. On this day Eastern Air Lines, Inc., founded in 1928 and an ever-popular fixture to millions of travelers in the United States, Mexico, the Caribbean and Latin America, vanished into history.

At 12:01 A.M., one of America's oldest and largest carriers shut down its operations. Forever. Although Eastern had been battling to stay alive under Chapter 11 of the Bankruptcy Code since March 1989, few people were prepared for the suddenness of the shutdown and its far-reaching financial, social and political implications.

One person who was prepared, however, was Francisco A. Lorenzo. Eastern was a dying horse even when Lorenzo's Texas Air Corporation acquired it back in 1986, and through bitter union strikes, multibillion-dollar losses and allegations of asset stripping and self-dealing, Lorenzo was eventually separated from Eastern in April

1990 when Martin R. Shugrue, Jr., Eastern's trustee, was appointed by the bankruptcy court to run the beleaguered carrier. Now, Lorenzo, sitting in his living room in Houston on January 19, could only feel somewhat absolved of the Eastern mess. Lorenzo's nemesis, Eastern machinists union leader Charles E. Bryan, had gotten his ultimate wish. Lorenzo was out and Eastern was dead.

Lorenzo also had to think to himself, somewhat amused, that Eastern's creditors would have been much better off had they accepted his offer to pay them thirty-five cents on the dollar back in April 1990 to take Eastern out of bankruptcy. He could feel this way because, due to Eastern's shutdown and ensuing liquidation, the creditors would end up receiving not even one cent for every dollar they were owed.

But all of this did not change the tragic fact that on January 19, 1991, almost 180 jet and turboprop aircraft flying Eastern's distinctive "two blue hockey sticks" livery, parked on the tarmac at airports in New York, Atlanta and Miami, would never again fly under those colors.

Neither did it change the fact that almost twenty thousand hard-working Eastern employees, who hours before had held exciting jobs, suddenly found themselves unemployed in the midst of a deep recession. Pilots, flight attendants, station and ramp agents, mechanics, reservation agents and managers alike were all suddenly introduced to long unemployment lines in cities across America.

How could an airline which at one time during the 1980s boasted over $4 billion in revenues suddenly be relegated to the junk heap with little more than $115 million left in the till to pay over $1 billion in unsecured creditors' claims?

Thousands of travelers who had purchased tickets on Eastern for travel on January 19 found themselves stranded in airports across America, left to their own devices to reach their final destinations. Although Eastern had established a $150 million ticket-refund protection program, ticketholders would spend many months of frustrating work trying to get their money back from the liquidating carrier.

There were other disappointments and casualties as well. At the time of the shutdown, Eastern was being operated by a court-appointed bankruptcy trustee, Martin Shugrue. Despite his heroic efforts, innovation and impassioned calls to fight on, Shugrue could only watch as Eastern evaporated into thin air. Although Shugrue had pulled out all the stops to keep Eastern flying, as events unfolded it became clear that forces were arrayed against him from the very start, ensuring that Eastern would ultimately crash and burn.

On this fateful day, however, not everyone was in the grips of melancholy. Charlie Bryan, head of the International Association of Machinists District 100, Eastern's mechanics union, had led almost nineteen thousand Eastern union employees in a strike against Eastern in the early days of March 1989, and the airline filed for bankruptcy several days later. Now, almost two years after the strike began, Bryan and his fellow union members rejoiced as news reports flashed across the country announcing the shutdown of the airline. On this fateful day, Charlie Bryan and his cohorts celebrated their success.

Judge Burton R. Lifland of the United States Bankruptcy Court for the Southern District of New York was the bankruptcy judge overseeing the Eastern case. Judge Lifland's chambers and courtroom command a sweeping, almost transcendent, view of New York harbor and the Statue of Liberty from the sixth floor of the old Custom House building located at Bowling Green in lower Manhattan. It was in this sixth-floor courtroom that Lifland, less than sixty days before Eastern shut down, had, over strenuous objection from Eastern's creditors, allowed Eastern to spend $150 million of creditors' money to fund its final eight weeks of operations. Had Lifland not allowed this money to be spent, and instead allowed the unsecured creditors to shut Eastern down in late November 1990 as they had pleaded, Eastern's unsecured creditors would have been able to recoup substantially more than what they actually ended up with. Instead, more than half of what was set aside to pay them, $150 million, was totally squandered to keep Eastern in the air for fewer than sixty final, agonizing days.

On January 19, the wisdom of Judge Lifland, already highly suspect, was proven to be seriously lacking.

The Eastern bankruptcy is widely considered to be one of the most complex and the most contentious bankruptcy proceedings in the history of American business. Although Eastern had been embroiled in bitter labor-management disputes amid continuing and substantial losses since the mid-1970s, from the beginning of the bankruptcy, labor problems and large losses were combined with avarice, poor judgment and animosity among many of the key players. It was, therefore, inevitable that the carrier would meet a sudden and ignoble end.

Key questions arise. Did over sixty years of history have to end this way? Could Eastern have been saved? Who is to blame for Eastern's demise? What lessons can be learned? The majority of the press reports at the time focused on Frank Lorenzo's supposed union bashing as the key factor leading to Eastern's demise. Charlie Bryan and the unions would have people believe nothing less than that Frank Lorenzo killed Eastern. But the record of events clearly reflects that Eastern was already in a deadly freefall well before Lorenzo acquired it in February 1986. Also, Lorenzo had absolutely no control over Eastern from the time of the appointment of the trustee in April 1990 until the carrier's shutdown in January 1991. Was Eastern already dead when the trustee was appointed, or could it have been saved?

In an instant, an airline that was at one time the second largest in the free world, in terms of passengers carried, ceased to exist.

1

THE DOWNWARD SPIRAL

Contrary to popular belief, Eastern's numerous problems did not begin with the arrival of Frank Lorenzo on the scene back in 1986. Rather, Eastern was knocked to the canvas by the debilitating punch of the Airline Deregulation Act of 1978 and the carrier's inability to adapt to the new market forces created by the legislation. After all, deregulation spelled the end of protected routes and guaranteed profits gleaned from inflated airfares—in short, the way airlines, including Eastern, traditionally made money. In order to understand the situation Eastern found itself in due to deregulation, a basic understanding of the overall structure of the airline industry and its changes since 1978 is especially helpful.

The history of the U.S. airline industry since deregulation in 1978 has been extremely tumultuous. Several hundred airlines have started and gone out of business since deregulation due, primarily, to their inability to adapt to the fast-paced changes brought on in a deregulated environment. Since late 1990, large airlines such as Continental, Midway, TWA, America West and Pan Am have filed for bankruptcy. In November 1991, Midway shut down and was liquidated. In December 1991, Pan Am, which not too long ago was the world's largest airline, shut down and was liquidated as well. All of these events have their cause in a common nexus: the inability of carriers to successfully adapt to deregulation and its competitive implications.

Soon after deregulation there was a substantial increase in the number of airlines. In the early 1980s low-cost, no-frills, nonunion carriers such as People Express, the first airline launched after deregulation, achieved a substantial market presence by offering heavily discounted fares which were significantly below those charged by the major carriers. As People Express grew (it became a billion dollar company in sales within five years), fare wars blossomed, leading inevitably to huge losses throughout the industry through the first half of the 1980s.

By the mid-1980s the major airlines (American in particular) were able to develop sophisticated revenue management computer systems that enabled them to price, in real time, an airline seat that otherwise would have gone empty at the low fare offered by, say, People Express. This was a watershed technological achievement in the industry, the industry's most important technology improvement since the switch from propellers to jet engines which began in the late 1950s.

Revenue (or yield) management is the reason why you can be sitting on an airplane having paid $99 for your ticket and the person sitting next to you paid $499 for his. If you can plan your trip several weeks in advance and know exactly which flight you want to take, you will likely be able to buy an "excursion" fare at a highly discounted price. On the other hand, a person, such as a business traveler, who finds out at 9:30 A.M. that she has to be in Chicago by 3:00 P.M. the same day usually has little flexibility and must pay the regular fare, which is almost always two to three times higher than the lowest excursion fare.

Yield management is the process whereby airline computer pricing systems automatically manage the inventory of seats that will be sold on a certain flight at various fares. Usually starting a year in advance of a particular day and flight, the computer constantly juggles the level of fares and the number of seats available at those fares to maximize revenue for that particular flight. The computer can predict, through complicated advanced mathematical formulas based on optimization theory, that there will be a certain number of people who need to travel at the last minute and will therefore be content with paying the high fare. Thus, it sets aside a certain number of last-minute seats and fares in anticipation of selling those seats at higher fares, thus maximizing revenue for that particular flight. If, close to the date and time of departure, the computer does not believe it can sell those remaining seats at high fares, it will make those seats available at lower fares.

People Express, which did not have a yield management system, merely sold all of its seats at one extremely low fare. For example, a usual People Express fare from Newark to Chicago was $69 one way when the prevailing fare on, say, United or American was $269. What yield management allowed the major carriers to do was, at the last minute in the booking cycle, sell all of its remaining empty seats at the $69 fare—thereby eliminating any price advantage that People Express might have otherwise had. After all, American was much better off if a seat that would otherwise have gone empty is sold for $69. This is because airline seats are highly perishable commodities. Once the door is closed and the aircraft pushes back from the jetway, the revenue-generating capability of an empty seat on that particular flight is lost forever. Perhaps no airline executive in the industry understood the concept of inventory perishability better than American's chairman Robert L. Crandall. American's computerized yield management system was, and still is, considered to be the best in the business. In fact, Crandall made a name for himself early in his career as a manager in the management information systems department at TWA.

Because of this powerful technological weapon in the hands of the majors, and unable to compete with them on customer service and passenger amenities, People Express and most other low-fare start-ups were forced out of business in the mid-1980s. Their only competitive weapon, price, had been completely neutralized. Although most airline industry "experts" say that the advent of the frequent-flyer program and "better and smarter" airline management was the key to driving the low-fare mavericks out of the marketplace, in my view it was the unmatchable yield management capability of the majors that struck the decisive blow.

Thus, beginning in 1985, the U.S. airline industry began to consolidate significantly as most of the new low-fare carriers, no longer able to compete with the majors, were forced to merge with more established airlines or simply were forced out of business altogether. Some of the key industry consolidation activity in 1985 and 1986 included former corporate raider Carl Icahn's acquisition of TWA and then TWA's successive purchase of Ozark Airlines; Delta's merger with Western; Northwest's merger with Republic; USAir's acquisitions of Piedmont and Pacific Southwest; and American's acquisition of Air California. Also during this period, Texas Air, which had earlier acquired Continental Airlines, acquired Eastern.

By the late 1980s, after this first phase of industry consolidation, the seven largest carriers (Eastern was ranked number three in terms of passengers carried before the Texas Air acquisition in 1986) controlled over 90 percent of the U.S. airline market. To finance all of these acquisitions, carriers loaded up on debt (mostly junk bonds, which were a prevalent source of financing at that time), made multi-billion-dollar purchasing commitments for new aircraft and expanded their route systems almost at a geometric rate. The capital structures of most airlines at this time consequently became very weak, ready to blow up at the first sign of an economic downturn or a major externality such as an oil shock. Too much debt and the resulting high-interest expenses put a major crimp in the operating cash flow of all overleveraged airlines. This was the lament of airline CEOs throughout the industry during the late 1980s even while the industry itself was generally profitable. While cash flow is the lifeblood of any business, it is particularly so in the airline industry. Airlines, with their unusually high proportion of fixed costs that must be covered regardless of the volume of business generated, constitute a business where cash is truly king.

The second wave of consolidation in the airline industry is still in progress but has its roots in the recession that the U.S. is presently struggling to throw off. Although recessionary data began creeping into the economy in late 1989, most economists believe that the recession became "real" in early 1990. As a result, airline industry passenger traffic growth in 1990 and 1991 decreased markedly from earlier years. Meanwhile, Iraq's invasion of Kuwait on August 2, 1990, and the resulting increase in oil prices, which doubled in just a matter of weeks, sent jet fuel prices skyrocketing, which caused airlines with already weak balance sheets and even weaker cash positions to hemorrhage.

As the likelihood of war became more certain, airline passenger traffic was weakened further as worries over personal security (which were largely unfounded) dampened the enthusiasm for air travel.

Within just a matter of months after the Iraqi invasion, the mountains of debt that several airlines had built in the 1980s began to crash down upon them. As stated earlier, Continental, Midway, America West, Pan Am and TWA were forced to declare bankruptcy or their intention to soon file for it. Of course, by late 1990 Eastern was already in bankruptcy, gasping for breath, and had only several weeks to live.

With so many airlines in dire straits, the few financially healthy carriers, such as American, United, Delta, USAir and Northwest, began picking up attractive strategic assets owned by weaker carriers who needed to raise much-needed cash. For example, American purchased Eastern's Latin American routes, United bought Pan Am's London and Latin American routes, and Delta purchased just about all of Pan Am's remaining assets.

The last decade has seen a tremendous amount of change in the U.S. airline industry that has caused much dislocation in the industry heirarchy. Eastern's problems began to surface in the early 1980s, and, unfortunately, nothing was done to arrest the downward spiral in which Eastern found itself by 1986.

When retired Air Force Colonel and former *Apollo 8* astronaut hero Frank Borman became president & CEO of Eastern in December 1975, Eastern had just registered an astounding net loss of around $50 million—the worst in its history up to that point. Yet it was a figure that would pale in comparison to the losses that the airline would suffer in future years. Borman, upon taking control of Eastern, immediately made some important changes. He moved Eastern's headquarters from Rockefeller Center in midtown Manhattan to Building 16 at the Miami International Airport. However, Borman's most important strategy was to negotiate substantially reduced labor costs with Eastern's three major labor unions.

Eastern's mechanics were represented by the International Association of Machinists and Aerospace Workers (IAM), its pilots by the Air Line Pilots Association (ALPA) and its flight attendants by the Transport Workers Union of America (TWU). During the late 1970s, Borman was able to negotiate union concessions, and, largely because of those concessions, Eastern actually was profitable from 1976 through the end of the decade, generating $363 million in operating income from 1976 through 1979.

However, the advent of deregulation and the growth of new industry upstarts such as People Express really began to take their toll on Eastern beginning in 1980. Even at that time, Eastern's route system focused on serving the east coast of the U.S., from the Northeast to Florida. When People Express started major fare wars in Eastern's bread-and-butter markets, offering $49 fares from New York to Florida, Eastern was unable to compete. Even with subsequent union concessions, Eastern still had a bloated cost structure that made it easy prey for low-cost, nonunion carriers such as People Express.

Amid and despite all of this industry upheaval, Borman managed to get along with Eastern's unions. During this period, Borman said, "Of all the unions I had to deal with, ALPA was the most open-minded. The local leaders of the IAM were tough but they were willing to listen and eventually came around." Borman's views are not surprising. Pilots are usually the most intelligent and businesslike employees of an airline. Their training and responsibilities in the cockpit require a certain temperament, one that is generally compatible with that of airline management with whom they usually identify. Flight attendants are hardly ever a force on their own, in fact, they almost always follow whatever the pilots decide to do. The IAM, on the other hand, was most troublesome to Borman. They had the most heterogeneous membership and thus the most to lose whenever concessions became necessary. The IAM represented not only highly paid and skilled aircraft mechanics but also the nonskilled, but nevertheless highly paid, aircraft cleaners, stock clerks, and others. With a split membership, the IAM could not easily allow its nonskilled workers to bear the brunt of any concessions on their own.

However, Borman's view of the IAM began to change drastically in 1980 with the election of Charlie Bryan as president of the IAM's District 100, Eastern's IAM local.

Charles Eustice Bryan began his career at Eastern in 1956 as a line mechanic. By 1980, when he ran for local IAM president, Bryan had already had some scrapes with Eastern management in general and Frank Borman in particular. Bryan disagreed with the concessions that labor, including the IAM, gave Eastern in the late 1970s. And although Bryan realized that Eastern had financial problems, he wasn't sure that Borman was the right man to tackle them.

When Bryan ran for local president in 1980 it was on a platform of trying to overturn one of the wage concession programs that Borman and the prior IAM leadership had agreed to earlier. This was the same wage package that had kept Eastern in the black, and protected IAM and other union jobs, for the previous several years. After Bryan won the election, he somewhat audaciously collected proxies from employees who had been given Eastern stock as part of earlier concession deals, thus nominating himself to a seat on Eastern's board of directors. Although he was unsuccessful in gaining a board seat at this time, Bryan earned for himself a national reputation as an activist union leader seeking a voice in the affairs of his company.

The uneasiness in the relationship between Borman and Bryan first surfaced in Las Vegas in 1980, where Borman and his wife, Susan, attended the national IAM convention. According to Susan Borman, Bryan, who was sitting at the Bormans' table, for some reason all of a sudden became obsessed with learning every minute detail about the *Apollo 8* mission. When talk turned to what was ailing Eastern, Bryan continued to focus only on *Apollo 8.* Because of this, Susan Borman became convinced that Bryan "didn't seem to give a damn about Eastern."

In 1980, Eastern incurred a net loss of $17 million. In 1981, it lost $66 million. Borman tried everything, but Eastern was just too much of a cash-devouring dinosaur to counter the likes of fleet-footed People Express and its $49 fares. In 1982, after acquiring the Latin American routes of bankrupt Braniff, Eastern lost $75 million. With almost $160 million in losses during the previous three years, and with Eastern's back against the wall, teetering toward bankruptcy, Borman felt that he had no choice but to go back to the unions for more concessions.

Throughout the early 1980s, Borman pushed Eastern to grow

since he knew, correctly, that Eastern would only become viable if it reached critical mass. Eastern was, in reality, too small to adequately cover its fixed costs. Unfortunately for Borman, the normal airline planning horizon of five to seven years to reach a size that would establish economies of scale ceased to make sense because the industry was changing so rapidly. Borman ordered over $2 billion in new Airbus A300 widebody aircraft, acquired the Latin American routes from Braniff, and began to diversify Eastern's route structure by establishing a hub in Kansas City and trying to attract more east-west traffic to counteract the seasonality of the north-south traffic flows that constituted Eastern's historic market. Needless to say, all of these activities cost money, which is why Eastern's long-term debt more than doubled from 1980 to $1.5 billion in 1983 and its interest expense grew at an alarming 45 percent annually from 1979 through 1983.

Given all of these problems, Borman's growth strategy in the early 1980s, while arguably well-conceived, was egregiously ill-timed. Eastern did not have the financial wherewithal to sustain such growth. Borman and Eastern would have been much better off to let the industry cycle turn against the discounters (People Express was already beginning to show signs of wear and tear by 1983), bide its time by focusing on its core markets, and expand during the industry shakeout that was sure to come soon, and which in fact did come in 1985 and 1986.

But in 1983 Borman did not have the benefit of seeing what was soon to happen in the industry, and at that time he was faced with a 1982 loss of $75 million and an even more dire prognosis for 1983. Thus, he went to the unions demanding massive cuts in pay and benefits, in addition to increases in productivity through changes in union work rules.

Facing bankruptcy, the possibility of liquidation and the resultant loss of jobs if concessions were not granted, both ALPA and the TWU went along with Borman's request resulting in substantial 18 percent pay cuts for their members. Charlie Bryan, however, not only refused to go along with the other unions but demanded a 30 percent wage *increase* for the IAM and threatened to strike if he didn't get it. Borman, quickly running out of cash, could not afford a strike and finally, at the 11th hour, caved in and gave Bryan and the IAM an unbelievable 32 percent wage increase over a three-year period. The deal with the IAM added over $170 million to Eastern's annual labor costs. As expected, the pilots and flight attendants, who had eaten hefty 18 percent pay cuts, were outraged. Borman said flatly afterward: "We were raped!"

In retrospect, Borman claims that Bryan masterfully manipulated the press in 1983 to accuse Borman of misrepresenting Eastern's financial problems so as to avoid IAM wage demands. Borman claims that Bryan "could sound so reasonable, sincerely cooperative and knowledgeable, that many reporters swallowed whatever he told them." Bryan's ability to use the press to make a demon out of management would serve him well in future battles with another Eastern chairman.

Bryan's demand for a wage increase while the other unions, who could easily see the handwriting on the wall, agreed to deep wage cuts is puzzling. Of course, Bryan had a fiduciary responsibility to his members to look out for and protect their interests. But a union leader also owes a larger duty to his membership to act responsibly so as to protect their jobs and the well-being of the company where they work. If Borman had rejected Bryan's outrageous demands, as he had every right to do, and put Eastern into bankruptcy, since the carrier had just about depleted its cash reserves, Eastern would likely have been liquidated back in 1983 and no jobs, including IAM jobs, would have remained. As such, Bryan's actions in 1983 were irresponsible. Although he got his wage increase, it was a gambit that placed the jobs of his membership at extreme risk.

Of course, after Bryan got a wage increase for the IAM, the pilots and flight attendants felt betrayed. Not only were they mad at Charlie Bryan for imperiling the company just so he could get fat pay increases for his members while everyone else swallowed deep cuts, but they were mad at Borman for having caved in to Bryan. An ALPA leader said afterward that "instead of calling him Colonel Borman, we now call him Colonel Sanders."

The IAM wage increase rendered the overall concession package largely ineffective and, mostly as a result, Eastern's loss more than doubled in 1983 to a whopping $184 million. Borman found himself in trouble again and was forced to go back to the unions just six months later for another round of concessions. At this point it was clear that Eastern's unions were bankrolling the company.

In January 1984, Borman presented the unions with another "crisis" demand for wage and work-rule givebacks, always using the threat of bankruptcy as a negotiating hammer. This was soon after Frank Lorenzo had put Continental into Chapter 11 in 1983 and had used the bankruptcy laws to throw out all of Continental's union contracts. With Continental as a precedent, this time even Bryan agreed to a deal where all Eastern employees, both union and nonunion alike, would take an additional 18 percent wage cut, worth almost $360 million to Eastern each year, and give productivity improvements in return for 25 percent of Eastern's stock and seats on Eastern's board of directors for employee representatives.

This arrangement lasted barely one year as airline traffic softened and Eastern continued to spend substantially more cash than it could generate from operations. In 1984 Eastern lost $38 million. Management felt that the prognosis for 1985, at the height of the mid-1980s fare wars, was ominous. Thus, Borman went back to the unions again for even more givebacks. Under this new agreement, the unions agreed to further wage cuts of up to 14 percent in addition to more work-rule changes. In return, Eastern established a profit sharing plan that vested if Eastern posted net profits of more than $90 million in any single fiscal year. Obviously, no vesting ever occurred under this plan which was conceived, as one pilot lamented, "in the midst of blatant stupidity."

Several factors combined to allow Eastern to actually make a profit during the first half of 1985. Obviously, the additional wage concessions helped. However, also aiding the brief respite from continued losses at Eastern was an overall increase in industry passenger traffic during this period as well as strikes at both United and Pan Am, which created a traffic windfall for Eastern. In fact, Eastern's managers thought things were looking so good by the fall that Eastern reversed the pay cuts that had been just recently agreed to and, in addition, granted 8 percent wage increases through 1987. However, these moves were extremely shortsighted and irresponsible on the part of management because within a matter of months traffic dropped precipitously and fare wars continued unabated, forcing Eastern to match even lower fares and causing a new cash crunch.

Thus, by late 1985, Eastern was back in its normal crisis mode, and its finances, according to Borman, had "decayed to the point of desperation." Borman not only had to renege on the wage increases that he had just announced weeks before, but he was also faced with having to demand new, massive cuts across the board from all employee groups once again.

For Eastern to have to fight crippling fare wars on its mostly low-fare leisure and tourist routes to Florida while all the while struggling under a massive pile of $2.5 billion in debt made the airline's prospects as an independent going concern extremely unlikely. Borman recognized this when he gave his ultimatum to the unions in late 1985. If he didn't get further wage concessions from them immediately so as to save Eastern, he would either sell the airline or "tank it."

Since the mid-1970s, and the ascension of Frank Borman to the top of Eastern, Eastern's employees had granted Eastern hundreds of millions of dollars in labor cost savings through concessionary collective bargaining agreements. It is clear that the pilots and flight attendants bore the brunt of the concessions and did so with the least acrimony. However, largely due to the 1983 wage increase, Charlie Bryan and the IAM certainly did not bear their fair share of cuts and, actually, took advantage of Borman's weak bargaining position to make out extremely well for themselves. There is nothing wrong with getting the better of the bargain in a negotiation, that is what negotiations are all about. But if Charlie Bryan's primary concern was the survival of Eastern and the job security of his members, then his extreme negotiating positions during the early 1980s were highly questionable.

Bryan's scorched-earth negotiating tactics pushed Eastern to the brink several times. Eastern survived only because of steep cuts agreed to by other employee groups and a whole lot of luck (such as strikes at competitors).

However, Eastern's continuous brush with death through the first half of the 1980s was equally the fault of Frank Borman's desire to grow Eastern through expansion without the financial underpinnings to sustain such growth. From 1979 to 1985, Eastern's revenues grew at a 10 percent annual clip, substantial growth for a company that had almost $3 billion in revenues in 1979. Had Borman waited just another couple of years before embarking on such an aggressive growth strategy, he could have picked up the pieces of several airlines that by 1985 had either filed for bankruptcy, were close to it or were begging for merger partners. For example, in late 1985 People Express beat out Frank Lorenzo and Texas Air in acquiring Frontier Airlines for a net cash cost of only $95 million. Frontier would have made the perfect merger partner for Eastern in 1985 because of its large presence in the western U.S., which would have countered Eastern's reliance on east coast traffic.

Borman's desire to grow at all costs in the early 1980s saddled Eastern with so much debt that the only option Borman had to keep the airline in business as an independent company was to go back continually to his employees for concessions.

Had Borman not overexpanded and had Bryan not overreached in his negotiating positions, Eastern could have been set straight financially, which would have allowed it to be a major player in the industry consolidation that began in 1985. Instead, strategic blunders by both men during the early 1980s caused Eastern's affairs to be in such horrific shape by the end of 1985 that Borman's threat to "fix it, sell it, or tank it" jibed nicely with the strategies of another airline chieftain who at that time was on the prowl for airline acquisitions.

2

THE END OF THE LINE

I first met Frank Lorenzo in the mid-1980s when he gave a speech at the Harvard Business School in Boston, where I was a student. Lorenzo received a standing ovation from the over one thousand students and faculty members assembled in Burden Auditorium to hear the man who at that time headed the largest airline company in the free world talk about the airline industry in general and Eastern in particular. Most of the audience felt that Lorenzo was a good public speaker. In fact, Lorenzo actually enjoyed returning to the school from which he received his M.B.A. in 1963. He got the most laughs from the crowd when he said, "I don't particularly admire Charlie Bryan."

During 1985, Lorenzo had made serious attempts to buy both Frontier and TWA, though in the end he was bested by his good friend and former associate Donald C. Burr of People Express and Carl Icahn. Burr got Frontier and Icahn acquired TWA. In fact,

Lorenzo lost TWA at the eleventh hour because TWA's unions, who were terrified at the prospect of working for Lorenzo, offered Icahn big wage concessions to come into the deal as a "white knight" at the last moment. Although Lorenzo's pride was slightly hurt by the TWA loss, an airline where Lorenzo had held his first job out of Harvard, he did come away with a $50 million profit from the sale of his TWA stock to Icahn in the takeover.

Nonetheless, two botched takeover attempts in rapid-fire succession did not sit well with the hard-charging, wheeling-and-dealing Lorenzo, particularly since Lorenzo realized that the only way his Texas Air Corporation, which owned Continental, was to be a survivor in the consolidating airline industry was to become a "megaplayer." Lorenzo always referred to his strategy as attaining economies of scale through "critical mass." Critical mass is nothing more than an airline having enough market power as evidenced by large numbers of aircraft, nationwide and international route systems and a sufficiently large frequent-flyer program such that travelers have a hard time going places without flying that particular airline to get there. Business school texts and strategic management consultants call this phenomenon "achieving economies of scale and scope."

By 1985, Texas Air had not attained critical mass because Continental, though a large airline, was not large enough to be a long-term player on its own. Lorenzo needed to increase substantially the size of his revenue base. The primary reason Lorenzo was interested in Eastern was that the addition of Eastern's $4.8 billion in 1985 revenues would almost triple Texas Air's revenues overnight. Also, by merging Continental and Eastern, Lorenzo could generate substantial cost savings by eliminating repetitive functions. The revenue and cost synergies would be tremendous, together worth up to $2 billion annually. An additional bonus would be if Eastern could be merged with Continental in such a way that Continental's nonunion status would be exported to the merged carrier so as to create one huge, low-cost, nonunion airline empire. Thus, Eastern and Continental made the perfect match for Lorenzo. Lucky for him, just at this time Frank Borman was looking to sell Eastern lock, stock and barrel.

By late 1985 Borman had made up his mind to find a buyer of Eastern. He retained the investment banking firm of Merrill Lynch & Company to drum up potential suitors. Both Ray Minella, a Merrill Lynch investment banker, and Borman went searching over almost all of corporate America for a potential savior, but there were no takers. Eastern was just too far gone. Edwin I. Colodny, president of USAir, told Borman he was not interested in buying Eastern because "your labor situation is out of control, I don't ever think we could work with your unions." Steven G. Rothmeier, president of Northwest, told Borman, "I just looked over your balance sheet. With your labor situation, there's no use in our even having lunch." Borman and Minella were so desperate that they even went to J. W. (Bill) Marriott, Jr., of Marriott Hotels, Fred Hartley of Union Oil, Barron Hilton of Hilton Hotels, Don Burr of People Express, and even Texaco. Why Minella would take Borman to see Texaco about buying Eastern baffles the imagination. In December 1985, Texaco was ordered to pay Pennzoil $11 billion, the largest court judgment in U.S. history, over the battle for Getty Oil. It is hard to believe that Texaco's management, staring down the barrel of having to write an $11 billion check, would even want to fly Eastern, let alone buy it!

In early December, Frank Lorenzo called Borman to determine if Borman was interested in selling Eastern's computer reservation system called System One. Continental did not own one of these extremely important computer systems and Lorenzo thought, with Eastern's cash running out, that Borman would jump at a deal to sell a key asset and raise some cash. When Borman asked Lorenzo if he would consider buying all of Eastern, Lorenzo became very interested. Borman promised to get back to Lorenzo.

Finally, after months of canvassing corporate America, Borman had found a potential suitor, one who, because of his past labor strategies, could be used as a very threatening "club" in future union negotiations. With Lorenzo firmly on record as a potential buyer, and having no other financing options available anyway, Borman went back to the unions for what he called "massive but necessary" concessions.

At Eastern in late 1985, both the pilot and flight attendant contracts were "open" (had expired), whereas the machinists contract wasn't due to expire until October 1987. Unlike in most other industries, labor relations in the airline industry are governed by the Railway Labor Act (RLA), an outmoded, inefficient and sometimes illogical law dating back to the early part of the century that establishes completely separate bargaining requirements for airline labor relations.

The RLA, enacted in 1926, created a special process for the peaceful settlement of transportation labor disputes, thus reflecting the tremendous strategic importance of the transportation industry in the national economy at the time. In 1936, the RLA was amended to also cover the then-fledgling airline industry. The RLA exists today pretty much in the same form as it did during the New Deal.

Under the RLA, once a union contract expires, all working conditions and rates of pay continue in effect until a new agreement is negotiated or the major dispute process has been exhausted. If a new agreement cannot be negotiated, then a party seeking to change pay, work rules or other working conditions must give advance written notice of that intention to the other party. The parties must then negotiate over the proposed changes. If the negotiations are unsuccessful, either party may then invoke the mediation services of the government's National Mediation Board (NMB), which tries to resolve the dispute. If mediation fails to produce an agreement, the NMB then offers "binding" arbitration to both parties, which can only occur if both consent. An unsuccessful proffer of arbitration releases the parties from mediation and triggers a thirty-day cooling-off period, after which the union may strike and the airline may impose its own rates of pay and work rules.

This time, with his back against the wall and Eastern running out of both time and cash, Borman decided to go for broke with the unions. In early January 1986, Borman retained the airline consulting firm of Avmark to perform a strategic analysis of how much Eastern needed to save in labor costs in order to survive. Avmark's president, Mort Beyer, is very knowledgeable about the market value of aircraft. However, more than once Beyer has been known to come back to a client with the answer that the client itself suggested at the outset. Eastern's managers had earlier completed an analysis that said Eastern needed approximately $700 million in annual labor cost savings to avoid bankruptcy and that a 20 percent across-the-board wage cut was necessary. After reviewing this analysis, Mort Beyer's recommendation to Borman, not surprisingly, was that Eastern needed to shave $700 million in annual labor costs, and the suggested amount of the necessary concessions was 20 percent. Thus, Borman had his mandate: 20 percent or bust!

Since the flight attendant contract was open, and flight attendants usually have the weakest bargaining position of any airline union, Borman initially demanded that they take 40 percent reductions in addition to major productivity increases. When the flight attendants balked, Borman was able to get the NMB to release Eastern and the TWU and start the thirty-day cooling-off period in a matter of only several weeks, a very short time. The flight attendants were therefore free to strike, and Eastern was free to impose its own contract terms upon them, on January 20, 1986.

As for the pilots, Borman walked into the Eastern MEC (Master Executive Council, the local ALPA governing body) and demanded 20 percent wage cuts, sharp reductions in benefits and pension contributions as well as more productivity. Several weeks later, the NMB released ALPA as well, and their cooling-off period was set to expire on February 26, 1986. At the same time he was hitting the pilots and flight attendants with his demands, Borman negotiated a deal with Eastern's banks so that they would not declare Eastern in default on its loans if Borman could negotiate steep concessions with all of Eastern's unions by February 23, 1986, a date conveniently set three days before the ALPA cooling-off period was scheduled to expire. This basically gave Borman sixty days to get his 20 percent concessions or have Eastern's loans called, which would force the carrier into bankruptcy and certain liquidation because the airline's cash position was perilously low by this time.

Eastern's immediate future rested squarely in the hands of Charlie Bryan and the IAM. Since the IAM contract was not set to expire until 1987, Bryan was under no obligation or duty to negotiate with Eastern, although everyone realized, including Bryan, that unless the IAM came up with its share of the 20 percent concessions by February 23, the banks would pull the plug on the whole company and that would be the end of the ball game. Borman requested 20 percent across-the-board wage cuts from the IAM in addition to increases in productivity, basically the same deal he offered to the pilots and, after modification, to the flight attendants.

As the February 23 deadline approached, Lorenzo and his chief lieutenants at Texas Air, Robert R. Ferguson, vice president of corporate development, and Charles T. Goolsbee, general counsel, were called into round-the-clock negotiations with Eastern and its financial and legal advisers. All the while, Charlie Bryan refused to budge on the 20 percent wage cut demand and, at the same time, hinted to some outside Eastern directors that he might agree to the cuts if the board of directors fired Borman. Bryan had officially linked concessions to the ouster of the chairman, president and CEO of the airline. A bold move even for Bryan. When word of Bryan's position leaked back to Borman, the Colonel blew his stack but vowed to himself that he would do anything to save the airline, perhaps even quit, if it meant getting the 20 percent cuts from all of the unions.

On Sunday, February 23, 1986, Eastern's board convened in the first-floor auditorium of Building 16, Eastern's corporate headquarters, located on the northern side of the Miami International Airport, to decide the fate of the airline. By this time, Eastern was in serious negotiations with both the pilots and the flight attendants at nearby hotels. Only Bryan refused to negotiate.

By Sunday afternoon, Lorenzo had negotiated a definitive stock purchase agreement offering to pay $10 per share in cash and securities for all of Eastern's outstanding common stock, representing a premium over the prevailing market price, for a total deal worth $615 million. Roughly two-thirds of that amount would be paid in the form of cash. The remainder would be in notes and preferred stock, some from Eastern itself. Although many believed this to be a low-ball bid, considering that Eastern was only hours away from Chapter 11, it was a fair offer. Lorenzo also put another condition on his offer. It had to be accepted by the Eastern board by midnight Sunday, that very day.

After Lorenzo's offer was presented to the board and the unions, Borman stood up in the auditorium and stated that if all three unions did not agree to the 20 percent concessions deal (which was worth about $450 million annually), the board would sell the airline to Lorenzo under the existing offer.

Larry Schulte, the Eastern ALPA MEC chairman, argued to his members that although 20 percent wage cuts were a steep price to pay, they were better off accepting the deal rather than risking a sale of the airline to Lorenzo. This argument seemed to carry water with the pilots who accepted the deal. Robert V. Callahan, head of Local 553 of the TWU, made a similar argument to the flight attendants who also agreed to the 20 percent cuts. At this point, Borman was almost there. All he had to do was convince Bryan that the airline could remain independent, out of Lorenzo's hands, if Bryan and the IAM would only join Eastern's other unions and agree to the 20 percent wage cuts.

Charlie Bryan was now at the crossroads. He could hold firm and see the airline sold to Lorenzo, who had become an anathema to labor because of Continental's abrogation of union contracts in bankruptcy, or he could play along, give Borman his 20 percent cuts, and live to fight another day with an independent Eastern. The choice seemed obvious: Why not just play along with Borman? After all, although Bryan's disdain for Borman was no secret, the old saying "the devil you know is much better than the devil you don't know" was applicable here. Everyone realized, and Bryan had to realize, that if Eastern was sold to Texas Air, the next logical step would be for Lorenzo to merge Eastern into Continental. At the very least, there would be fewer mechanics jobs for Bryan's IAM members in a merged carrier because it would make more sense for Lorenzo to hire mechanics off the street at $9.50 per hour rather than pay IAM-represented mechanics $16.50 per hour and up. Of course, an even darker possibility facing Bryan was that Lorenzo would attempt to break the IAM altogether and then throw the union off the property, in which case Bryan's members would not have any jobs at all. However, these very realistic scenarios evidently had no affect on Bryan and he chose to hold firm: no concessions!

As the evening wore on, just hours before the midnight deadline, it was clear to Borman that Bryan needed a push. During a break in the board deliberations downstairs, Borman invited Bryan up to Borman's office, located on the ninth floor of Building 16, where he did his best to convince Bryan that forty thousand jobs, the entire airline, were at risk but could be saved only if Bryan would agree to the 20 percent cuts. Bryan would not be moved. Borman then placed a call to the IAM's national headquarters in Washington. William "Wimpy" Winpisinger, the national IAM president in Washington, was not Bryan's boss but had a lot of influence with him. Even after several pleas from Winpisinger to accept the cuts, Bryan still adamantly refused.

When Borman and Bryan returned downstairs to the first floor, on Borman's suggestion, Bryan went off to huddle with two outside Eastern directors: Harry Hood Bassett and Peter O. Crisp. Bassett was chairman of the executive committee at Southeast Bank in Miami and Crisp was a close adviser to the Rockefeller family. Bassett and

Crisp offered to let Bryan nominate a vice chairman of the airline in return for the 20 percent wage cuts. Bryan refused but said that since the machinists had already found 5 percent in labor cost savings through productivity improvements, he was willing to look for an additional 15 percent in cost savings through additional productivity improvements. This was, of course, a hollow promise because the other unions were giving real 20 percent wage cuts, not just productivity improvements, and there was no guarantee that Bryan would be successful in delivering the other 15 percent in productivity improvements down the road. Bryan's position resulted in him playing Russian roulette with the airline's very existence and the lives of forty thousand employees. When Bassett and Crisp reported back to Borman and the board the details of Bryan's offer, it was rejected out of hand as being illusory.

Back in the auditorium, as midnight approached, tempers began to flare on all sides as everyone realized that the only stumbling block to keeping Eastern independent was Charlie Bryan. After several minutes of loud rancor, Bryan finally showed his hole card, which he had kept close to his vest during the past several weeks. Bryan offered to take 15 percent wage cuts if the board immediately fired Frank Borman. Upon hearing this, Borman sprang up, walked directly over to Bryan and asked him, "Charlie, are you going to cooperate or not?" Bryan didn't respond. Borman, pointing his finger in Bryan's face, snarled, "I'm going to tell the world you destroyed this airline." Bryan retorted, "I'll tell them you did, so where will that get us?"

Faced with this standoff, the board asked Eastern's chief financial officer, Wayne A. Yeoman, if Eastern could get by with 15 percent wage cuts, instead of 20 percent, across the board from all employees. Yeoman responded that it had to be 20 percent.

Amazingly, Borman put his immense pride aside and openly agreed to step down immediately as chairman, president and CEO if Bryan agreed to the full 20 percent wage cuts like the other unions had done. Unbelievably, Bryan refused to budge the other 5 percent, even when he could have had the head of his longtime nemesis on a silver platter. Borman said later that "Bryan was absolutely irrational, apparently willing to see Eastern go down the drain rather than give in."

Out in the lobby, Richard P. Magurno, Eastern's general counsel, walked up to Bryan and said, "Charlie, I'm trying to control my temper right now, but you've just destroyed forty thousand jobs. I want them all to know that one guy destroyed their jobs."

Bryan responded, "There are fifteen guys inside who did it," referring to the directors still deliberating.

Although Lorenzo had extended the midnight deadline by a few hours, there was really nothing left to discuss. Bryan wouldn't budge. At two-thirty in the morning on Monday, February 24, 1986, the board of directors, having no other choice, voted to sell the airline to Frank Lorenzo and Texas Air. After the vote, Bryan stated to several reporters, "For all his faults, Lorenzo is a businessman who has demonstrated he knows how to make money and how to run a successful company. I can work with Frank Lorenzo."

This episode shows that Charlie Bryan held the fate of an entire airline and its forty thousand employees in his hands, yet was willing to see the airline sold rather than cave in. The irony of the situation was that because of the earlier wage increases won by Bryan, even a 20 percent wage cut would have left the IAM members with a comparatively higher base pay than the flight attendants and pilots who had taken bigger cuts than the IAM throughout the early 1980s.

Nonetheless, Bryan showed himself to be a master of public relations, able to turn the media focus from one issue to another all the while enhancing the public perception of both himself and his union. In this capacity, he was the consummate union boss. Also, Bryan's high-profile activities at Eastern propelled him to the forefront of union activism. During the high-flying 1980s, with multibillion-dollar takeovers easily financed with junk bonds, employees for the first time became vocal stakeholders able to affect the outcomes of takeover deals. Bryan's involvement at Eastern seemed to have ignited a flurry of similar union activity through the late 1980s at other airlines as well as in other industries throughout America.

Soon after the Texas Air takeover, before he resigned as head of Eastern, Borman told a reporter that the IAM "had bled us dry for years." Although there is truth in this statement, Borman still cannot avoid responsibility and blame for what happened at Eastern during his watch. But even Borman's serious financial blunders could have been corrected had Bryan's demands been less outrageous. His rigidity, more than any other single cause, guaranteed that Eastern would soon reach the end of the line.

After the Eastern acquisition, which was legally completed on November 25, 1986, it could be said that Texas Air had finally attained the "critical mass" that Lorenzo felt was necessary to survive in the rough and tumble airline industry. Continental and Eastern together employed almost fifty thousand people, flew more than 450 jet aircraft and generated roughly $8 billion in annual revenues. Not bad at all for a company that was only formed in 1980 and which at the time owned a small, nonunion airline called New York Air.

Critical mass notwithstanding, Lorenzo well knew that Eastern would not be a viable company until its labor costs were substantially reduced and its bloated infrastructure streamlined. In contrast, Borman ran Eastern like a regulated utility, but the "slash and burn" atmosphere that characterized the deregulated airline industry during the 1980s required a lean and mean organization able to respond quickly to the constant changes occurring in the marketplace. Even after the 20 percent wage cuts that the pilots and flight attendants had accepted just before the takeover, Eastern's labor costs were still the highest in the industry, constituting almost 40 percent of the airline's total costs. By comparison, the airline industry average was 35 percent and Continental was at an extremely low 20 percent. With one of his airlines (Eastern) at the top of the cost spectrum and the other (Continental) at the bottom, it would be impossible for Lorenzo to get the revenue and cost synergies he needed to make the Eastern acquisition, and potential merger with Continental, provide strategic and economic benefit to Texas Air and its shareholders, to whom Lorenzo owed a fiduciary duty to maximize the value of their stock.

Thus, Lorenzo knew that he had to do whatever he could to bring Eastern's labor costs not only in line with the rest of the industry but, if possible, in line with those at Continental. With over $5 billion in debt, Lorenzo's entire Texas Air empire depended upon it.

Immediately after Lorenzo acquired control of Eastern, he installed Continental's former president Philip J. Bakes, Jr., a former chief counsel at the now-defunct Civil Aeronautics Board as well as a former aide to Senator Edward M. Kennedy, as president of Eastern. In early 1987, Bakes announced that he was looking to cut Eastern's $1.7 billion annual labor costs by over $500 million, or 30 percent. To do this, Bakes said he needed the pilots and flight attendants to renegotiate their contracts and accept 30 percent wage cuts while the IAM had to accept a whopping 50 percent cut in pay.

Not surprisingly, all three unions balked at this demand, which was a direct signal from both the marketplace and Lorenzo to union members that their old way of life was going to change under the new management structure. John J. Bavis, Jr., an Eastern pilot who took over Larry Schulte's place as head of the Eastern pilots union after the takeover, is reported to have said, regarding the wage demand, "This is crazy, how can they think they can get away with this?"

With similar responses from the flight attendants and, of course, the machinists, Lorenzo saw that the only way he was going to bring Eastern's labor costs in line with the rest of the industry was to begin reversing Borman's kamikaze expansion strategy. Thus, Lorenzo began to downsize Eastern in the hope of salvaging a core revenue stream which would result in Eastern breaking even on an operating basis.

He started by laying off almost 10 percent of Eastern's workforce, over four thousand people, such that by September 1987 Eastern had as many employees, thirty-six thousand, as it did in 1978.

When October came, it was time for Lorenzo to begin negotiating a new machinists contract. Contrary to popular belief, Lorenzo did not enter negotiations with the IAM to break the union. Rather, Lorenzo felt that if he could somehow force a steep wage cut on the IAM, by whatever means necessary, then the pilots and flight attendants would come around and accept their share of cuts, which would result in an Eastern with "market rates" of pay, almost matching those at Continental.

The proposal that Lorenzo and Bakes put to the IAM at the beginning of negotiations in October 1987 called for a 40 percent wage cut for baggage handlers and an overall cut of 50 percent in machinists' wages, roughly the same proposal valued at $265 million annually that was presented to the IAM by Bakes early in 1987. By this time, Eastern's unions in general and Charlie Bryan in particular had begun waging a secret war of attrition against Eastern management and Frank Lorenzo, refusing to be forced to accept lower wages. The prevailing union view at Eastern was that Eastern's wages were the highest in the industry and they were going to stay that way!

Thus, when Charlie Bryan received Eastern's offer he countered by demanding 10 percent pay hikes for the IAM over a two-year period. This demand, similar to Bryan's strategies with Borman earlier in the decade, was obviously intended to send a strong signal to Lorenzo that Bryan was prepared to go to the mat to prevent any deterioration in IAM pay scales.

After several weeks of getting nowhere, with both sides holding firm, Eastern demanded that the mediation board, as required by the Railway Labor Act, release the parties from further obligation to negotiate. Once released, the IAM could strike and Eastern could impose its own wage demands on the machinists. If the IAM called a strike, Lorenzo not only could impose lower wages but could be rid of the union altogether just by hiring permanent replacements. The key to this strategy, obviously, was the pilots. If the pilots refused to cross IAM picket lines, Eastern wouldn't fly. Bakes and the rest of Eastern management continued to assure Lorenzo that the pilots, because of their animosity toward Charlie Bryan for having received 32 percent wage increases in 1983 as well as causing the airline to be sold to Lorenzo in the first place, would decide to cross IAM picket lines in the event of a strike, even if the sole motivation for doing so was out of spite. If they did, the IAM would face certain destruction since maintenance could easily be contracted out to independent third parties and Eastern, courtesy of its pilots, would be able to fly through a strike unimpeded.

Unfortunately for Lorenzo, Bakes's assessment of ALPA sentiment was largely incorrect. Although Bavis, the pilots' leader, disliked Bryan (whom he accused of being a "socialist") and in fact seemed to approve of pilots crossing IAM picket lines, most of the pilots were upset with what they considered to be harrassment and retribution by management for the pilots' failure to agree to the earlier wage-cut demands. Nonetheless, Bakes continued to assure Lorenzo that the pilots would cross an IAM picket line, and Lorenzo, relying on this assessment, decided that he would be better off if the IAM did strike so he could impose lower wages and rid himself of the union altogether. In the beginning it seems quite certain that Lorenzo did not go into Eastern with the express desire to kill the IAM. However, that in fact became the goal only after it was made clear that Bryan was not going to negotiate substantial wage cuts in good faith.

All through late 1987 and early 1988, Eastern management made elaborate preparations for the IAM strike that it knew was soon to come. Meanwhile, both Eastern and Texas Air continued to lose money, lots of it. Eastern's large losses, due largely to annual $300 million interest payments on its huge debt, were compounded by expensive strike contingency plans. The only delay was the National Mediation Board (NMB), which would not declare an impasse and release the parties so as to start the thirty-day clock. As long as the NMB refused to act, Lorenzo had to continue with his expensive strike contingency plans such as providing for replacement maintenance.

Since Eastern, Continental and Texas Air were all losing money at this time, Lorenzo was forced to resort to selling off Eastern assets to generate sufficient cash to sustain its operations. Texas Air's debt of over $5 billion was already at dangerous levels, and continuing strike contingency plans systematically ate up millions of dollars of additional cash each month. By transferring assets out of high-cost Eastern into low-cost Continental, Lorenzo reasoned that he could carry out a de facto "merger" of Eastern into nonunion Continental without having to worry about Eastern's unions.

While risky, if handled correctly this was a brilliant strategy. Eastern's assets, as those in any corporation, must be used by management to maximize the rate of return on investment to the common stockholders. Texas Air owned all of Eastern's common stock, which meant that if Texas Air thought it could utilize Eastern assets more efficiently and more profitably in a lower-cost environment, which it obviously could, then Texas Air management could effectively argue that it had a fiduciary duty both to the company and, in turn, to its shareholders to make the attempt.

The asset-shuffling strategy was risky principally because it provided a public relations forum for the unions to charge that Lorenzo was "stripping" Eastern in order to break the unions. Transferring Eastern assets to Continental and other Texas Air subsidiaries was both logical and legal, but the public relations risks of the strategy were severe. As it turned out, Charlie Bryan was able to use his superior public relations skills to paint Lorenzo as a "devil" who was "stealing" assets in order to kill Eastern.

To this charge, Lorenzo responded rather logically, "We didn't buy Eastern in order to kill it."

By late 1988, Lorenzo was unable to make any progress whatsoever with Charlie Bryan and the IAM. Sensing that further negotiations, or even attempts to negotiate, would be futile, Lorenzo turned his attention to the mediation board with the expectation of soon being released from further negotiations, which would start the thirty-day clock. Unfortunately for Lorenzo and Eastern, Walter C. Wallace, the NMB member in charge of the Eastern negotiations, kept delaying in releasing the parties, all the while hoping for a "miracle" settlement. Wallace should have realized that both sides in the battle had dug in their heels, and further delay was, therefore, both useless and counterproductive. However, Wallace, feeling that he could come through with some last minute heroics, continued to pressure both Eastern and the IAM to reach an agreement.

At the same time that Lorenzo was pressuring Wallace for a release, the IAM made what can only be described as a major strategic blunder. John F. Peterpaul, the head of the IAM's transportation division in Washington and Bryan's boss, met with Wallace and told him that the union had decided to call secondary boycotts if there was an IAM strike at Eastern.

Secondary IAM boycotts would pose major problems throughout the country. Basically, a secondary boycott is a strike by a union against companies with which it does not have a dispute. The machinists represented almost a hundred thousand workers in the airline industry. In a secondary boycott, almost every major airline would be faced with a machinists strike, resulting in substantial disruptions to the nation's air traffic system. Additionally, the IAM represented almost twenty thousand rail workers. Secondary strikes against the major interstate and commuter rail systems in places like Chicago, New York and Washington, together with air traffic slowdowns, would cause the country to grind to a virtual standstill.

By using the threat of secondary strikes, the IAM was attempting to exploit a little-known provision in the Railway Labor Act. After the NMB releases the parties from negotiation, the thirty-day clock does not have to begin if the NMB concludes that a strike (or threat of secondary strikes) would adversely affect the nation's transportation system. In such a case, the NMB can request that the president appoint a three-person Presidential Emergency Board (PEB) to take over the negotiations. The PEB has the authority to delay the start of the thirty-day clock for an additional sixty days while it tries to work out a settlement. If either party rejects the PEB's settlement offer, then the matter goes to the Congress, which, through legislation, mandates a settlement both parties are required, by law, to accept.

The IAM's call for a PEB was a big mistake for several reasons. First, it would bring the White House directly into the middle of what was already a nasty labor-management battle and turn it into an equally nasty political battle. Second, although emergency boards were a fairly common occurrence in railroad disputes, they were a very rare thing in the airline industry. Third, the decision to appoint a PEB would be made by the incoming forty-first president of the United States, George Herbert Walker Bush, who was considered no friend of the labor movement and who, as vice president in 1981, assisted President Ronald Reagan in breaking the air traffic controllers union during the PATCO strike.

These factors made it clear that the odds were high President Bush would not call for an emergency board if asked. More importantly, by using the threat of secondary strikes, Peterpaul and the IAM quickly lost most of their public support, which up until that time they had acquired by virtue of their successful public relations campaign against Lorenzo. After all, it would be very difficult to convince a New York City commuter that the reason he or she can't get to work one morning is because of Charlie Bryan's disputes with Frank Lorenzo at an airline thirteen hundred miles away down in Miami.

On January 6, 1989, William Winpisinger, the IAM national president, sent a letter to Wallace at the NMB promising to call secondary boycotts on the nation's airlines and railroads in the event of an IAM strike at Eastern. On January 31, the NMB finally proffered a final settlement to both Eastern and the IAM suggesting binding arbitration. Eastern immediately refused and Wallace began the thirty-day clock, which was set to expire at 12:01 A.M. on March 4, 1989.

Finally, Lorenzo had a definitive date for his much-anticipated showdown with Charlie Bryan. If the IAM struck on March 4, according to Lorenzo's plan, the pilots would cross the IAM picket lines, Lorenzo would impose new wages and work rules on the mechanics, the IAM would be barred from the property and Lorenzo would be forever rid of Charlie Bryan. Eastern's labor costs would be in line with those in the rest of the industry, and the airline could then be easily merged into Continental, creating a single low-cost industry giant to wreak havoc against the other higher-cost megacarriers such as United, American and Delta. This was Lorenzo's vision.

Days before the March 4 deadline, Wallace formally requested that President Bush appoint an emergency board. Bush, after huddling with his top legal and political advisers, correctly concluded that what was really going on at Eastern was a classic labor-management dispute that could not and should not be settled by the political process but, rather, through direct bargaining between the parties. After announcing on Friday, March 3, just hours before the strike deadline, that he would not intervene, the president instructed his secretary of transportation, Samuel K. Skinner, to take whatever actions were necessary to prevent secondary strikes from disrupting the flow of interstate commerce. Skinner, now the White House chief of staff, immediately announced that if secondary strikes were called, he would at once file legislation on Capitol Hill to outlaw secondary strikes altogether. "The legislation is all ready to go, sitting on the corner of my desk, and can be filed on the Hill within fifteen minutes," Skinner told reporters.

It appeared that Lorenzo had the political situation covered. Now all he had to do was make sure that what Eastern president Bakes kept telling him was true, that Eastern pilots would cross IAM picket lines! The best way for Lorenzo to guarantee this key result was to offer the pilots a reasonably attractive deal that they could live with. Now the spotlight switched from Bryan to Jack Bavis, the pilot union leader at Eastern. It was his responsibility to recommend action on the Lorenzo offer and determine if the pilots would call a "sympathy" strike and honor IAM picket lines. At this moment, the future of Eastern rested squarely in Bavis's hands.

Just days before the March 4 deadline, Lorenzo sent a fifteen-minute video by Federal Express to the homes of each of Eastern's 3,500 pilots announcing the terms of the deal he wanted them to accept. The basis of the offer was job protection for the pilots in the event Eastern was merged with Continental or declared bankruptcy. A five-year contract was offered that even called for gradual pay increases while at the same time asking for a small cut in benefits totalling $64 million annually over the five years. Overall, given the alternatives that the pilots faced if they sided with Charlie Bryan and refused to cross IAM picket lines, this appeared to be a very reasonable offer.

Bavis, advised by his lawyer Bruce Simon of Cohen, Weiss and Simon and his financial adviser Farrell P. Kupersmith of Touche Ross & Company, the accounting firm, rejected the Lorenzo offer out of hand as a "gimmick." According to Bavis, the primary reason he rejected the offer was that the job protection guarantees promised by Lorenzo could be wiped out if Eastern was put into bankruptcy. Although this scenario was possible, it was highly unlikely. Under the Bankruptcy Code, collective bargaining agreements cannot be repudiated unless there has been a full and fair opportunity for further bargaining and hearings in open court. A bankruptcy filing does not automatically render previously negotiated contracts worthless. Bavis's decision to reject the offer focused on a small probability that was substantially overshadowed by the certainty that Eastern would sink, and the pilots would be out on the street, if the pilots did not cross the picket lines.

Bavis should have stepped back from his advisers and considered more thoroughly the possible strategic outcomes of his actions.

His failure to do so was a sin that would later plague the Eastern creditors. Had he recommended to his members that they accept the Lorenzo offer, his members would have had jobs and Eastern would have easily been able to fly right through the IAM pickets and, perhaps, could have avoided bankruptcy altogether with the resultant $150 million in annual savings from not having to pay IAM wages. Also, with the IAM and Bryan off the property, Bavis and ALPA would have immediately catapulted themselves to the apex of union leadership at Eastern with the potential actually to help shape overall corporate policy goals. Finally, Bavis would have been able to exact "sweet revenge" against Bryan for all of the problems caused by Bryan and the IAM going back to the early 1980s. Bavis should have thought about all of these things when his lawyer and accountant advised him to reject the Lorenzo offer and honor IAM picket lines. Bavis's decision cost his membership over three thousand jobs and was the single most important factor why Eastern declared bankruptcy a few days after the IAM strike began.

After ALPA rejected the Lorenzo offer and Bavis told his members to honor IAM picket lines, which were scheduled to go up at midnight, Lorenzo made one last-ditch effort to make peace with Bryan and the IAM. Late in the evening before the strike deadline, Lorenzo made a serious offer to Bryan to accept $125 million in annual wage concessions instead of the earlier demand for $150 million. Bryan refused. The strike began the next day and both the pilots and flight attendants, calling sympathy strikes, refused to cross IAM picket lines all across America. On the morning of Saturday, March 4, 1989, Eastern was virtually grounded.

With all but just a handful of Eastern Air Shuttle flights grounded, its cash position deteriorating by the hour, and with no labor relief in sight, Eastern had no choice but to file for bankruptcy. It did so on March 9, 1989, in the United States Bankruptcy Court for the Southern District of New York. Judge Burton R. Lifland, long known for his procompany stance in bankruptcy cases, was assigned to the Eastern case. From this moment on, neither Lorenzo nor Texas Air had unfettered control over Eastern. That control was transferred to Judge Lifland and, to a lesser extent, Eastern's creditors. This made Lorenzo's task of extracting some value out of Eastern for Texas Air shareholders even that much more difficult.

Although a host of problems led Eastern into bankruptcy, the event that precipitated the Chapter 11 filing was ALPA's rejection of Lorenzo's offer and its decision to honor IAM picket lines. Any reasonable analysis of the last-minute Lorenzo offer to the pilots shows that the Eastern pilots were a lot better off accepting the deal, crossing IAM picket lines and allowing Eastern to keep flying as a lower-cost airline while saving their jobs and, in fact, getting pay increases to boot! Although Bavis was no fan of Lorenzo's, he should have cut through the Bryan-inspired anti-Lorenzo rhetoric and accepted Lorenzo's offer. Given Eastern's financial condition at that time, Bavis should have jumped at the deal!

3

BANKRUPTCY AIN'T SO BAD

By 1989, perhaps no chief executive in America was as familiar with the pitfalls, and possibilities, of bankruptcy as Frank Lorenzo. He was well prepared for the Eastern bankruptcy because of his experience with Continental Airlines back in 1983.

A business experiencing severe financial difficulties may seek relief from creditors by filing a petition for voluntary reorganization under Chapter 11 of the Bankruptcy Code. The purpose of Chapter 11 is to allow a company to reorganize its finances and operations, come up with a plan to pay its creditors, and emerge from bankruptcy as a healthy company. Congress thought this a better solution than to force all bankrupt companies to liquidate, sell off their assets to pay off creditors and lose forever the benefits of that employer in the community.

Once a company files a Chapter 11 petition, it becomes a "debtor-in-possession," or "debtor," which means that existing management is allowed to continue to operate the company during the pendency of the bankruptcy case. The Bankruptcy Code also allows a debtor to reject, or "throw out," certain kinds of "executory" contracts such as collective bargaining agreements. The process by which this can occur was changed by Congress in 1984 due to Lorenzo's ingenious use of Chapter 11 with Continental Airlines in 1983.

When Lorenzo's Texas International (later changed to Texas Air) acquired Continental in late 1982, Continental was already an airline in deep financial trouble. Continental's long-term debt totalled $642 million, yet it had only $142 million in shareholders' equity. By the end of 1982, Continental had incurred a net loss of almost $42 million and had spent $90 million just to meet that year's interest payments on its huge debt load.

During the first half of 1983, Continental lost another $84 million. The company was constrained in its efforts to return to profitability by its heavy debt and by labor contracts mandating some of the highest labor costs in the industry. For example, Continental's cost per available seat mile, a standard industry cost measure, was 17 percent higher than the industry average in 1983. During the summer of 1983, Continental's losses mounted even further: another $30 million lost from June to August for an eight-month loss of $114 million. Faced with these mounting losses, Lorenzo sought wage and work-rule concessions from Continental's unions to help stem the flow of red ink.

In August, Continental's machinists, who were also represented by the IAM, went on strike because Lorenzo refused to accept their demand for a 36 percent wage increase with no work-rule concessions. Coincidentally, this was at the same time that Charlie Bryan was demanding similar IAM wage increases from Frank Borman at Eastern. During August and September, seemingly oblivious to the airline's quickly deteriorating condition, Continental's flight attendant and pilot unions rejected Lorenzo's plea for $100 million in temporary concessions. Later, in September, all three unions rejected an offer from Lorenzo that would have reduced labor costs $150 million annually for several years in return for stock and profit sharing.

On September 21, 1983, because of continued union intransigence, Stephen M. Wolf resigned as president of Continental (he is now chairman & CEO of United Airlines). At the same time, Continental's board of directors discovered that if Continental were to meet its current payroll, debt service and some back payments to vendors, the airline would run out of cash within nine days.

After a personal plea to the pilot union by Lorenzo on the carrier's precarious cash position, and after no union response, Lorenzo was forced to put Continental into Chapter 11 on Saturday, September 24, 1983.

After the Chapter 11 filing, Continental ceased all operations and over the weekend laid off 65 percent of the workforce, over nine thousand employees. At the same time, Continental unilaterally threw out its collective bargaining agreements with the unions and imposed new work rules and substantially reduced wage rates. Pilot salaries, on average, were cut in half, and all other employees who remained, including top management, took at least a 15 percent pay cut. Lorenzo, the airline's chairman, cut his own salary by 83 precent.

By the following Monday morning, Continental began flying again as a smaller, lower-cost, nonunion carrier able to operate free from the shackles of excessively burdensome and inflexible labor agreements. Lorenzo's strategy worked. By 1985, Continental was making money and its seat-mile costs had been reduced by almost 30 percent. Continental ultimately emerged from Chapter 11 in September 1986 as a healthy airline.

Largely because of the intense lobbying by labor in reaction to Lorenzo's unilateral abrogation of Continental's collective bargaining agreements, in 1984 Congress amended the bankruptcy laws making it much more difficult for debtors to void their union contracts. The goal of the 1984 amendments was to force employers and unions to bargain over modifying or rejecting labor contracts while the employer is still in Chapter 11. Although companies may no longer reject contracts unilaterally, they still may apply to the bankruptcy court for full rejection of those contracts under certain circumstances.

Thus, Lorenzo's decision to put Eastern into Chapter 11 in early March 1989 sprang from an intimate knowledge of bankruptcy law and the possibility of eventually rejecting Eastern's very costly and burdensome labor agreements. Even after the bankruptcy filing, Lorenzo's goal was to propose a plan of reorganization to pay off Eastern's creditors, negotiate lower wages and then merge Eastern into Continental. The problem was that immediately after the bankruptcy, Eastern's unions began to agitate for Lorenzo and Texas Air to be separated from Eastern.

Immediately after Eastern filed for bankruptcy, ALPA moved for the appointment of a trustee to operate the airline. Such an appointment would literally remove Lorenzo and Texas Air from any control over the affairs of Eastern. Under the bankruptcy law, the court may appoint a trustee to run the company if there is evidence that current management has engaged in fraud, dishonesty, incompetence or gross mismanagement. This is a rash action taken only in very special circumstances because it is presumed that management knows more about operating the company than lawyers or accountants, the kinds of people usually chosen by judges as bankruptcy trustees. Nevertheless, the pilots, after having blown their last decent chance to help save the embattled airline, now were determined to do everything in their power to make life as difficult for Lorenzo as possible.

Farrell Kupersmith, the ALPA accountant, gave as his principal reason for the motion to appoint a trustee the allegation that "Eastern management is controlled and dominated by Frank Lorenzo and Texas Air through an interlocking directorate, and through the installation of managers in positions of authority at Eastern who owe their allegiance to both Texas Air and Lorenzo."

While true, these allegations had absolutely no bearing on the reasons for the appointment of a trustee and, in fact, merely belabored the obvious. Texas Air acquired all of the common stock of Eastern so that it could control Eastern. Companies certainly do not pay to acquire other companies so that control cannot be exerted. After all, why else would a company acquire another company if it could not control the affairs and management of the acquired company after the purchase? This argument of Kupersmith's was, to be generous, specious.

The other principal reason for ALPA's motion for a trustee arose from several transactions that Texas Air consummated with Eastern from the time of the acquisition in 1986 up until just before the bankruptcy in 1989. Most of these transactions, which later became known as the "prepetition transactions" (because they occurred before Eastern filed its bankruptcy petition), involved the sale or transfer of assets from Eastern to Texas Air, Continental or other entities controlled by Texas Air. ALPA's contention was that these asset sales and transfers occurred at less than fair market value, thereby were financially harmful to Eastern, and were done with the intent to strip assets so as to kill the unions.

According to Kupersmith, "Lorenzo-directed management has not acted to benefit Eastern in the past, and will not investigate, attempt to recover, or litigate highly questionable transactions that have occurred between Eastern and its affiliates." For example, Kupersmith alleged in an affidavit that Eastern: (1) made loans to Texas Air at no interest or without adequate security, (2) made "irrational" investments into Texas Air affiliates for the sole benefit of Texas Air, (3) made "exorbitant" payments to Continental for strike-related services and (4) entered into joint business ventures that favored Texas Air at the expense of Eastern.

Although a corporation is under no legal duty or obligation to deal with its wholly owned subsidiaries on a purely "arm's-length" basis with respect to intercompany transactions, Kupersmith's allegations that Eastern received less than fair market value in several of these transactions appeared to have some merit. For example, in November 1986, Eastern accepted a $16 million noninterest-bearing "due on demand" receivable in lieu of cash for certain merger-related expenses from Texas Air. Eastern held the note for almost two years without requiring Texas Air to make a payment, foregoing approximately $2.8 million in annual interest. In contrast, Texas Air made immediate demands on Eastern for $4.8 million in fees and expenses relating to the proposed, but aborted, sale of the Eastern Air Shuttle in July 1988. This entire amount was collected by Texas Air by September 1988.

Another example offered by Kupersmith was the purchase of Eastern's computer reservation system, System One, by Texas Air in April 1987. Eastern received a $100 million convertible subordinated 6 percent debenture due in the year 2012 from Texas Air for System One. The deal produced no cash and was far less than what System One would have been worth in the open market.

These allegations seemed to strike a nerve with Judge Lifland. However, because the appointment of a trustee was so unusual, particularly so early in a bankruptcy case, Lifland was hesitant. Yet Lifland could not totally ignore the ALPA allegations that Eastern management, because of its loyalties to Lorenzo and Texas Air, could not necessarily be trusted to act in the best interests of Eastern's creditors and public shareholders (although Texas Air owned all of Eastern's common stock, its preferred stock was publicly held).

Lorenzo, trying to stall for time so that he could put together his own reorganization plan and still keep Eastern under the control of Texas Air, made another brilliant bankruptcy move. Lorenzo countered the ALPA motion for a trustee with his own motion for the appointment of an examiner, allowed under the bankruptcy law, to investigate and report on ALPA's allegations of prepetition irregularities.

This was the compromise that Lifland was looking for and he moved on it without delay. Within ten days after the ALPA motion for a trustee, Lifland approved the appointment of a Washington lawyer, David I. Shapiro, as the examiner in the Eastern case. Shapiro, who had worked on the Agent Orange mass tort litigation, was given a mandate by Lifland to "preserve Eastern as a viable operating airline and to prevent the often bitterly opposed parochial interests of management and the unions from destroying it." Lifland further stated his general position in the case: "Eastern is a wasting national asset. Planes are not flying and I want planes flying again."

This would be the overarching policy upon which Lifland would base all of his decisions in the Eastern case. Unfortunately, however, Lifland's policy was fatally flawed. Eastern was not a "national asset." By 1989, there was substantial overcapacity in the U.S. airline industry, and other airlines were already in the process of filling the void left by Eastern's grounded flights. Eastern was certainly not the sole, or even primary, provider of airline service in this country. It's largest hub, Atlanta, was already adequately served by Delta, and its Northeast-to-Florida routes were being served by several other carriers. Had Eastern disintegrated immediately after the bankruptcy filing, the American public would have been no worse off from a consumer-welfare standpoint as other airlines would have easily filled the void. Although airfares would probably have increased initially, the law of supply and demand in the airline business would have quickly brought both fares and service back to reasonable levels, as it has since Eastern's shutdown in early 1991. Lifland's lofty view of himself as overseeing a bankruptcy case that would potentially affect the entire nation was just plain wrong and was probably ego driven. Before long, many other people would pay a high price for Lifland's lofty, self-serving views.

In addition to investigating and reporting on the prepetition transactions, as well as attempting to negotiate a labor settlement that would end the strikes against Eastern, Shapiro was given a more important mandate by Lifland. Shapiro was authorized to find someone immediately who would buy Eastern as a going concern. Since the airline was still grounded at this time, and was quickly losing value as airplanes sat on the ground and expenses mounted, the task of finding a buyer took on a sense of urgency.

Peter V. Ueberroth, the former baseball commissioner who had done an outstanding job running the 1984 Summer Olympics in Los Angeles, had actually been offered the job of chairman or president of Texas Air, Eastern or Continental by Frank Lorenzo back in November 1988, while Lorenzo was waiting for the NMB to release Eastern and the IAM from negotiations. Ueberroth declined, saying that he wasn't good at working for other people. Ueberroth had also had several contacts with Eastern's union leaders, Bryan and Bavis, about helping the unions with a bid to buy Eastern. So Ueberroth was already familiar with the situation at Eastern when he entered the negotiations to buy it immediately after the bankruptcy filing in March 1989.

In early March, Ueberroth and his partner, J. Thomas Talbot, a former airline executive who is now involved with troubled Hawaiian Airlines, met with Lorenzo and decided to attempt to buy Eastern. They then met with the ALPA representatives and discussed a deal in which the employees of Eastern would own a large portion of the new company in return for substantial wage and work-rule concessions. Ueberroth also brought in Martin R. Shugrue, Jr., a former president of Continental, who would actually run Eastern after the acquisition.

On April 6, less than a month after the bankruptcy filing, an agreement was announced for the purchase of Eastern as a going concern by a new corporation that was to be controlled jointly by Ueberroth, Talbot and Eastern's employees. The new corporation was called the Eastern Air Lines Employees and Service Company and was to be owned 30 percent by management, 30 percent by Eastern employees and 40 percent by public shareholders. It would purchase all of Eastern's common stock from Texas Air, together with several other Texas Air assets, for $464 million. However, the purchase agreement had one huge condition: that Ueberroth's group reach labor agreements with all three Eastern unions no later than midnight, April 11 (less than a week away), that would be satisfactory both to the Ueberroth group and to Texas Air.

Ueberroth and Talbot next began marathon negotiations with all three Eastern unions at IAM headquarters in Washington. Shapiro took it upon himself to be the official "overseer" of the discussions, to make sure that everything possible was done to reach an agreement and get Eastern sold. After several days, the unions said that they would grant Ueberroth major wage and work-rule concessions in return for 30 percent of Eastern stock. However, they placed a totally unreasonable condition on their concessions. Since it would take approximately sixty days for the sale to be consummated and approved in bankruptcy court, the question arose as to who would be in control of Eastern for that interim sixty-day period? The unions were adamant that their concessions would apply only if Lorenzo was somehow removed from Eastern during those sixty days.

Lorenzo's reply to this condition was, obviously, shock and surprise. How could the unions expect Lorenzo to give up control of the airline before the deal had been completed and he had been paid? After all, nothing prevented Ueberroth, during those sixty days, from changing his mind and backing out of the deal, leaving Lorenzo, Texas Air and the creditors to clean up the mess left behind. Lorenzo summed it up fairly clearly: "When you sell a house, you don't hand over the keys until the closing, until you've been paid."

Initially, the subject of interim control was not addressed so that Ueberroth and the unions could put the finishing touches on the labor agreements. The final negotiating sessions lasted around the clock and, in the early morning hours of April 10, just a day before the deadline, comprehensive back-to-work and concessionary labor agreements were signed.

Basically, the labor agreements granted the Ueberroth group an astounding $1 billion worth of concessions over a five-year period. The IAM gave the bulk of the concessions, totalling approximately

$166 million of the total annual savings of $210 million. Evidently, Charlie Bryan didn't have any problem giving Ueberroth $166 million in annual concessions while stuffing Lorenzo's last-minute, pre-bankruptcy request for only $125 million annually. The desperation in the union position was obvious. They were locked out of their jobs and off the property. Although other potential suitors such as Hyatt Hotel magnate Jay Pritzker, TWA chairman Carl Icahn, and others were circling around Eastern, the Ueberroth deal was obviously the unions' last and best hope to buy Eastern and beat Lorenzo. The fact that Bryan gave Ueberroth more in concessions than Lorenzo had asked for makes one wonder just how much Bryan's animosity toward Lorenzo colored his negotiating demands. Thus, for the unions, it was Ueberroth or nothing!

With these new labor agreements in place, all parties, consisting of Ueberroth's group, the unions, Shapiro and a bushel of investment bankers and lawyers, returned to New York to tackle the issue of interim control, the last sticking point. Texas Air did not want to entrust Eastern to a new, and unproven, management team until after Eastern had been irrevocably sold and Texas Air had been irrevocably paid. If the Ueberroth group were to walk away from the transaction after an unsuccessful start-up attempt during the interim period, Lorenzo would be left with an asset worth substantially less than it was at present. The Ueberroth group, on the other hand, refused to close the deal until after it could assess the potential costs and the likelihood of success of an attempt to "ramp up" Eastern's operations after the strike was over. Finally, the unions all agreed that they were not going to call off the strike and return to Eastern if Lorenzo was still in control of the airline.

In an attempt to solve the interim-control problem, Shapiro suggested, with the agreement of both Ueberroth and the unions, that a trustee be appointed for the sixty days. While solving the concerns of both Ueberroth and the unions, a trustee would not do anything for Lorenzo and Texas Air. In fact, Lorenzo would face the same problem of giving up control of his asset for a period of time without ever knowing for sure whether he would actually be paid for it. Lorenzo and Texas Air dismissed the idea immediately.

Nonetheless, Lorenzo offered a compromise. Texas Air would keep Eastern grounded for thirty days. The unions wouldn't have to come back to work for Lorenzo because Eastern wouldn't be flying. During those thirty days, Ueberroth could complete his due diligence of Eastern and decide if he was actually going to go forward with the deal. But this offer died also. Finally, in the waning moments with the April 11 deadline approaching, Texas Air agreed to discuss relinquishment of control of Eastern before the closing if Ueberroth entered into a binding, noncancellable agreement, subject to appropriate protections. Ueberroth, finally realizing that he was not quite sure what he was getting into, began to have second thoughts about the entire deal and refused. That was the end of the negotiations, and Shapiro finally reported to Judge Lifland that the deal was dead. Outside the courthouse, Ueberroth curtly told the group of assembled reporters: "We are deeply disappointed that this transaction lapsed. Our agreement with Texas Air is finished, terminated, and is over." With that, Ueberroth got on a plane back to California.

The unions, who had just days earlier trumpeted in press reports that Ueberroth was coming in to save the airline, were silent in shock and disbelief. They had come so close yet, at the end, the deal fell apart. Why?

After the deal died, everyone cast blame on everyone else. Shapiro blamed Ueberroth: "He didn't want to risk his 'golden boy' image if the start-up failed." Texas Air's lawyers, led by the nation's leading bankruptcy attorney, Harvey Miller of the law firm of Weil, Gotshal and Manges, blamed Shapiro: "Shapiro shouldn't have suggested a trustee." Not surprisingly, the unions blamed Lorenzo.

But the real blame for the deal's collapse must rest squarely on the shoulders of the unions. Their ridiculous demand that Lorenzo give up complete control of the airline before the closing was not only unreasonable, but could have opened up Lorenzo and Texas Air to shareholder lawsuits if control had in fact been given up and then Ueberroth backed out of the deal before closing, leaving Texas Air with additional liabilities and an asset worth even less than before. Lorenzo, for his part, appeared to have been completely reasonable during the negotiations, even offering to discuss a preclosing transfer of control. Unfortunately, events moved too quickly to allow for such a compromise.

All the unions had to do was agree to remain on strike while Ueberroth spent thirty days to complete his due diligence. If he then decided to close the deal, the unions could have called off the strike and returned to work only after Lorenzo had completed the sale of the airline. The unions allowed themselves to be pigeonholed into thinking that they would have to return to work immediately. That was the basis of the stumbling block which eventually killed the entire deal. It's amazing that with all the lawyers and financial advisers involved, such a simple solution could not have been reached. The unions' complete and irrational hatred of Frank Lorenzo so clouded their vision that they cut their own throats by making any deal to buy Eastern impossible.

On April 17, Lorenzo announced in a press release that "Eastern is no longer for sale." However, largely due to Judge Lifland's private proddings, Shapiro continued to pursue a sale of the airline on his own. Although several other groups put forward bids, none was substantial. The best bid was made by Jay Pritzker valued at $400 million in cash plus assumption of certain liabilities, clearly insufficient to get Eastern up and flying again. By mid-May, even Pritzker went away and the result was that Eastern was still grounded, its unions were still on strike and, most importantly, the airline, though in bankruptcy, was still under the direct control of Frank Lorenzo and Texas Air. Shapiro then turned his attention to investigating the prepetition transactions. It would take him an entire year to complete the investigation and file his report.

After it became clear that there would be no buyer of Eastern, Lorenzo began putting together a plan to get Eastern flying again, albeit as a much smaller airline. The operating strategy was to rebuild Eastern's large Atlanta hub in addition to continued Northeast-to-Florida flights. As a result, the airline would be rebuilt to roughly 60 percent of its prestrike size. The financial strategy, though, was more intriguing. Lorenzo decided that the best way to save Eastern was to sell off roughly $2.5 billion in nonstrategic assets (such as the Latin American division) and use those proceeds not only to fund Eastern's continued losses as it operated, but also to fund a plan of reorganization in which Eastern's creditors would be repaid and Eastern would emerge as a wholly owned subsidiary of Texas Air, which then could be merged into Continental.

From an operational standpoint, Eastern immediately began recruiting new pilots to fly in the place of the ALPA strikers. It hired and trained new, non-IAM, mechanics as well as non-TWU flight attendants. And all within a period of roughly sixty days. By early summer, Eastern was slowly building back its schedule with a much smaller, nonunion and lower-cost workforce. The credit for building back so quickly must go to Eastern President Bakes, who, while misreading the position of the ALPA pilots prior to the strike, was able to ramp up the airline quickly and with a minimum of disruption to both employees and passengers.

At the time, which was early summer 1989, Lorenzo's operational strategy of focusing on the Atlanta hub was a good one. During 1989 the airline industry had the best financial year in its history, traffic was strong (the recession had not yet kicked in), and Eastern's presence in Atlanta was well known, though not as dominant as Delta's. For years, Eastern had battled Delta for dominance at Atlanta's Hartsfield International Airport. At its height, Eastern had over 400 daily departures out of Atlanta whereas Delta had over 460. Though Eastern did well in terms of traffic in Atlanta, the hub was rarely, if ever, profitable because of the high overhead costs of other

Eastern operations allocated to the Atlanta hub. However, the hub historically had operated at break-even or better on a purely cash basis, which was important for Lorenzo if he was going to try and rebuild Eastern and bring it out of bankruptcy.

The key to Lorenzo's overall financial strategy was the Eastern creditors. When a company files for bankruptcy, the claims of its creditors take precedence over those of its shareholders. Moreover, in a bankruptcy where the company is highly leveraged, as with Eastern, it is normal for creditors to be ultimately paid only a fraction of what they are owed, and the shareholders usually end up with absolutely nothing at all.

Since the goal of Chapter 11 is to assist bankrupt companies in reorganizing their finances, a company in bankruptcy must propose a plan of reorganization soon after it files a Chapter 11 petition. In other words, it must state how it plans to emerge from bankruptcy, pay off its creditors and claims against it, and operate after bankruptcy. It is through a plan of reorganization that the ownership of the company postbankruptcy is ultimately determined.

Obviously, Lorenzo's goal was to put together as quickly as possible a plan that would repay the creditors sufficient amounts so that Texas Air could retain the bulk, if not all, of Eastern's common stock after it emerged from bankruptcy. Lorenzo and his lieutenants, led primarily by Robert R. Ferguson, Lorenzo's key strategist at Texas Air and now CEO of Continental, thus began putting together at once a plan of reorganization that they would sell to the Eastern creditors.

A committee of unsecured creditors, usually picked from among the seven largest, is appointed soon after a company files for Chapter 11. On the Eastern committee sat its largest and most powerful creditors. Among them were Airbus Industrie and Boeing, the airplane manufacturers; General Electric and Rolls-Royce, who made the engines on most of Eastern's Boeing and Airbus aircraft; AT&T, Marriott, Citicorp, even Lintas, Eastern's advertising agency. However, also on the committee were all three unions because when Eastern filed for Chapter 11 it owed its employee pension plans almost $1 billion.

The chairman of the Eastern creditors' committee was the president of the U.S. subsidiary of Airbus, Alan S. Boyd. It was Boyd who convinced U.S. airlines such as Eastern and Pan Am to take a chance in the 1980s on the new generation aircraft that the European consortium was just then introducing to airlines across the world. Boyd, a very intelligent businessman in his own right, would unfortunately come to rely primarily on the advice of his lawyers and investment bankers in areas that required just plain business common sense. He would do this to the tremendous detriment of both himself and his fellow creditors.

While Lorenzo began putting together a reorganization plan for the Eastern creditors, the Eastern unions became increasingly desperate. With no buyout in sight and Eastern consistently building back its operations with nonunion replacement pilots, mechanics and flight attendants, some union leaders began thinking seriously about calling off the strike, waving the white flag and returning to work, if Lorenzo would have them. The biggest proponent of this strategy was Bavis, the pilot leader.

Bavis had quickly gotten religion. He saw that it would not be long before Eastern would be flying its full schedule on the new, downsized business plan and that such flying would be done entirely with nonunion pilots and ALPA members who crossed the picket lines. The best way to protect what little prospect his ALPA members had of ever flying for Eastern again was to eat crow and get back in the cockpit before it was too late. In fact, over eight hundred union pilots had by this time already crossed the picket lines and returned to work, obviously preferring to make a living and support their families rather than support the egotistical ravings of Charlie Bryan.

During August, the Eastern Master Executive Council (MEC) held a strategy session in which Bavis, supported by Henry Duffy, the national ALPA president, as well as Shapiro lobbied for calling off the strike and returning to work. Charles H. "Skip" Copeland, a militant on the MEC from New York who wanted to do everything in his power to drive Lorenzo from Eastern, reacted angrily to Bavis's plea and stood firm, the strike should continue! The Eastern ALPA rank and file sided with Copeland, and largely as a result of his suggestion to call off the strike, Bavis was replaced by Copeland in early September as the head of the MEC.

Although the pilots had at least discussed the possibility of returning to work during the summer, Charlie Bryan and the IAM would hear nothing of it, wouldn't even consider the idea. Bryan felt that the only way he would call off the IAM strike and return to work was if Lorenzo was gone. Although his members' strike benefits would soon run out and many of them would be forced to subsist on food stamps, Bryan was determined not to be seen as caving in to Lorenzo. "Only one kind of man walks away from this type of fight," Bryan boasted.

By October, the pilots' situation became so desperate that even the militant Copeland began to change his mind. However, he convinced the Eastern MEC to try one last "Hail Mary" play. During the summer the unions had been lobbying some members of Congress to sponsor a bill that would have forced President Bush to appoint an emergency board which would then impose a labor settlement at Eastern. This effort was a complete waste of both time and union resources since there was no doubt that the bill had little chance of passing, and even if it did, it would not pass with the necessary two-thirds majority required to override what would certainly be a swift and unequivocal presidential veto.

When the futility of this effort finally became apparent to the unions, they settled on a compromise solution. They asked Congress to pass a bill that would establish a bipartisan commission that would recommend a labor settlement. The bill passed both the House and the Senate and then went to the White House. Copeland and the other pilot leaders decided to hold off on any decision to end their strike until they saw what would happen to the bill sitting on the president's desk.

Not surprisingly, President Bush vetoed the bill on November 21, saying that it would "hinder saving Eastern Air Lines and the jobs of its employees." In a note of appreciation, Lorenzo, a big Texas backer of the Bush-Quayle campaign in 1988, thanked the president for having "the courage and a clear vision of the need to keep the airline industry competitive."

Two days later, ALPA threw in the towel and officially called off its sympathy strike against Eastern. Interestingly, the hard-liner Copeland, fighting to the bitter end, abstained from the MEC vote. Although symbolic of the union's total and complete defeat, the return-to-work vote had no practical effect since by that time Eastern had over 1,800 nonunion pilots (including 800 ALPA strikers who crossed picket lines) already flying for the airline, which had reached almost 60 percent of its prestrike size. The next day, the flight attendants called off their sympathy strike as well.

Only Charlie Bryan and the IAM, who were the root cause of the strikes in the first place, refused to give in. Bryan claimed, "We're not going to go back or go away, that's for sure!"

While the Eastern unions were spinning their wheels in their unsuccessful attempt to regain their lost jobs, Lorenzo and Bakes were putting together the finishing touches on their proposed plan of reorganization, which they would attempt to sell to the creditors. Although Alan Boyd of Airbus was chairman of the creditors' committee, the real decision makers for the creditors turned out to be their legal and financial advisers.

Bankruptcy, particularly in large cases, is truly a feast for lawyers. In the Eastern case several large law firms represented Texas Air and Eastern. In addition, there were lawyers for the creditors, for Eastern's preferred stockholders, for the examiner and for the investment banks, consultants and accountants. There were also lawyers for many of Eastern's more than one million individual creditors and claimants.

The legal feast on the Eastern carcass was so great that from the time Eastern filed Chapter 11 in April 1989 until the case was close to being closed in March 1992, legal and other professional fees for all parties involved totaled well over $100 million, or roughly $5 million per month or over $31,000 per hour (assuming an eight-hour work day). And the interesting part about bankruptcy law is that most legal fees in a bankruptcy case, even those incurred by others, are ultimately paid by the estate of the bankrupt company.

In large bankruptcy cases, soon after a creditors' committee is appointed by the United States Trustee (an official appointed by the Justice Department to help administer cases), there is a mad dash by all the major bankruptcy law firms, most of which are located in New York City, to pitch their legal services to the committee. Joel B. Zweibel, then the head bankruptcy lawyer at Kramer, Levin, Nessen, Kamin and Frankel on Third Avenue, was the lucky jackpot winner in the Eastern "bankruptcy lottery." He and his firm were chosen by Boyd and the committee to be lead counsel for the creditors. Zweibel had made a name for himself representing creditors in large bankruptcy cases such as Texaco. Both Zweibel and his assistant, Adam C. Harris, would make decisions of questionable value throughout the Eastern bankruptcy. Although Zweibel and Harris's role was to act as legal advisers, they ended up making high-impact business decisions which I thought should have been made by Alan Boyd and the creditors themselves.

The creditors also decided to retain a major Wall Street investment bank, Goldman, Sachs and Company, as their financial advisers. The primary reason that they chose Goldman was that Wall Street's highest rated airline stock analyst, Michael Armellino, worked there at the time. Also on the Goldman team was a Harvard classmate of mine, Barry S. Volpert. Although knowledgeable about corporate finance and restructurings, the Goldman team was completely overshadowed by Arthur Newman, managing director of the restructuring and reorganization group at Chemical Bank, and now a managing director at the Blackstone Group in New York. Newman's analysis and insight throughout the Eastern case were particularly keen.

Goldman charged the committee a monthly retainer, which was ultimately paid by Eastern, of $150,000, whereas Chemical's monthly retainer amounted to $100,000. There is no doubt that the committee could have saved itself, and ultimately Eastern, $150,000 a month by letting Goldman go and relying on Art Newman's advice. However, even the monthly retainers of Goldman and Chemical combined paled in comparison to what Zweibel and his law firm charged. Zweibel's personal billing rate was $375 per hour. During an average month, Zweibel's firm submitted bills for anywhere from $500,000 to $750,000 in legal fees, plus an additional $100,000 in expenses including limousines, expensive dinners and airline tickets.

But even Zweibel's huge legal fees were only a drop in the bucket when compared to those charged by the lawyer for both Texas Air and Eastern whom the bankruptcy bar calls the "Big Kahuna" of bankruptcy attorneys: Harvey R. Miller of the law firm of Weil, Gotshal and Manges. Weil Gotshal, located on Fifth Avenue in the General Motors Building, is considered to be the nation's preeminent bankruptcy law firm, and Miller is considered to be the nation's top bankruptcy lawyer, as evidenced by his billing rate of $400 per hour (conveniently set $25 per hour more than Zweibel's).

Miller and Zweibel usually find themselves on opposite sides of the same large bankruptcy cases. While Zweibel focuses on the rights of creditors, Miller and Weil Gotshal usually represent bankrupt corporate debtors. In fact, it was Miller who had advised Lorenzo during Continental's successful bankruptcy proceedings.

During an average month, Weil Gotshal submitted legal bills totaling over $1 million in addition to another $500,000 in expenses, for a total of $1.5 million per month. Even Judge Lifland, a close friend of Miller's, would soon complain about the "outrageous" legal expenses that Eastern, and ultimately its creditors, would have to pay in the case.

Thus, with all of this high-priced legal and financial talent on board, Lorenzo and the creditors began to negotiate a plan of reorganization. The goal of the creditors was to maximize the amounts ultimately paid to them while Lorenzo sought to minimize the amount of cash he had to pay while also maintaining control over Eastern.

In mid-April, about a month after the bankruptcy filing, Texas Air presented its first business plan for Eastern to the creditors. The plan proposed that the Atlanta hub be rebuilt to approximately 60 percent of its prestrike size. It also proposed that the creditors would be repaid in full, receiving 100 cents on the dollar for their claims, through the sale of over $2 billion in certain "nonstrategic" Eastern assets. The plan even showed that Eastern would be marginally profitable in 1990. The key to this plan, however, was the sale of Eastern's South American routes to American Airlines. Without the cash from the route sale, the financial projections in the plan would be missed by a wide margin.

The major decision creditors must make in a bankruptcy case is whether they would receive more from the liquidation of the company or from its reorganization. During the spring and summer of 1989, airline stocks were reaching new highs due to a surge in traffic and a sudden interest in airlines as merger or takeover candidates. For example, during this period Alfred A. Checchi succeeded in acquiring Northwest Airlines and Marvin Davis started a bidding war for control of United Airlines. Given this frenzied environment, the Eastern creditors thought that the airline had a decent chance of surviving. Also, the promise by Lorenzo to pay them 100 cents on the dollar was too good to be true. Thus, the creditors embraced the April business plan.

The plan of reorganization calling for paying creditors 100 cents on the dollar was filed on July 21, 1989. However, within a couple of weeks after filing the plan, Lorenzo and Texas Air began to see two huge cracks forming in the plan's edifice. First, it became apparent that the actual amount of creditors' unsecured claims against Eastern was substantially higher than originally thought when Eastern filed for bankruptcy back in April, perhaps another $150 million higher. Second, the South American route sale to American for roughly $350 million, the proceeds from which formed the entire financial basis of the plan, suddenly died.

Lorenzo and American's chairman Robert Crandall have never been friends. The two Texas rivals, Texas Air (now called Continental Airlines Holdings, Inc.) is headquartered in Houston while American is based in Dallas, have consistently jockied for position as the "biggest" airline in Texas. When Lorenzo merged Continental, People Express, Frontier and New York Air on a single day in February 1987, creating one single large carrier, Crandall was said to have remarked, "I hope he falls flat on his face!"

Continental had earlier filed a lawsuit against American alleging several hundred million dollars in damages arising from American's allegedly biased listing of Continental's flights in American's Sabre computer reservation system. In fact, when I worked at Continental in 1987 in the planning department, I had come up with the damages calculation for this lawsuit. When American agreed to buy the South American routes, it made the dismissal of the lawsuit a key condition. During face-to-face, and often acrimonious, negotiations between Lorenzo and Crandall, the deal stalled and Lorenzo pulled back, announcing that Eastern would continue to operate the routes. Without the $350 million from the route sale, the idea of paying the creditors 100 cents on the dollar became ludicrous.

With the South American route deal to American suddenly off, Lorenzo went back to the creditors in late August and presented a second business plan. This new plan confirmed that without the route sale, Eastern would never be able to pay its creditors 100 cents on the dollar. Instead, the plan provided that Eastern would operate the South American routes, build up Eastern's Miami hub to feed those routes while continuing with the simultaneous build up of the Atlanta hub. Over the strong objections of the creditors, Eastern implemented the Miami build up through the third and fourth quarters of 1989.

By late 1989, Eastern's losses had grown enormously due largely to a downturn in industry traffic. Also, the overall economic climate was adversely affected by the October stock market crash, which in turn was caused primarily by the collapse of a union bid for United Airlines. That deal fell through because of the refusal of a consortium of banks led by Citibank to provide financing. All of these factors conspired to turn Eastern's financial statements into a sea of red ink.

For example, while the August plan called for losses in December 1989 to be only $33.5 million, December's actual loss was over four times that amount, or $138 million. The vast majority of this negative variance was attributable to the start-up costs associated with the Miami hub and South American operation.

Throughout that fall, the creditors, looking at larger and larger losses each month, got fed up and contacted Crandall at American themselves trying to unload the South American routes. After much haggling again between Lorenzo and Crandall, a deal was finally struck in mid-December whereby American agreed to pay Eastern $350 million for the routes and Continental agreed to settle the computer reservations system (CRS) lawsuit against American, which it had refused to do earlier in the year.

The key reason for Lorenzo's change of heart was that Eastern's losses were increasing at such an alarming rate that even he was taken by surprise. Lorenzo now knew that the only way to salvage some cash out of the rapidly diminishing Eastern estate was to sell one of the few valuable assets that the carrier had left. That's one of the reasons why he was willing to forego possibly hundreds of millions of dollars in the CRS lawsuit. However, such damages were, at best, uncertain.

By the end of December 1989, Eastern's losses for the year had totalled a staggering $900 million, at the time the largest single airline loss in the history of aviation. Lorenzo, starting to feel that perhaps Eastern was not salvageable as a going concern, in addition to running into serious liquidity problems at both Continental and Texas Air, promised to put together a third business plan for the creditors that he would present to them in January. However, Lorenzo knew that this new plan would be a far cry from the plan proposed back in the summer calling for paying creditors 100 cents on the dollar.

In retrospect, Lorenzo probably should have accepted Crandall's deal for the South American routes back in the summer. Had he done so, the deal would have closed by the end of 1989, Eastern would have received the cash and Lorenzo would have been able to take Eastern out of bankruptcy soon thereafter. However, as 1990 approached, and the economy began to look, smell and sound as though it were truly in a recession, Eastern's fortunes became even more grim. So grim that, in fact, several Texas Air insiders felt that even with the route sale to American and the $350 million it would bring, Eastern probably would not make it through the first half of 1990.

In late January 1990, Lorenzo presented to the creditors his third business plan for Eastern. This plan showed Eastern operating the Atlanta hub, which by this time was at 65 percent of its prestrike levels, and the de-hubbing of Miami in conjunction with the sale of the South American routes to American. The result was that Eastern would be basically an airline with a competitively inferior hub in Atlanta against that of giant Delta and would also have heavy flying from the Northeast to Florida. Such a route structure, given the problems that the industry was facing in 1990, clearly was not sustainable. However, the creditors, at this point grasping for straws without any financial or strategic direction whatsoever, accepted the plan and awaited a proposal from Lorenzo as to how much on the dollar they would receive.

On February 22, the creditors accepted a deal that would pay them just 50 cents on the dollar, a far cry from the 100 cents they were promised just six months earlier. However, both the world and Eastern had changed substantially since then. Under the new plan of reorganization, the creditors would receive $490 million, of which only $300 million would be in cash, and that cash would come from the proceeds of the route sale to American. The remaining $190 million in value would be paid in the form of notes from both Continental and Eastern, guaranteed by Continental and secured by Eastern's Atlanta hub. The notes would pay interest at the annual rate of 15 percent over an eight-year period.

However, this plan was highly conditional. It required, for example, that Eastern satisfactorily settle its labor disputes with the pilots and the flight attendants. It also was predicated upon a satisfactory settlement with the examiner, Shapiro, of the prepetition transactions. Shapiro's report was due in a matter of days. It was also conditioned on the sale of System One, the CRS subsidiary, to Electronic Data Systems (EDS). Since all of these conditions were dependent upon third parties, and were therefore outside the exclusive control of either Texas Air or the creditors, the odds that the deal would fail were relatively high.

Nonetheless, this was a great deal for Lorenzo since he would acquire control of Eastern and take it out of bankruptcy literally for no money down. Although the creditors were not too enthusiastic about the deal, particularly given all the conditions attached to it, their only alternative was to liquidate Eastern. Goldman Sachs had done a cursory financial analysis that said the creditors wouldn't get more than 40 cents on the dollar, and maybe even 20 cents, in the event of a liquidation. Against an optimistic 40 cents in liquidation, Lorenzo's 50 cents didn't look so bad, even with all of the conditions attached to the deal.

Although several creditors refused to support the proposal, the unions, GE and Rolls-Royce among them, the full committee voted to approve the plan. The next key issue was the examiner's report and his findings.

Immediately after the Ueberroth deal to buy Eastern failed, Shapiro turned his attention to investigating the prepetition transactions, the allegations that Lorenzo engaged in asset stripping at Eastern. Shapiro and his law firm, Dickstein, Shapiro and Morin in Washington, D.C., spent almost an entire year interviewing hundreds of witnesses and reviewing thousands of documents. Finally, on March 1, 1990, Shapiro filed his five-inch-thick report.

Shapiro first stated that his efforts to resolve the existing labor disputes in a manner that would permit the retention of all or much of Eastern's prestrike workforce were unsuccessful. Shapiro said, "It was not humanly possible to overcome the unions' and Mr. Lorenzo's intransigence based on a long history of mutual hostility."

This statement, like many of Shapiro's proclamations in the Eastern case, was melodramatic and failed to address the key issue in the labor dispute. Although the pilots and flight attendants called off their strikes and offered to return to work in November 1989, they conditioned their offer on the immediate firing of the replacement workers, or "scabs," and the reinstatement of the strikers. The unreasonableness of this offer was obvious. Eastern was able to hire and train quickly thousands of replacements to get the airline flying again only by giving assurances that the replacements would not be fired if the strikers ever agreed to return to work. Nobody would have come to work at Eastern without such protection. Eastern could not go back on its word to the permanent replacement workers upon which Eastern's fate rested during the early poststrike days. Furthermore, Eastern had in fact rid itself of the unions. Why then would it allow the unions to reestablish a presence on the property?

Union leaders either seemed to miss these points or chose to ignore them. At any rate, the unions refused to come back unless the replacements were fired and Eastern refused to take back the strikers unless the replacements were guaranteed seniority and were not themselves replaced. The obvious result was a standstill that did not affect Eastern in the least since the airline continued to operate on a daily basis with the permanent replacement workers. The unions sued to force Eastern to rehire their members.

The other, more important piece of Shapiro's report concerned the prepetition transactions. Shapiro found that there would be "reasonable grounds" for asserting claims on behalf of Eastern against Texas Air or Continental with respect to twelve of the fifteen prepetition transactions that had been identified. It was Shapiro's contention that these transactions provided Eastern with less than fair consideration or "reasonable equivalent value." According to Shapiro, the twelve claims, if asserted, would have an aggregate value ranging from $285 million to $400 million. Although denying the validity of Shapiro's claim, Lorenzo and Texas Air agreed to settle the dispute by paying the creditors $280 million of which $133 million was to be in cash.

In return for the settlement payment, Shapiro agreed to recommend against the appointment of a trustee to run Eastern. "The appointment of a trustee could so disrupt Eastern's business and its ability to sell tickets as to make its continued viability as an air carrier untenable," claimed Shapiro. "The risks of a trustee should not be undertaken." Within a month, Shapiro would be singing a completely different tune.

The press trumpeted Shapiro's findings as proof of the unions' claims that Lorenzo had in fact stripped assets from Eastern to benefit Texas Air and Continental. However, Shapiro made it clear in his report that he made no finding as to whether the allegations were true or could be proved in a court of law. In fact, in a letter to Speaker of the House Thomas S. Foley dated after the report was filed, Shapiro explained the nature of his report and stated that the report "did not make a judgment as to the validity of [any such claim] or [the] likelihood of success ... In short ... [the Examiner] did not find on the merits against Eastern, Continental or Texas Air."

In fact, Shapiro's valuation methods were highly suspect since there were few, if any, reasonable fair market corollaries by which

Shapiro could have valued the truly unique intercompany transactions that were the subject of his analysis.

Shapiro's analysis was flawed, in my view, because in attempting to place a singular value of up to $400 million on the prepetition transactions, he did not place a counterbalancing value on all of the benefits Eastern received from Continental and Texas Air, either directly or indirectly, by virtue of its position as being part of the Texas Air group of companies.

For example, Eastern had access to aircraft hull and liability insurance rates under the Texas Air umbrella insurance policy that were substantially lower than the rates Eastern would have had to pay were it to go out in the market and insure on its own, assuming an insurance carrier would have even written Eastern a policy given the carrier's deteriorating financial condition.

Another, more important example stems from Eastern's involvement with the OnePass frequent-flyer program. OnePass allowed passengers who accumulated mileage on Eastern flights to redeem those miles for free trips on Continental flights, and vice versa. Largely due to Eastern's shrinking route system, many business travelers flew Eastern primarily because they could redeem their OnePass miles on Continental to such exotic places as Mexico, the Caribbean, Latin America and the South Pacific. Although Eastern paid a fee to Continental of approximately a penny per passenger mile flown to participate in OnePass, the incremental revenue that flowed to Eastern by virtue of the program was estimated to be in excess of $350 million per year.

Shapiro's analysis made little attempt to value these types of benefits that flowed to Eastern by virtue of its ownership by Texas Air, benefits that were easily worth more than $400 million annually to Eastern. These were certainly enough to offset the up to $400 million that Shapiro claimed Eastern might have been owed in a one-shot payment.

Although all seemed to go well for Lorenzo regarding the settlement with Shapiro, things were not going so well at Eastern. The problem was simple: the serious and very public financial and labor problems at the airline drove the business traveler away. Business travelers are very important to an airline's financial health because they pay much higher fares and are more frequent customers. Eastern was unable to attract the business traveler and had to rely, instead, on the leisure traveler who paid $79 fares to fly to Florida.

The result was that Eastern found itself in a death spiral, its financial fortunes deteriorating daily. Thus, by late March, Lorenzo was forced to throw out the proposed reorganization plan agreed to less than a month earlier that would have paid creditors 50 cents on the dollar. A new plan was required given Eastern's ever-sagging financial fortunes.

In January 1990, Eastern's business plan projected that Eastern would lose $145 million for the entire year. However, things were getting so bad so quickly that Eastern had already lost that much by late March. Thus, when Lorenzo presented his most recent plan for Eastern, the carrier's 1990 projected losses had more than doubled to $330 million. In addition, Eastern needed $80 million from an escrow account set aside to pay creditors just to keep flying for the next couple of months.

But these increased losses were just a drop in the bucket to the creditors compared to Lorenzo's next bombshell: the February agreement calling for paying creditors 50 cents on the dollar was off! A new deal would have to be struck given the current financial condition of the airline.

Not surprisingly, the creditors were furious. Some creditors immediately began calling for the liquidation of Eastern, but that view was given short shrift since the creditors' financial and legal advisers felt that there was a better chance of higher repayment if Eastern continued as a going concern. Judge Lifland also wanted Eastern to keep flying, seeming at times to view himself as the airline's rescuer rather than the creditors' guardian.

Finally, after more than a year in bankruptcy proceedings, the creditors decided to take some initiative on their own. Up until this point, they had been passive reactors to Lorenzo's and Texas Air's plans, largely on the advice of their lawyer, Zweibel. Now, largely under the direction of Airbus's Boyd, they wanted to put the pressure back on Lorenzo.

Based on Eastern's worsening financial and operating condition, the fact that a plan of reorganization proposing payment of 50 cents on the dollar would not be filed, and Eastern's need to withdraw $80 million from the escrow account (where the asset sales proceeds were placed ultimately to pay off creditors) just to fund its losses for the second quarter of 1990, the creditors demanded that Texas Air fund all of Eastern's losses until a reorganization plan was approved based on the 50-cent deal. If Lorenzo refused, the creditors would play their hole card. They would ask Lifland to appoint a trustee and strip Lorenzo of control over Eastern.

In early April, not to be outdone, Lorenzo came back with his response. Now he was proposing a reorganization plan that paid creditors 25 cents on the dollar, of which only 5 cents would be in cash and the other 20 cents would be in the form of notes from Continental and Eastern. As a sweetener, Lorenzo also offered to fund a $14 million Eastern pension plan payment that was due in April and to fund up to $25 million in Eastern losses in excess of those projected in the most recent business plan.

The creditors unanimously rejected Lorenzo's proposal and further directed Zweibel to file a formal motion for a trustee who would close the sale of the South American routes to American, which had just been approved by the court but needed regulatory approval, and to pursue the sale of Eastern as a going concern or "otherwise maximize recoveries" for creditors. Zweibel filed the motion with the bankruptcy court on April tenth.

Although they requested a trustee, the creditors stopped short of calling for the immediate liquidation of Eastern. Lifland had made it abundantly clear that he favored a sale of the carrier as a going concern so as to, ostensibly, save Eastern and the jobs of its employees. A call for a trustee who would operate Eastern as opposed to someone who would merely liquidate had a much better chance of success in Lifland's courtroom. Also, even though Lifland had approved the South American route sale to American, the sale still required approval from the Department of Transportation (DOT). If Eastern were liquidated before the sale was completed, the DOT would probably kill the deal and the creditors would be left holding the bag on worthless assets for which American had otherwise agreed to pay $350 million.

Lifland set a date for hearing the creditors' trustee motion of Friday, April 13, 1990 , in his courtroom located in room 623 of the bankruptcy court in lower Manhattan. The hearing would also incorporate the allegations made in ALPA's trustee motion, which had been filed immediately after Eastern declared bankruptcy back in March 1989. Together, these motions for the appointment of a trustee put Lorenzo and Texas Air on the defensive.

The bankruptcy law provides that a judge "may" appoint a trustee where it is in the interests of creditors to do so. However, the law states that a trustee "must" be appointed if there is reason such as fraud, dishonesty, incompetence or gross mismanagement. The creditors' motion, drafted by Zweibel and Harris, rested on several reasons why they thought Lifland was mandated to appoint a trustee.

Zweibel's first argument in favor of a trustee belabored the obvious. That Eastern's continuing and "devastating" losses were extremely damaging to the airline's unsecured creditors. From the start of the case in March 1989 through April 1990, Eastern had withdrawn $320 million from the special escrow account, set aside to pay creditors, just to fund its operations. With the pending request for an additional withdrawal of $80 million from escrow, that brought the total to $400 million. In addition, from the beginning of the case through April 1990, Eastern had incurred a staggering net loss of $1.2 billion.

Although true, this allegation did not justify the appointment of a trustee based solely on "incompetence" or "gross mismanagement" on the part of Eastern or Texas Air. After all, it was the creditors who had approved the withdrawal of the $320 million from escrow to keep the airline flying. As for Eastern's financial performance, although the retention of the South American routes during the latter half of 1989 increased the airline's losses over what they otherwise would have been, the company's labor problems, more than anything else, caused the $1.2 billion loss. Few travelers were willing to endure continued and vocal IAM picket lines at airports across America just to fly Eastern when other airlines offered the same product at the same fare without the worry accompanied by flying an airline whose financial and labor situation was so strongly in doubt.

Zweibel's next argument for a trustee was the contention that Texas Air had demonstrated its inability to project the results of Eastern's operations to the point where the creditors had lost all confidence in the management ability of both Texas Air and Eastern officers.

From the beginning of the Eastern bankruptcy case, Lorenzo had presented five business plans to the creditors. In each case, within a relatively short period of time after presenting a particular plan, Eastern fell far short of its projections. For example, there was a negative swing of $184 million in the mere two months from the January 1990 to the March 1990 projections for Eastern's total losses for the year. The inability of Texas Air to predict accurately Eastern's losses, even for short periods of time, rankled the creditors and led them to lose all confidence in management.

Although this argument had some merit, it must be understood that the airline industry, by its very nature, is so dynamic that plans concocted just months before can be rendered moot by a single competitive stimulus in the marketplace, for example, a new competitor, a major price change, etc. This reality of airline planning, when coupled with the quickly deteriorating finances of Eastern, combined to make Eastern's effective planning horizon basically thirty days. In fact, but for the $320 million in escrow withdrawals, Eastern would have never gotten off the ground after the strike and would have been liquidated soon thereafter.

In addition, the creditors' financial advisers, Chemical Bank and Goldman Sachs, approved each and every plan that Lorenzo presented to them. If such high-priced financial talent thought that Lorenzo's projections were reasonable, as they did and as they told their clients, then caveat emptor, let the buyer beware! Zweibel and the creditors had five separate occasions to disagree with Lorenzo's plans and push for a trustee or to liquidate. They chose not to. Any attempt to blame Texas Air for inaccurate projections thus became self-serving. This argument, however, more than any other, seemed to hold the most water with Lifland.

Finally, Zweibel alleged that Texas Air was "unreasonably delaying" Eastern's Chapter 11 case based on the delayed South American route sale. Also, since the February plan to pay creditors 50 cents was off, the proposed settlement of the prepetition claims, which was conditioned on the acceptance of a reorganization plan, was dead as well. Zweibel claimed that a trustee was needed simply to move the route sale along and reach a definitive settlement with Shapiro over the prepetition transactions.

On the merits, this basis for the creditors' trustee motion was questionable. However, Zweibel and Harris did wax eloquent in their motion. "There should be no mistake that it is the unsecured creditors of this estate who are being asked to fund the continuing fantasies of Eastern and Texas Air.... Texas Air has admitted to this Court and others that the value of its common stock has been wiped out. The same holds true for all series of Eastern's preferred stock. Thus, it is the creditors who are the only group bearing the weight of the continuing staggering losses. Those creditors have now said, 'No more!'"

"No more cash from escrow to fund losses which only increase with the passage of time, resulting in a substantial impairment of their potential recoveries. No more business plans constantly reconfiguring the airline and containing projections which bear no relationship to reality, and which do not address the fundamental issue of producing a viable entity. And no more time for this company's management and its sole common equity holder (Texas Air) to protect their own interests at the expense of the unsecured creditors. It is time for the destiny of Eastern to be determined by an independent trustee acting for the interests of unsecured creditors, not the vanished interests of Texas Air."

In a stirring denouement, Zweibel wrote, "Texas Air and Eastern have regularly blamed others for their missed projections, dismal performance and regular reneging. First it was the unions; next the activities of the examiner; then the Preferred Stockholders' Committee; on occasion, the Court, and now this Committee. This finger-pointing is truly a pathetic effort to hide the real culprits, who can be found in the executive offices in Miami and Houston."

All of the creditors applauded Zweibel's motion. The Pension Benefit Guaranty Corporation (PBGC), the federal agency that oversees and insures employee pension plans, did not oppose the motion for a trustee so long as the result would not be the break-up of Eastern's so-called "controlled group." Eastern was a member of a group of companies controlled by and under common control with Texas Air, Continental, SystemOne and other Texas Air subsidiaries. Under the Employee Retirement Income Security Act of 1974 (ERISA), Eastern and all other companies in the controlled group were jointly and severally liable for Eastern's unfunded pension plan liabilities totalling almost $1 billion. If Eastern's pension plans were terminated and the PBGC were unable to look to the Texas Air companies for payment, PBGC and, ultimately, taxpayer losses would be enormous.

In fact, when Lifland agreed to appoint a trustee, his order specifically stated that Eastern's controlled group would not be affected. It was this ruling, in large part, that forced Continental to file for Chapter 11 bankruptcy in December 1990, when the financial burden placed on Continental by the Eastern pension plan liability became too much for the struggling carrier to bear.

The Eastern preferred stockholders, mostly public shareholders who had their own committee, also approved of Zweibel's motion for a trustee but with the express condition that such a trustee be ordered by Lifland to continue to operate, rather than liquidate, the airline. "The Preferred Committee is hopeful that, with an independent, competent operating trustee in charge of the airline, adequately funded, a real possibility exists to reorganize the airline" or sell it.

The reason for the preferred stockholders wanting an operating trustee was obvious. If Eastern were in fact liquidated, although ahead of the common stockholders in order of payment, the preferred stockholders would not receive any money unless and until the unsecured creditors had been repaid in full. Since the unsecured creditors were now looking at being paid 25 cents on the dollar, or less, the preferred stockholders had a shot at being paid only if Eastern was somehow sold as an operating entity. Thus, they had nothing to lose by playing along! They even offered their own plan of reorganization, which included $70 million in concessions from the unions. But that was a wasted exercise since the unions were in no position to give concessions due to their being locked out of the property.

Given all of these forces arrayed against him, Lorenzo unleashed the legendary Harvey Miller and his legions at Weil, Gotshal and Manges to craft what was sure to be a stirring, yet very costly, legal response and put an end to all of this talk about appointing a trustee. Unfortunately for Lorenzo, and the $1 million monthly fees Eastern was paying Weil Gotshal, his law firm landed on the assault beaches without any weapons!

Harvey Miller himself spent relatively little time on the Eastern case. He is known as a "rainmaker," someone who attracts business because of his reputation but who then pushes the actual work off on other more junior partners and associates. A senior attorney at Eastern, referring to Miller's continued unavailability, said: "I don't even know if there is a Harvey Miller!"

The lawyer charged with the day-to-day handling of the Eastern case at Weil Gotshal was Bruce R. Zirinsky. An intense and intelligent man who could be abruptly rude without giving it much thought, Zirinsky is more skilled as a litigator than as a negotiator. Zirinsky and another junior partner at the firm, Deryck A. Palmer, one of the firm's few black attorneys, were instructed by Miller to draft a memorandum in response to Zweibel's motion calling for a trustee. For the money that was spent, the Weil Gotshal response failed to address Zweibel's arguments—arguments that, on their face, sounded pretty convincing. Rather, Zirinsky and Palmer based their entire argument largely on the contention that a trustee would "impede Eastern's reorganization" and that existing management's experience "is essential for a prompt and successful reorganization."

Instead of providing credible responses to Zweibel's charges, Zirinsky and Palmer focused on applauding Eastern's military charter work: "A [Department of Defense] survey found a company with vastly improved morale ... The company continues to maintain some of the strongest dispatch, charter and safety programs in the industry."

Weil Gotshal was clearly grabbing for straws. Unfortunately for Lorenzo, his law firm left him open to a chorus of accusations that, when allowed to fester unopposed, mandated Lifland, and for that matter any reasonably objective person, to agree with the creditors' motion for a trustee.

When the trustee hearing began in Lifland's courtroom on Friday, April 13, 1990, there were over forty lawyers who had filed appearances in the case representing twenty-two of the nation's leading law firms, in addition to the packed gallery of reporters, Texas Air and Eastern executives, employees and other interested observers.

However, the key players in court were Zirinsky and Palmer of Weil Gotshal representing both Texas Air and Eastern, and Zweibel and Harris of Kramer Levin on behalf of the unsecured creditors.

The hearings dragged on for several days, but what was more interesting were the secret, behind-the-scenes negotiations going on outside of the courtroom between Lorenzo and the creditors. Lorenzo saw this as his last and best opportunity to salvage the situation. After the hearings began, Lorenzo raised his offer from 25 cents to 27.5 cents on the dollar as a payout to creditors. They refused. Lorenzo then upped the ante again to 30 cents, but this time he added an attractive sweetener. Texas Air would pay half of the $80 million that Eastern sought to withdraw from the special escrow account just to keep operating. The creditors flatly refused again.

However, there seems to be no objective reason for them to have done so. The only important condition on the offer was that Lifland approve the settlement of the prepetition claims by June 30, certainly well within the range of possibilities even for Judge Lifland's crowded docket. A payment of 30 cents on the dollar is not particularly bad in any bankruptcy, let alone in the volatile airline industry where values can plummet overnight, not to mention with a company such as Eastern that was only weeks away from running out of cash and shutting down completely. Once an airline shuts down and its planes stop flying, the value of the entire entity tends toward zero. Thus, an offer of 30 cents for Eastern at this critical juncture, given the carrier's huge losses and its tenuous cash position, was a very attractive offer. Then why didn't the creditors go for the deal?

It appeared that the creditors' financial advisers, led by Art Newman of Chemical Bank, secretly favored taking Lorenzo's offer because they knew, even if they were extremely lucky to find a buyer for Eastern as a going concern, they would be hard-pressed to get more than 30 cents on the dollar given Eastern's dire condition. However, the creditors' lawyer, Zweibel, made it clear to everyone on the committee that he thought 30 cents was way too low and that they should hold out for the prospect of a higher return under an independent operating trustee.

This was a vain hope at best. The airline's condition was already critical. By the spring of 1990 the recession was beginning to take hold and airline traffic was going into a freefall. If anything, Eastern's value would steadily decrease thereafter, no matter who was in charge.

Not only did the creditors reject Lorenzo's 30 cent offer, but they kept demanding that Lorenzo go back to his earlier offer of February when he planned to pay them 50 cents. This position, also championed by Zweibel, was totally unreasonable given the drastic change in Eastern's circumstances from February to April. Much can happen in a matter of eight weeks to a company that is deteriorating so rapidly. In fact, Eastern's estimated loss for all of 1990 almost doubled between January and March. By April it had almost doubled again. A strong argument could have been made by April that the company wasn't worth 5 cents, let alone 50. Nonetheless, the creditors continued to cling blindly to an earlier offer that had no present economic justification, and in fact that wasn't even on the table.

After another day of hearings on the motion for a trustee, the creditors, feeling that the situation was quickly slipping out from under their control, did an about-face. Creditor financial expert Newman, realizing that Zweibel's continued demand for 50 cents wasn't getting the creditors any closer to a deal, took direct control of the negotiations and convinced his clients to propose a more reasonable counteroffer.

Newman told Texas Air that the creditors would accept 37.5 cents on the dollar as opposed to Lorenzo's standing offer of 30 cents. However, their acceptance was conditioned on them receiving 8 percent of Texas Air stock and 19 percent of Eastern stock as part of the transaction.

Although on its face the creditors' counteroffer seemed reasonable enough, Lorenzo was forced to reject it because of the messy corporate control issues that would have resulted if Eastern was not a wholly owned subsidiary of Texas Air after the reorganization. If the creditors had ended up with 19 percent of Eastern's common stock, then the intercompany transactions that Lorenzo had planned for Eastern post-reorganization, including a merger of Eastern into Continental, would have been very difficult to achieve.

First, intercompany transactions where minority shareholders are involved are subject to a higher and tighter legal standard. The key reason why Lorenzo's prepetition transactions involving Eastern were perfectly legal was that Texas Air owned all of Eastern's common stock and therefore owed no fiduciary duties to minority stockholders because there weren't any. More importantly, if the creditors were 19 percent holders of Eastern common stock post-reorganization, they could hold up Lorenzo's plans for a merger of Eastern into Continental by demanding inflated payment terms before tendering their stock.

Thus, for these reasons primarily, Lorenzo did not accept the creditors' counteroffer of 37.5 cents when it involved such a large chunk of Eastern stock.

Late in the evening of the last day of the trustee hearing, Lorenzo himself finally took the stand. Up until this moment, the results of the previous several days of negotiations with the creditors had remained confidential. Lorenzo, in open court, then recounted the various last-minute offers and counteroffers and then made it clear to Lifland and Zweibel, who was cross-examining him, that the 30 cent offer was still on the table and that he was ready to go forward with it. In response to a question from Zirinsky about the ability to restructure the terms of the offer, but not the 30 cent amount, Lorenzo stated: "But even with regard to the subject of consideration, if the committee would like to restructure and rearrange the debt shares, we are prepared to do that."

The hearing adjourned without further progress. About 7:30 P.M., when the hearing resumed, the examiner stood up and, in a characteristic long-winded polemic, supported the creditors' motion for a trustee. Shapiro blamed Lorenzo and present management for Eastern's huge $1.2 billion in losses since the beginning of the case. He also blamed Lorenzo's negotiating tactics for the failure of the parties to reach a settlement on a reorganization plan for Eastern. "The issue in reality, and I say this more in sadness than in anything else, is really Mr. Lorenzo. Can anyone blame the creditors for being outraged?" This was a complete change from Shapiro's statement just a month before that the appointment of a trustee would seriously harm Eastern.

Shortly thereafter, Lifland called another recess and told those assembled that he would have a decision within the hour. Around ten o'clock, Lifland returned with a fairly lengthy document from which he began to read, a document which he obviously could not have written during the hour recess. Lifland's words and tone were both scathing and condescending to Lorenzo.

> Throughout this case, Eastern has continually made operating projections which it has failed to achieve with the resultant losses being borne by the unsecured creditors.... Eastern has also come to a number of agreements with the Committee concerning potential plans of reorganization but Eastern has been unable to meet the terms of such agreements.
>
> This Court finds by clear and convincing evidence that the appointment of an operating trustee is warranted. Eastern's inability to formulate a business plan and make operating projections which have a longevity of more than several months, along with the continuing enormous operating losses being sustained by the estate, mandate that this Court order the appointment of a trustee for incompetence.
>
> With Mr. Lorenzo at the throttle, or hovering over it, Eastern has used $1.2 billion to "fuel" this reorganization trip. The time has come to replace the pilot to captain Eastern's crew.... Eastern's owner-manager, as personified by the Chairman of the Board of both the parent and the Debtor, is not competent to reorganize this estate.

Lifland then continued to describe the type of trustee he wanted to run the struggling carrier. "This Court has always considered that a trustee, if appointed, would be empowered, and indeed mandated, to operate and manage the airline as a going concern. The interests of creditors, preferred shareholders, employees and the flying public are better served by an order appointing an operating trustee rather than allowing the liquidation of assets of the estate." Lifland further stated that the trustee should be "an eminently qualified person" who has experience in running a troubled airline.

Since Lifland wanted the new trustee to operate Eastern and not liquidate it, Lifland had no problem approving the release of the \$80 million from the escrow account that Lorenzo had earlier requested so that Eastern could fund its operations. But this time the \$80 million would be used by the trustee, not Lorenzo.

When Lifland finished, Harold D. Jones, the United States trustee who is appointed by the Department of Justice to help the court in administering bankruptcy cases, stood up and announced: "The individual that I have selected and would request this Court to approve is Martin R. Shugrue, Jr."

Shugrue, who had been president of Continental, was objected to by Weil Gotshal's Zirinsky allegedly because of the requirement that a trustee be a "disinterested person." Zirinsky's real aim, however, was to raise the "disinterested person" issue with the hope that Lifland would delay his decision for a day or two to research the law, which in turn would give Lorenzo one last window of opportunity to negotiate a deal with the creditors and avoid a trustee altogether.

Lifland, seeing right through Zirinsky's patently obvious strategy, would not delay any further. He abruptly cut Zirinsky off and declared, "I do so order Mr. Shugrue's appointment."

The appointment of Shugrue marked the end of Frank Lorenzo's control over Eastern Air Lines. Under the bankruptcy law, once a trustee is appointed, the trustee has the legal authority to act as a one-person chairman, president, chief executive officer and board of directors. Shugrue's only boss was Judge Lifland. Without control of Eastern's board, Lorenzo, even though he owned all of Eastern's common stock through Texas Air, had no authority or control over the airline. In short, both he and Texas Air were shoved completely out of the picture.

When news of Shugrue's appointment flashed across the country, one man was ecstatic: Charlie Bryan. Since the strike, Bryan had felt neglected. He was no longer in the center of events, no longer the driver of other people's (other than his members') destinies. Bryan was no longer involved in "life or death" negotiations or decisions because Eastern, for obvious reasons, did not even attempt to negotiate to end the strike and bring the IAM back on the property. In essence, Bryan was on the outside and nothing he could do could get him back on the inside. Thus, when Lorenzo, too, was thrown out, Bryan saw this as a kind of poetic justice. As Bryan saw it, Lorenzo had forced Bryan out and now Judge Lifland had forced Lorenzo out.

Bryan had high hopes that Shugrue, who announced soon after his appointment that achieving labor peace at Eastern was a top priority, would agree to Bryan's settlement terms so that Bryan could triumphantly lead all of the unions back onto the property. Although both ALPA and the TWU had called off their strikes months before, they were still refused access to the airline because of the issue of the status of the permanent replacement workers Eastern had hired to fill the union spots. Bryan's hope was that he would lead the march back to Eastern to a chorus of accolades that labor, and Eastern's unions, had finally beaten Lorenzo. Or so he thought!

The appointment of the trustee ended what had been more than a decade of greed, incompetence and personal animosity surrounding Eastern. The travails of the airline up to this crucial point had, in essence, almost guaranteed that it would end up in the hands of a court-appointed receiver.

On the day of Shugrue's appointment, April 19, 1990, Lorenzo had finally lost his battle to somehow create a large, low-cost, nonunion "megacarrier" out of a combination of both Eastern and Continental. His Eastern stock, already worthless from the day Eastern filed for bankruptcy, did not even allow him access to or control of Eastern under the regime of the trustee. In fact, soon after the trustee was appointed, Texas Air stopped including Eastern's financial results in its consolidated financial statements, reflecting that, for all intents and purposes, Texas Air no longer owned Eastern. If Lorenzo wanted to acquire assets of Eastern henceforth, he would have to bid on them in open court just like any other potential suitor.

Was Lorenzo at fault for the events that led up to the appointment of a trustee? Partially. Although he made several offers to the creditors which he felt, and which the objective evidence shows were in fact, reasonable, Lorenzo should have recognized that his adversaries' intense dislike of him meant that he would have to sweeten any deal to get Zweibel's blessing. For example, when the creditors told Lorenzo that they would accept 37.5 cents if it included 19 percent of Eastern stock, Lorenzo should have countered that he would increase the cash portion of the deal from the 5 cents ($49 million) at which it had been previously valued to, say, 10 cents (or roughly $100 million) in return for the creditors receiving no Eastern stock at all.

Although a more expensive deal up front, it probably would have carried the day and saved Lorenzo much more than that in excess costs and aggravation down the road. Even Zweibel would have had a problem convincing his clients, the creditors, not to accept 10 cents in cash out of a total of 37.5 cents as part of a reorganization plan. Lorenzo would have gotten Eastern and then been able to merge Eastern any way he saw fit into Continental, probably by liquidating Eastern as a corporate entity and transferring its key assets and nonunion personnel to Continental. Texas Air would have maintained its "critical mass" and Lorenzo would probably still be in control of his empire today. A little bit more cash, even though the financial analysis may not have warranted it, would have gotten Lorenzo home. Lorenzo's top strategist, Robert Ferguson, should have convinced Lorenzo that this was the only way he was going to put together a deal that allowed him to keep Eastern. Instead, the deal fell through and, eventually, Lorenzo lost control of everything.

Soon after the trustee was appointed, Texas Air changed its name to Continental Airlines Holdings Inc. (CAHI) to reflect that Eastern was no longer part of the empire, and the principal operating subsidiary of the holding company was Continental. Largely due to the problems at Eastern, and the unions' public relations smear campaign aimed at Continental, Continental had continued to hemorrhage red ink since the Eastern bankruptcy began. Carl R. Pohlad, the Minneapolis investor and trusted friend of Lorenzo's who also serves on the board of CAHI, said that the entire issue had boiled down to Lorenzo's personality and continued affiliation with the airline. "Frank's image has hurt the company to the point where the situation may be irreversible if something isn't done soon," Pohlad is reported to have lamented.

Lorenzo agreed that his continued presence at Continental made it almost impossible for Continental to shake the Eastern legacy, which many believed had a lot to do with Continental's huge losses. As part of an overall recapitalization of Continental, Lorenzo agreed to step down, his shares in both Jet Capital Corporation, the personal holding company through which he controlled Texas Air, and Continental were bought out. Scandinavian Airlines System, already a substantial owner of Continental stock, kicked in additional funds for a larger stake in the airline. Lorenzo would remain on the board of Continental, but he would not sit on its powerful executive committee.

With the amount of money Continental paid for his stock, the price for which was a hefty 180 percent premium over the then prevailing market price for Continental stock, Lorenzo received around $30 million to leave Continental. "Not a bad severance package," one senior Texas Air official close to Lorenzo commented afterward.

Upon Lorenzo's departure, Continental named former Delta CEO Hollis L. Harris as chairman and CEO of Continental. Harris, a slow-talking southern good ol' boy, was expected to bring some Delta–type stability to Continental, as one board member put it.

It was soon determined, however, that Lorenzo's presence wasn't at the root of Continental's problems. They were much deeper. Continental was still suffering from the "big bang" as many senior Continental managers referred to it. It relates to the merger on February 1, 1987, in which Lorenzo combined Frontier, New York Air, People Express and Continental into one single airline on a single day. The service disruptions from that event are now legendary, and the key result was that the business traveler deserted Continental completely. Even though the service problems had been fixed since early 1990, and in fact Continental arguably offers some of the best service among U.S. airlines as of this writing, it has been extremely difficult for Continental to convince business travelers of this. Thus, although Continental has among the lowest costs of any major airline, it also has the lowest yields, or revenues, per passenger mile, due to the large number of leisure travelers and the lack of business travelers who fly the airline. Continental's difference between costs and revenues per mile is too small to allow the carrier to make any money. This was and continues to be Continental's major problem.

Harris, who was used to the type of company such as Delta, which basically runs itself, was like a fish out of water in the slash-and-burn kind of atmosphere that pervaded Continental management. Within three months of taking over, Harris found Continental on the verge of bankruptcy. Instead of paring down the company to shave costs, Harris looked to expand without any major long-term strategy. Furthermore, he was unable to make the very tough choices about the company's future that were required and to act decisively once those choices were made.

Faced with deteriorating finances at Continental, which were exacerbated by the Eastern pension plan liabilities that the PBGC foisted on Continental, Harris put the carrier into Chapter 11 in early December 1990.

Through the early part of 1991, Harris made absolutely no progress in turning Continental around. In fact, Continental lost almost $300 million in the first half of the year. In mid-August, Harris distributed a message on the Continental employee call-in hotline. He intoned mysteriously that Continental employees needed to "pray for the airline's survival three times a day. We're at war with forces within and outside the company." The very next day, the board ousted him, and Robert Ferguson, Lorenzo's former financial strategist who doesn't mind making tough decisions, took over as CEO. Regarding the voice-mail message, all Harris would say afterward was "I just thought it was the right thing to do."

Continental's future survival as of early 1992 is by no means certain. Given the situation, Lorenzo would have been much better off had he done what was necessary to mollify the Eastern creditors back in April 1990. So, Frank Lorenzo was partially to blame for the appointment of a trustee.

However, most of the blame for the condition of Eastern which led to the appointment of a trustee must fall on the lawyer for the creditors' committee: Joel Zweibel. Zweibel, who started the Eastern case while working for the law firm of Kramer Levin, soon after the trustee was appointed transferred, with all of the Eastern work, to the law firm of O'Melveny and Myers. The law firm, as it turned out, where Judge Lifland's first cousin was also a partner.

Zweibel had the committee eating out of his hand. Whatever he said took on the aura of law. Few would openly challenge him in committee meetings. According to one important committee member: "Zweibel ruled the committee as his personal fiefdom." Basically, whatever Zweibel recommended, the committee adopted as its official policy. Thus, Zweibel was largely responsible for the committee's various positions on the several reorganization plans that were offered by Lorenzo.

Although Lorenzo could have sweetened the pot on the creditors' last offer of 37.5 cents by offering more cash, Zweibel should have recommended to his clients that they take Lorenzo's earlier offer of 30 cents and be happy about it. By mid-April, Eastern had run out of cash. But for the $80 million withdrawal from the escrow account that Lifland approved in conjunction with his appointment of Shugrue, Eastern would have had to shut down and begin liquidating that very week. In addition, there were no other offers on the table from any credible parties to buy the airline as a going concern. These facts made Eastern absolutely worthless. In fact, Eastern had a substantial negative net worth.

Given the situation, why didn't Zweibel recommend to the committee that Lorenzo's 30 cents was better than the 5 cents they would likely see in a liquidation? (The actual payout will not even be one cent.) One committee member says that he wanted to take Lorenzo's offer "and run" because "I estimated the potential payout in liquidation, even then, to be de minimus." However, "Zweibel kept hammering away that Lorenzo's offer was illusory, or had too many conditions, or wasn't a real 30 cents.... After a while, it was plain, at least to me, that he wasn't going to accept anything Lorenzo offered unless it met his own specific criteria."

But a more important question must be asked. Would the creditors have been much better off just liquidating Eastern back in the summer of 1989, after the last of the credible bids to buy Eastern fell through? Eastern's assets certainly would have fetched substantially more then, during the height of the airline takeover craze, than they did after the shutdown in 1991. The Atlanta hub, South American routes, modern Boeing 757 and Airbus A-300 aircraft, Miami maintenance base, attractive landing and takeoff slots at New York's LaGuardia and Washington's National airports, all would have generated proceeds at or more than their fair market values during the first half of 1989. Had the creditors sold those assets then, they would easily have received 100 cents on the dollar, and even the preferred stockholders would have received some payout. Then why didn't they push for liquidation soon after the bankruptcy filing?

The creditors' financial advisers put together a preliminary liquidation analysis soon after the bankruptcy filing that showed a potential payout, at that time, of at least 60 cents. It is very unusual for any bankruptcy to pay creditors such a high percentage of their claims, let alone an airline bankruptcy. Why didn't Zweibel push his clients to take the 60 cents at that time? Although there were several complex reasons why Eastern probably would not have been liquidated immediately, for instance Judge Lifland's insistence that he would keep Eastern flying at all costs, nothing prevented Zweibel from at least recommending liquidation at that time to the committee due to the extremely high expected payout.

A member of the creditors' committee stated bluntly: "As soon as we saw those early liquidation numbers, many of us began to quietly make a case for immediate liquidation. Zweibel counseled against this course of action because he felt we could sell the airline as a going concern and get full value, not just the 60 cents which was anticipated."

How Zweibel could have thought that someone would buy Eastern lock, stock and barrel after all other bidders had tried and abandoned the idea, after the PBGC claim of up to $1 billion was still unresolved, is difficult to see. Perhaps Zweibel truly felt that he could somehow miraculously engineer a sale of the airline as a going concern where all other efforts had failed. However, all subsequent events proved such hopes to be futile.

Eastern's long and tortuous trek through the abyss of bankruptcy had reached a critical crossroads. Did the appointment of a trustee mark the end of the road or did it give Eastern one last shot at survival? Just about everybody believed that Eastern was dead and gone and that the trustee would just oversee a funeral procession. As one member of the creditors' committee put it: "As soon as Lifland appointed the trustee, I immediately began to redeem all of my Eastern frequent-flyer miles. It was only a matter of time."

All but a handful of people truly believed that to be the case. The distinct minority was lead by the man whom Lifland had appointed as trustee, Martin R. Shugrue, Jr., who honestly believed that Eastern still had some life left in it.

As it turned out, Shugrue was right. Eastern in fact did have some life left in it. That is, until the corporate bungling and personal animosity reached such despicable levels that even Shugrue ultimately had to throw in the towel.

4

AND HE SHALL LEAD THEM

Martin Roger Shugrue, Jr., or "Marty" as he prefers to be called, grew up as the son of a Providence, Rhode Island, policeman. After graduating from Providence College with a degree in economics he became a naval aviator. One of his biggest thrills while in the Navy was participating in the air-sea rescue of the *Apollo 8* capsule when it splashed down in the Pacific in 1968, the same capsule that included astronaut and future Eastern Chairman Frank Borman. Twenty-three years later, when Shugrue was trustee of Eastern, he joked with Borman, "Colonel, if I had known then what I know now, I would have left you in the damn ocean."

After the Navy, Shugrue went to work for Pan American World Airways as a pilot, where he also became a member of ALPA. He spent several years piloting the Boeing 707, the first commercial passenger jet, which Pan Am inaugurated into service in the early 1960s.

A very engaging person who has a way of making friends with

everybody, Shugrue left the pilot ranks in a few years after being furloughed and, largely due to his personality, entered Pan Am management. During a period of roughly twenty years, he worked his way up through the bloated and bureaucratic Pan Am infrastructure. He served as director of performance measurement, director of organizational planning, staff vice president of corporate personnel, managing director of the eastern-central U.S., managing director of the United Kingdom and Western Europe, vice president of industrial relations, vice president of personnel, senior vice president of administration, senior vice president of marketing and, finally, vice chairman and chief operating officer.

During most of the 1980s, Shugrue was the number two executive at Pan Am reporting to C. Edward Acker, Pan Am's chairman and chief executive officer. Acker had made a name for himself while at Air Florida, although many industry observers claim that he drove that carrier into bankruptcy. He is now CEO of a commuter airline called Atlantic Coast Airlines. Nevertheless, upon his arrival at Pan Am, Acker was heralded as a savior for the then ailing, and now liquidated, once mighty aviation pioneer.

The primary cause of Pan Am's legendary financial problems stemmed from the lack of a sufficiently large domestic route network to feed passengers to its once far-flung international system. Although Pan Am has now been liquidated, up until 1978 both Pan Am and TWA had an absolute stranglehold among U.S. carriers in international aviation. After deregulation, other carriers such as United, American, Northwest, USAir and Delta began to acquire smaller airlines and build up large domestic hubs. Later, these airlines began to expand overseas. During all of this activity, Pan Am was left behind without any major domestic route network. It attempted to build a domestic route network in 1980 with the acquisition of National Airlines, but this turned out to be an unmitigated disaster for Pan Am.

Pan Am paid $400 million for National in January 1980 although the airline, based in Miami, offered little strategic value to Pan Am.

National's primary north-south East Coast route system, in addition to its Houston minihub, generated little incremental passenger feed to Pan Am's international routes. Furthermore, National's fleet of McDonnell Douglas wide-body aircraft was wholly incompatible with Pan Am's fleet of Boeing wide-body aircraft. Pan Am would have been much better off if it had spent the $400 million on buying another airline better suited to Pan Am's needs, such as Eastern with its huge Atlanta hub. Even spending the $400 million on building its own domestic hub structure would have been better for Pan Am than wasting that amount, and much more, on National.

The National merger was a disaster for Pan Am because not only did it exacerbate Pan Am's already serious financial woes, but it resulted in the most bungled attempt to integrate the workforces of two merged carriers in the history of the airline business.

Acker didn't arrive at Pan Am until after the National merger was just about completed in early 1980 but he was responsible for its implementation. As the bungled handling of the National merger caused Pan Am's financial problems to escalate immediately and substantially, Acker found himself scrambling to generate cash. He decided that his only choice was to begin a major sell-off of Pan Am's key assets.

In 1980 and 1981, Acker sold Pan Am's 50 percent interest in Falcon Jet, Pan Am's landmark office building at 200 Park Avenue, in midtown Manhattan, and the internationally famous Intercontinental Hotel chain. As Pan Am's financial problems continued unabated into the mid-1980s, Acker continued to sell off the crown jewels of the empire. The most important of these was Pan Am's historic Pacific Division, which was sold to United for a paltry $750 million in 1985.

The asset sales did absolutely nothing to solve the inherent structural problem of Pan Am, a substantial lack of domestic feed. Shugrue, who pleaded with Acker to do something to solve the airline's structural problem, was helpless to take any action other than voice his displeasure with Acker's strategy. The Pan Am board of directors gave Acker carte blanche to do with the airline as he saw fit, which unfortunately had nothing to do with solving the key problem.

For example, in early 1986 Acker purchased a Northeast commuter airline called Ransome Airlines, which Acker then named Pan Am Express. Acker's intent was to have Ransome collect passengers from the northeast and feed them into Pan Am's international jet hub at New York's JFK International Airport. Unfortunately, this strategy did very little to solve the feeder problem. What Pan Am needed was substantial feed from a large jet hub providing several thousand passengers a day to the international routes rather than the relatively insignificant several hundred passengers a day that a commuter operation provided.

Also in 1986 Acker spent almost $100 million to acquire assets from New York Air, which became the Pan Am Shuttle. The Pan Am Shuttle served the Boston–New York–Washington corridor in competition with the Eastern Air Shuttle. Shugrue was against this acquisition as well because, again, it did nothing to solve Pan Am's primary problem of a lack of domestic feeder traffic. Although the Shuttle gave Pan Am a high profile in important markets and allowed Shuttle travelers to earn Pan Am frequent-flyer miles which, ostensibly, gave them an incentive to fly Pan Am overseas, the acquisition did little to solve the airline's core problem. Not being in charge, Shugrue could only sit by and watch.

By 1987, Pan Am had lost over $1.5 billion since Acker's arrival in 1980, and this was after accounting for the gains from all of the asset sales. In December 1987, Jay Pritzker, who owned the Hyatt Hotel chain as well as Braniff, proposed a merger of Braniff and Pan Am. Given Braniff's financial condition at the time, it would soon go into bankruptcy and be liquidated, the benefits to Pan Am of such a proposed merger were dubious at best. Because of this, and the fact that Braniff's domestic operations were too small to help Pan Am anyway, Shugrue had substantial reservations about the idea. Nevertheless, Acker jumped at the deal and went ahead full blast to get it done.

As part of his proposal, Pritzker asked Pan Am's unions for substantial wage concessions. The issue came down to the Pan Am pilots who were trying to decide whether to give Pritzker concessions, and therefore go for the merger, or hold back and take their chances with Acker. One Pan Am pilot union leader referred to this dilemma as a "damned if you do, damned if you don't" scenario. By late December, as the merger deadline drew near, Shugrue, no longer able to sit by silently, came out publicly against the merger. Shugrue and Acker, who never truly got along with each other anyway, were now open adversaries.

In the end, Pritzker backed away from the deal, and the unions, who were fed up both with the fiasco over the Pritzker deal as well as with the billion-dollar losses since Acker's arrival, pressured the Pan Am board to make some drastic changes. Pan Am board member William T. Coleman, Jr., a former secretary of transportation in the Ford administration and noted civil rights attorney, negotiated a deal with Pan Am's unions that called for wage and work-rule concessions in return for the sacking of Acker. Unfortunately for Pan Am and Shugrue, Shugrue was included in the purge.

Just about everyone following the Pan Am situation at the time was surprised that Shugrue, who was very popular with the unions, found his head on the same platter as Acker's. After the incident, the unions stated that it was their intention to remove Acker but not Shugrue. In retrospect, Shugrue was removed because, although he courageously opposed a deal that would have certainly ruined Pan Am by merging it with failing Braniff, his position necessarily put him at odds publicly with the airline's chairman in addition to several board members who favored the Pritzker deal. It is unclear whether Coleman himself supported the Pritzker deal or not. What is certain is that Coleman felt that a clean sweep of the top levels at Pan Am was necessary to make labor peace and get much-needed concessions.

During the Pritzker debacle, Shugrue received a telephone call from Frank Lorenzo. Lorenzo told him, "Marty, you're dead. You can't publicly fight the board like that and expect to survive. I've got something for you." Lorenzo was looking for a replacement for Thomas G. Plaskett, Continental's president whom Lorenzo had hired away from American less than a year earlier. Lorenzo was disappointed with Plaskett for bungling the "Big Bang," the single-day merger of Continental, Frontier, New York Air and People Express on February 1, 1987. While Continental was suffering from major operational glitches each day, hundreds of flights cancelled and mountains of lost baggage, Plaskett was allegedly playing golf during the workday instead of closely monitoring the quickly deteriorating situation. Lorenzo needed an executive with a strong operations background and thus offered Shugrue the job of president at Continental.

By coincidence, at the same time Shugrue took Plaskett's place as president of Continental, Plaskett took the places of both Acker and Shugrue and became chairman, president and CEO of Pan Am. This type of executive musical-chairs is common because of the few qualified executives in the industry who, it is thought, have the necessary credentials to run a large carrier. I do not necessarily agree that only long-time airline executives can run an airline. Alfred A. Checchi, the chairman of Northwest, had absolutely no airline experience before he took over Northwest in 1989. Not only has Northwest creatively paid down a large part of its over $3.6 billion in acquisition debt, but it is growing through strategic acquisitions and partnerships. Checchi is the perfect example of a smart non-airline executive adding value in the industry.

Regarding the executive shuffling between Pan Am and Continental, Plaskett definitely got a better deal than Shugrue. At Pan Am, Plaskett was given the chairman and CEO titles and reported to a sleepy board of directors populated mostly by men in their late sixties. At Continental, Shugrue was made president but Lorenzo kept the titles of chairman and CEO. As Shugrue would quickly learn, it didn't matter what his title was at Continental, everyone in the organization knew who the real boss was.

I first met Shugrue after he had just arrived as president of Continental. I was on the verge of leaving Continental at the time, where I worked in the planning department. I looked forward to returning to the Northeast in my new job as assistant to the president of MasterCard International in New York. Before I left Continental, though, most of the middle and senior managers with whom I worked questioned whether Shugrue, or anyone else for that matter, would be able to do anything to fix the serious operational and financial mess in which Plaskett had left Continental.

Shugrue's most important contribution to Continental upon his arrival was that he instituted much-needed financial and operational monitoring and control systems. Also, he wasn't afraid to cut flights where necessary or add flights where there was a market opportunity. Most Continental executives agree that Continental's improved quality of service is in large part attributable to the triage that Shugrue first applied after taking over in early 1988.

Lorenzo's management style at Continental took the term *hands-on* to new heights. Lorenzo was chairman, president and CEO of Texas Air, the holding company. However, Lorenzo would also assume various titles at Continental, one of Texas Air's operating subsidiaries, depending upon his mood or the airline's most recent financial results. Sometimes he would be content to be just chairman of Continental and let someone else be president and CEO. Other times Lorenzo would assume the titles of both chairman and CEO and let someone else be president. One time he got so fed up that he took all three titles: chairman, president and CEO. Every Monday morning some fellow Continental executives and I took bets to see which title Lorenzo would have by the end of the week.

Regardless of his actual title, Lorenzo would take it upon himself to make direct operating decisions at the airline, many times without the knowledge of the person who he himself had given the authority and responsibility to make those decisions. Lorenzo's view, which arguably had some merit, was that this type of management style kept everyone, including the CEO, on their toes and hopping. One thing that you could definitely not say about Continental was that it was bureaucratic or lethargic.

When I was working in Continental's planning department, Plaskett was president and Douglas Birdsall was senior vice president of planning, which included pricing. Birdsall, a former president of New York Air, is one of the smartest marketing and planning executives in the industry. He left Continental soon after I did and went to a large travel service company called Travelmation, located in Stamford, Connecticut. Birdsall would many times be called into Lorenzo's office on the fifteenth floor of the American General Center, Continental's corporate headquarters in Houston, and be given a direct order by Lorenzo to cut all fares nationwide, across-the-board, by 40 percent effective immediately. A flurry of activity would ensue on the twelfth floor, where all the planning and marketing staff were located, as over a hundred thousand fare changes had to be processed in addition to the creation of new advertisements that were to run in over a hundred newspapers. By midnight, if we were lucky, we would usually finish implementing the new price structure and marketing campaign.

However, the president of the airline, in this case Plaskett, would sometimes only find out about the new fare strategy when he opened up the next morning's newspaper and saw the ad that had been developed, without his knowledge, the night before. One senior Continental executive claimed, when reminded of this example, "But with Plaskett it really didn't matter because he was out on the golf course anyway!"

Shugrue complained that these, and other similar activities by Lorenzo, actually undermined Shugrue's ability to manage the airline effectively. Shugrue was not alone in this sentiment. Since 1984 Continental has had seven different presidents in as many years, largely due to Lorenzo's style of management. Nevertheless, as unorthodox as it may have been, Lorenzo's management style actually provided Continental with the unique advantage of being able to make decisions quickly in a fast-changing marketplace. In addition, the fast-paced environment at Continental left no room for the stultified bureaucracy found at other large airlines such as Eastern or Pan Am. Even middle managers, such as myself, had a lot of latitude to make quick decisions without seeking several layers of approval. This type of entrepreneurial environment actually allowed me to devise one of the most successful marketing strategies in Continental's history. One that would also be used by Shugrue later on at Eastern.

My primary responsibility while in the planning department in 1987 was to oversee the marketing and overall corporate strategy for a new hub that Continental had just decided to open in Cleveland. At the time, Continental had only a handful of flights in Cleveland while the big guy in the market was USAir. We faced two huge problems: (1) Because of the major service disruptions caused by the Big Bang, business travelers avoided Continental altogether; and (2) USAir's large market share in Cleveland seemed almost impenetrable. One day, Birdsall came into my office, which actually consisted of half of a conference room table, and said, while handing me a file bulging with papers, "Fix Cleveland!"

Using a Harvard Business School tool called a five-forces analysis, in which the structural components of the marketplace are identified, I saw that our best hope was to exploit USAir's key competitive weakness: USAir aircraft, at that time, did not have a first class cabin. Continental's aircraft did.

I immediately put in place a program, just in Cleveland, where any traveler who arrived at a Continental gate with a full coach ticket, who most likely was a business traveler anyway, would be automatically upgraded to a first-class seat. Before long, hundreds of USAir passengers, with full coach tickets, started showing up at Continental ticket counters just so they could fly first-class on Continental rather than coach on USAir.

At the same time I enlisted the help of Continental's senior vice president of marketing, James V. O'Donnell, to come up with a catchy name and advertising slogan for the new Cleveland campaign. O'Donnell, who now runs his own marketing consulting firm in Houston and was formerly president of the advertising firm of Scali, McCabe and Sloves/Southwest, is a great "guerilla marketer." Someone who can craft an award-winning ad campaign within a matter of hours. O'Donnell decided to call the program *YONEPASS* after the *Y* designation for coach class and the OnePass frequent-flyer program of Continental. O'Donnell also came up with the slogan "Nuts to USAir," based on the fact that for the same ticket you could fly first-class on Continental and get first-class service instead of flying coach on USAir where all you would get is a bag of peanuts.

To top it all off, we called a major press conference in downtown Cleveland to announce the new campaign and trucked in a baby elephant named Connie Continental. At the press conference, in front of all the reporters, Connie would shake her head as if saying no when offered a bag of USAir peanuts, and would shake her head as if saying yes when offered a *YONEPASS* ticket on Continental.

USAir did get some revenge, though. The next day, a group of USAir ticket agents in Cleveland walked up to the Continental ticket counter and unleashed a fusillade consisting of bags of USAir peanuts, all in good fun I suppose.

The *YONEPASS* program was so successful in Cleveland that Continental adopted it nationwide beginning in January 1988, and it continues to be the airline's major marketing strategy to this day. Several Continental executives say that *YONEPASS* is responsible for almost $400 million in additional revenue to Continental each year. As for Cleveland, it is now one of Continental's largest hubs with over two hundred flights per day throughout the country and into Canada. USAir, in the face of Continental's dominant market position in

Cleveland, is now but a shadow of its former self there in terms of market share.

This type of action, and result, was possible at Continental because lower-level managers, such as myself, were allowed to take the initiative, something which I later discovered would never be allowed within Eastern's bloated infrastructure.

Shugrue's overall strategic efforts at Continental hadn't been given the time to become effective by late 1988 when Lorenzo started to become impatient with the lack of perceived progress. Unfortunately, the service disruptions caused by the Big Bang had set the airline back three years. Yet, at the time, nobody realized it. Lorenzo, who is normally extremely impatient when it comes to bad news, wanted answers and an immediate change in Continental's fortunes. An impossible goal but one that Lorenzo attempted to attain anyway.

So, in early 1989, Lorenzo began to look around for another executive who he thought would somehow miraculously reverse Continental's fortunes overnight. In February, Lorenzo picked D. Joseph Corr, who at the time was an executive vice president at TWA, to become Continental's new president and CEO.

Shugrue had lasted in the position as Continental president exactly a year and a day. However, as of early 1992, Shugrue still holds the record for having the longest tenure of any Continental president since the airline first emerged from bankruptcy in the mid-1980s. This is because by October 1989, barely six months after taking over at Continental, Corr had resigned.

After leaving Continental in February 1989, Shugrue became a consultant, and his first client was Al Checchi, who at the time was preparing a blockbuster bid to acquire Northwest Airlines. After his successful bid, Checchi offered Shugrue the job of president and CEO of Northwest. However, Shugrue, who likes living in the temperate climes of Houston with his family, turned down the job at Northwest's headquarters in Minneapolis because, he said, "I didn't feel like shoveling snow in Minnesota all year long."

As the summer of 1989 approached, I began to itch to get back into the rough-and-tumble atmosphere of the airline business. Although I liked my job at MasterCard, the organization had the lethargic characteristics of a bank, which is understandable since MasterCard is actually a not-for-profit association owned by the banks that issue the association's credit cards. At about the same time, Shugrue was finishing up his consulting work for Checchi on the Northwest deal and was looking for something else to do himself.

In early June I contacted Shugrue and told him of the business plan that I had put together for a bid to acquire struggling Hawaiian Airlines. I asked him if he was interested in mounting a bid, and he agreed to review the business plan and make a decision within a couple of days.

Having already made up my mind to proceed with finding investors for the deal, come hell or high water, I immediately tendered my resignation from MasterCard and began putting together a deal team. In addition to myself and Shugrue, who soon accepted, the team included Richard ("Dick") Allen, a former senior Continental operations executive who is now an executive at Ogden-Allied, and another senior executive from Continental who still works there.

Hawaiian was owned by its seventy-year-old patriarch, John H. Magoon, Jr. The airline suffered heavy losses primarily because it had an outdated fleet of Lockheed L-1011 wide-body aircraft, which it used to compete against the major carriers flying between various points on the U.S. mainland and Honolulu. Flights from the mainland U.S. to Hawaii are unprofitable for just about all airlines because the fares, almost all leisure-driven, are too low for the large amount of distance traveled (for example, it's almost five thousand miles from Chicago to Honolulu). The major airlines offer service to Hawaii primarily to add value to their frequent-flyer programs as an award destination. Hawaii is an attractive "loss leader" in the airline business.

Hawaiian's problem was that its cost structure mandated that it had to make money flying from the mainland U.S. to Honolulu, the only airline in the market that faced such economic necessity. Thus, everytime a new low-fare vacation package deal to Hawaii surfaced, Hawaiian saw its revenues plummet without any corresponding decrease in costs. The result was financial chaos.

The business plan that I put together for our proposed acquisition called for scrapping the L-1011s, getting out of the mainland U.S. market altogether and focusing on Hawaiian's bread-and-butter interisland routes as well as some special routes from Hawaii to the South Pacific. I labeled this strategy "retrench and harvest," which meant that we would refocus the airline on its base business and reap the advantages from doing so. Aloha Airlines, Hawaiian's only other interisland competitor, was solidly profitable because it stayed away from the mainland U.S. markets.

Magoon, Hawaiian's owner, was offered earlier in the year $45 per share in cash by a unit of PacifiCorp, a utility based in Portland, Oregon. Incredibly, Magoon spurned this exceedingly rich offer and, in an article in *Forbes* magazine, steadfastly claimed, "I'm holding out for fifty dollars a share."

We spent the entire summer putting together financing for our bid and were ready to submit a fully financed offer of $25 per share when we read in the newspaper one day that Magoon had signed a deal with Peter Ueberroth and Thomas Talbot at $22 per share. Ueberroth and Talbot, having come so close with Eastern just months before, finally succeeded in getting an airline. However, unfortunately for both them and their investors, Hawaiian is now in worse shape than it ever was under Magoon.

Instead of refocusing and downsizing the business, Talbot, as president, continued to compete in the mainland U.S. market and proceeded to get stomped by the mega carriers. Hawaiian lost $115 million in 1990 and suffered similar losses in 1991. It was many times on the verge of liquidation as its primary lender, Security Pacific, threatened to close off all of its credit lines. Furthermore, as if to add insult to injury, in early 1991 a popular television show did a story on

Hawaiian alleging that the carrier's maintenance practices were among the worst in the airline industry. Although Northwest injected some capital into the company in early 1991 in return for some key Hawaii-to-Australia routes, Hawaiian will probably ultimately go the way of Eastern, Midway and Pan Am.

After the Hawaiian deal, in the early fall of 1989, Shugrue received another telephone call from Frank Lorenzo, who at the time was battling with the Eastern creditors over various reorganization proposals. Lorenzo told Shugrue that the Texas Air board of directors had ordered a consulting study on the feasibility of merging Continental and Eastern. Lorenzo wanted Shugrue to undertake the study because Shugrue had been president of Continental and had done due diligence on Eastern for Ueberroth and therefore knew both airlines extremely well. Shugrue, who was paid $100,000 for the sixty-day project, accepted and asked me to join the effort. My fee was $20,000 plus expenses. We began the last week of September 1989 under orders to have a finished product by Thanksgiving, which would then be presented to Lorenzo and the Texas Air board during their early December board meeting scheduled to be held at the Ritz-Carlton Hotel in Naples, Florida.

Lorenzo chose Shugrue for another, more important reason than his knowledge of the operations of both airlines. If word had gotten out during that time that Lorenzo was seriously looking at merging Eastern and Continental, Lorenzo would have been placed in a very uncomfortable position. First, the Eastern creditors, upon discovering the plan, would have immediately upped the ante in terms of the compensation they were willing to take from an Eastern reorganization plan. After all, a merged Eastern and Continental would have been worth much more than just Eastern by itself. Second, and perhaps more important, Lorenzo would have faced serious problems with the "single carrier" case that was then pending before the National Mediation Board. The Eastern unions claimed that Lorenzo and Texas Air were managing Eastern and Continental as a "single carrier." If that was actually the case, then the Eastern unions would have had the right to hold elections at Continental with a view to representing both Continental and Eastern employees. Obviously, that would have meant the end of the low-cost, nonunion Texas Air empire. Any talk of a potential merger of the two carriers would have given the NMB a "smoking gun" with which potentially to rule in the unions' favor. At least that was the fear of Texas Air's general counsel, Charles T. Goolsbee.

Lorenzo felt more comfortable having Shugrue perform the merger study, rather than a consulting firm, primarily because of the necessity to maintain top confidentiality.

The study was given the secret code name Project Red to maximize confidentiality. The project team, consisting of four people, leased its own suite of offices several floors above those of Texas Air's in a downtown Houston skyscraper. Lorenzo wanted the team to operate independently of the influences of Continental, Eastern or Texas Air but not be too far away from the nerve center of the Texas Air empire.

In addition to Shugrue and myself, the Project Red team consisted of a handful of functional experts. John B. Adams, a senior vice president of Texas Air and Lorenzo's chief labor strategist, engineered Texas Air's labor strategy at Eastern after the takeover. Adams, though vilified by the Eastern unions for his actions in dealing with them, was a cool-headed and reasonable guy who stuck to his guns. Unfortunately, Adams had received so many death threats due to his work at Eastern that he moved his family out West and commuted to Texas Air's headquarters in Houston. The other full-time team member was Steven Westberg, a director of finance at Texas Air. Westberg's finance and control background was instrumental in valuing the cost advantages to a merger of the two airlines. Involved on a limited basis was Gregory D. Aretakis, a vice president of planning at Continental who is an excellent market planner and scheduler; James M. Stevens, a Continental marketing vice president who brought some overall financial and marketing strategy to the project discussions; and Clark H. Onstad, Texas Air's regulatory and legislative vice president in Washington. Although Shugrue, as project leader, reported directly to Lorenzo, general management oversight of the project team was provided by both Goolsbee, Texas Air's general counsel, and Robert D. Snedeker, Texas Air's chief financial officer. Knowledge of the project was strictly limited to these individuals.

Since I was the only member of the Project Red team who did not live in Houston, for the full sixty days of the project I lived in the Doubletree Hotel in downtown Houston, which was connected to the building where our offices were located. Because Lorenzo wanted to maintain top secrecy about our activities, I was not allowed to request travel passes on Continental, which required going through the Continental and/or Texas Air administrative infrastructure. So each weekend when I commuted back to my home in New York, I purchased a regular ticket on Pan Am and flew into JFK, although LaGuardia is much closer to the city.

After the first month, when I submitted my expense vouchers, Lorenzo saw how expensive it was for me to buy full coach tickets on Pan Am and he blew his stack. One day he came storming up to our offices, with my expense report in hand, and marched right into Shugrue's office. I could hear Lorenzo through the wall screaming at Shugrue, "Tell Robinson to keep his expenses down." Lorenzo, whom Shugrue called the King of the Universe, though never within earshot, then stormed out but smiled and said hello to me before he left. Afterward, Shugrue sauntered into my office and, with his trademark smirk, said, "Robinson, keep your fucking expenses down." Amazingly, that very day I received travel pass clearance on Continental.

My primary job on the project was to devise a computer model that would estimate the revenue benefits, or synergies, that would result from a merger of Continental and Eastern. I was also responsible for the overall writing and coordination of the final product. We finished just before Thanksgiving 1989, and the results were very well received by both Lorenzo and the Texas Air board of directors.

Our job was not to recommend a specific course of action but, rather, to identify the costs and benefits of a merger were one to occur as well as outline how a merger could be implemented. We found that a merger would result in approximately $1.6 billion in additional annual revenue synergies to the merged carrier over a five-year period. Furthermore, after spending $350 million in one-time merger-related integration costs, Texas Air would reap almost $500 million over five years in cost savings from a merger. In short, a merger of Continental and Eastern would put Texas Air on solid financial and market footing with benefits to the tune of almost $2 billion annually.

We wrote, "Our analysis shows that operating one large airline system is more advantageous to Texas Air than the present method of operating two separate and distinct airline systems. In fact, there are very substantial benefits available to a merged company." However, we also warned that "significant contingencies impacting Texas Air's ability to achieve the potential merger-related revenue and cost benefits identified in the study are, among others, the bankruptcy proceedings of Eastern, proposed legislative initiatives adverse to Texas Air and its subsidiaries, potential adverse legal decisions in several major ongoing legal cases, and, perhaps most importantly, improper merger planning and implementation resulting in employee disharmony, operational discontinuities and marketing mishaps, all resulting in Texas Air not being able to offer a competitive post-merger product."

Both Lorenzo and the Texas Air board of directors, after reviewing our analysis, decided that a merger made all the sense in the world and was the preferred course of action to take. However, before Eastern could be merged with Continental, it had to be under Texas Air's sole control. This, in turn, wouldn't happen unless and until the Eastern creditors had agreed to a plan of reorganization that was ultimately approved by Judge Lifland. Unfortunately for Lorenzo, as he entered 1990, it was becoming more and more difficult for him to reach an agreement with Eastern's creditors as to the structure of a reorganization plan.

As 1990 progressed and the likelihood of a consensual deal with the creditors all but evaporated, Lorenzo formally dropped the idea of a merger of Continental and Eastern. Instead, he hoped that he would be able to make a deal with the creditors that allowed him to take Eastern's best assets: Atlanta hub, Airbus A-300 aircraft, LaGuardia and Washington-National slots, without the union employees.

After the completion of Project Red, Shugrue and I formed an airline consulting firm in which we analyzed various aviation opportunities for investors, mostly regarding smaller commuter airlines. One such project was our analysis of the viability of a Florida commuter operation based in Miami. Bar Harbor Airways, a commuter airline that was at the time jointly owned by both Continental and Eastern and which operated as Continental/Eastern Express, had a Miami operation that did not fit into Continental's strategic plans and therefore was offered for sale by Continental. After we put together a business plan for an investor who was interested in acquiring the Florida operation, the investor at the last minute got cold feet and backed out of the deal. Nonetheless, the analysis we had done on Bar Harbor's Florida routes would come in very handy in a couple of months.

Throughout the early spring of 1990, Shugrue was becoming impatient with consulting and was looking to get back into the airline business. He said, "This consulting stuff is for wimps and eggheads. I'm best at running companies."

During the weekend of April 13, when the hearings on the creditors' motion for a trustee began, Shugrue was in New York. He had just been contacted by a group of very wealthy Japanese investors who wanted him to lead their effort in launching what would be a mammoth takeover of United Airlines. The investors were interested in United because of the carrier's Pacific Division, which it had acquired from Pan Am, as well as the substantial decrease in the price of the carrier's stock caused by the aborted union takeover attempt back in the fall of 1989. In the spring of 1990, United shares were relatively cheap and that, evidently, caught the eyes of the Japanese investors who had already lined up billions of dollars in financing to do the deal.

When in New York, Shugrue, a Republican, usually stays at the Union League Club on Park Avenue. The Union League was formed at the beginning of the Civil War in most northern cities and acted as an auxiliary of the Republican party. Its main goal was to provide local popular support for President Lincoln's political and military strategies during the war. This was important for the Union effort because, particularly in New York, antiwar and proslavery Democrats, or "Copperheads," had a strong following and wanted to use their base of support to force the Lincoln administration to recognize the legitimacy of the Confederacy and negotiate a settled peace. In recognition of its past, the main reading room of the Union League Club has oil portraits of every Republican president.

Shugrue called a strategy session at the Union League Club to discuss how to proceed with the Japanese-backed United effort. In addition to myself, lawyers representing the Japanese investors as well as the investors' U.S. financial advisers were present. Shugrue also enlisted his top confidant and adviser, the man whose advice is always consulted before Shugrue makes a major move, Berl Bernhard.

Bernhard, a rather laid-back and good-natured fellow, is chairman and a name partner of the influential Washington-based law firm of Verner, Liipfert, Bernhard, Mcpherson and Hand. A Phi Beta Kappa graduate of Dartmouth and then Yale Law School, Bernhard has spent many years in public service, first as the staff director of the U.S. Commission on Civil Rights, appointed by President Kennedy, then as a special consultant to Secretary of State Dean Rusk in the mid-1960s and, finally, as national manager of Maine Senator Edmund S. Muskie's unsuccessful 1972 presidential campaign. (To this day, Bernhard steadfastly maintains that Muskie didn't cry during the New Hampshire primary when it was reported that Muskie's wife had used obscene language while campaigning.) Bernhard, who lives in Annapolis, is also considered to be a world-class yachtsman, having won several Bermuda races. Bernhard and his law firm had represented Pan Am while Shugrue was vice chairman and had also represented Continental while Shugrue was president. Bernhard's already strong influence with Shugrue would become even more evident as the Eastern case progressed.

It was during the United strategy session at the Union League Club that Shugrue became aware that things were starting to heat up down at the bankruptcy court hearing. It became apparent that Lifland was seriously considering appointing a trustee to run Eastern, and, in fact, Lifland had told Harold Jones, the U.S. Trustee, even before the hearing began to start looking for possible candidates.

Jones immediately thought of Shugrue as his choice for trustee for several reasons. First, Jones had been impressed with Shugrue's handling of the Ueberroth bid to buy Eastern just a year before. In fact, it was Shugrue who had actually negotiated the $1 billion concessions package with the Eastern unions as part of the Ueberroth takeover attempt. Second, Shugrue had done the Texas Air merger study of Continental and Eastern and therefore was very familiar with Eastern's situation. Third, it just so happened that Shugrue was one of the few former major airline CEOs, besides Acker and Corr, of course, who didn't have a full-time job running a major airline and was therefore available. Finally, and perhaps most important, since Shugrue had worked for Frank Lorenzo and got along well with him, Jones thought that the appointment of Shugrue would avoid any strenuous objections from Texas Air to the appointment of a trustee. On this last point, Jones was correct.

Shugrue was summoned down to the Custom House building,

where the bankruptcy court is located, to meet with Jones to discuss the possibility of his becoming trustee and, of course, Bernhard was by his side. After a brief meeting, Jones was convinced that Shugrue was the man for the job and told Shugrue to remain in New York because the trustee hearing could break open at any moment.

Events moved so fast and furiously that, within a matter of forty-eight hours, Lifland had ordered that Shugrue be appointed to run Eastern. During the days immediately preceding Shugrue's appointment, I was instructed by Shugrue to start putting together a business plan and acquisition model for the United deal. Before I could even get my computers set up to begin work, Shugrue had been appointed trustee. Obviously, that put an end to Shugrue's potential involvement with the United effort and the Japanese investors. After seeing their lead man in the U.S. dragged off to run another airline, the Japanese suddenly got cold feet and lost interest in the United deal entirely.

Steve Wolf, United's chairman, did not know how close he came to being taken over. The Japanese were fully financed and were resolute, until Shugrue's withdrawal, to consummate the acquisition. There would have been absolutely nothing United could have done to thwart the Japanese-backed bid.

On April 19, 1990, news of Shugrue's appointment as the trustee of Eastern flashed across the country. Eastern's final chapter had begun.

After satisfying all of the procedural requirements associated with becoming a bankruptcy trustee in the Eastern case, for example posting a $9 million performance bond, and negotiating his monthly draw of $35,000, Shugrue settled into a position truly unique in all of corporate America because the Eastern case was unlike any other bankruptcy.

Under the bankruptcy law, once a trustee is appointed in a Chapter 11 case, the existing board of directors and, therefore, management is completely ousted. Shugrue became a one-man chairman of the board, board of directors, president and chief executive officer. The other senior managers at Eastern, chief operating officer and below, thus served only at Shugrue's pleasure and could be removed by him at any time. As far as Eastern executives and employees were concerned, there was no doubt at all who the real boss was.

From a management reporting standpoint, as an officer of the court, Shugrue answered only to Judge Lifland. However, Shugrue was under an overall affirmative legal duty to administer the Eastern estate so as to maximize value for the airline's unsecured creditors. As such, Shugrue's job was politically sensitive because his official boss, the judge, had no legal or economic stake in the outcome of the case whereas the real stakeholders, the creditors, didn't have any official control over the trustee. Yet if Shugrue was going to get anything done at Eastern at all, it was paramount that he get the approval of the creditors, over whose objection Lifland would unlikely rule.

But the judge and the creditors weren't the only "masters" that Shugrue had to worry about pleasing. He also owed a legal duty to Texas Air and, therefore, Lorenzo. Although Eastern's Texas Air–dominated board of directors had been ousted by virtue of Shugrue's appointment, Texas Air still owned all of Eastern's common stock. As such, Texas Air was still an important stakeholder in the Eastern Chapter 11 proceedings. Maybe not as important as the unsecured creditors, who receive priority status in bankruptcy over shareholders, but important nonetheless.

In addition, the examiner in the case, because of the influence he had with Judge Lifland, was also a key player whom Shugrue had to coddle. David Shapiro, the Washington lawyer who had investigated the prepetition transactions, was able to convince Lifland to make him the court's special adviser in the Eastern case after filing his report. Why Lifland needed a special adviser is unclear. The Eastern case, though complex, already had hundreds of lawyers, investment bankers, consultants and accountants involved supposedly rendering "professional" advice to their clients. If Lifland, as the federal bankruptcy judge hearing the case, wasn't supposed to have any interest in the case, then why did he need a special adviser? Perhaps Lifland felt that he needed someone to render objective advice in the face of obviously biased information being fed to him from all of the various parties.

Finally, Shugrue also had to be very concerned about the unions. The unions had to be dealt with on two separate bases. First, ALPA, IAM and the TWU were all among the largest unsecured creditors of the estate and therefore had representatives on the creditors' committee. If they didn't like something that the trustee was doing, they had the capacity to foment rebellion against the trustee within the committee, which would obviously make Shugrue's job that much more difficult. Also, as members of the creditors' committee, the unions had access to highly confidential financial and strategic information about Eastern's ongoing operations. That access would prove to be a useful weapon for the unions as they began publicly to call for Eastern's liquidation.

The other basis for Shugrue's concern about the unions stemmed from the realization that true labor peace would never really come to Eastern unless and until Shugrue negotiated a settlement with all three unions regarding the issue of permanent replacement workers and the rehiring of the strikers. Shugrue felt, correctly, that the traveling public would never really feel comfortable flying Eastern again until the labor animosity had been extinguished. According to Shugrue, "We need to have a picture of me and Charlie Bryan hugging on the front page of *The New York Times*."

The requirement that Shugrue balance the competing needs and parochial interests of all of these various interest groups, in addition to the highly public nature of the Eastern case, made his job, without a doubt, the most difficult in corporate America at the time.

However, before Shugrue could focus on dealing with these various stakeholder issues, he first had to stabilize the quickly deteriorating condition then existing within Eastern's executive ranks and management structure.

Luckily, when Lifland approved Shugrue's appointment as trustee he also approved the request for Eastern to withdraw $80 million from the special escrow account. Otherwise, Eastern would have run out of cash and been forced to close down within seventy-two hours of Shugrue taking over. With an $80 million nest egg to start off with, Shugrue could focus his attention for the first several days on fixing the serious problems existing on the ninth floor of Building 16 at the Miami International Airport, Eastern's senior executive suite.

Upon Shugrue's arrival at Building 16 the day after he was appointed, it was obvious that Eastern was on the verge of complete and total collapse. The executives as well as all twenty thousand rank-and-file employees were completely demoralized and disillusioned. After all, they were experiencing a long and bitter IAM strike coupled with continued agitation by ALPA and the TWU. On top of that, a federal criminal grand jury in New York was in the process of investigating Eastern and several employees, including a vice president, for faulty maintenance practices. Everyone knew that an indictment was imminent. What wasn't known for sure was who would be indicted, how far up the chain of command the indictments would go and how far-reaching the charges would actually be. In a business built on consumer confidence, such as an airline, it is exceedingly difficult to maintain such confidence when you are about to be indicted for faulty maintenance practices. Also, Eastern at this time was losing over $1 million per day with absolutely no strategic or financial plan to stem the losses. All of these major problems, any one of which could easily have brought down mightier corporations than Eastern, when combined with the daily barrage of bad press about the struggling carrier, resulted in a siege mentality encompassing the ninth floor of Building 16.

Shugrue's most immediate task was to clean the ninth floor of deadwood, those senior executives either whose presence would be continually disruptive to the reorganization process or who did not add much, if any, value to Eastern's ongoing operations. The first one on the chop list, and the easiest decision to make, was Phil Bakes, Eastern's president and CEO.

From the moment Shugrue was appointed trustee, and therefore assumed the titles of president and CEO, Bakes was no longer needed. More importantly, Shugrue wanted to send a message to everyone, both inside Eastern and out, that he was completely in charge and was wiping away any ties to the old Texas Air–dominated regime at Eastern. This immediately earned Shugrue points with Eastern's unions, who had always looked upon Bakes as a Lorenzo clone anyway. Bakes himself agreed that he had to go, though he had done a credible job just keeping Eastern intact during the strike. Shugrue walked into Bakes's office and announced that a change had to be made. "I completely understand, Marty," said Bakes. "In order for you to be successful, you have to nuke any references or ties to the old TAC (Texas Air Corporation) establishment." Shugrue agreed, thanked Bakes for his understanding and immediately showed him the door. Shugrue then took over Bakes's office, Borman's old office and the only one on the ninth floor with a private bathroom.

The next decision that had to be made was what to do with Joseph B. Leonard, Eastern's executive vice president and chief operating officer. This one was tricky. On the one hand Leonard, now a senior executive at Northwest, is an excellent operations manager who worked his way up through Eastern's maintenance organization and therefore had his finger on the pulse of Eastern's operational infrastructure. Shugrue, who had just arrived in town, needed a tough operations manager to keep him informed of what was going on inside the belly of the beast. On the other hand, it was on Leonard's watch that the destructive and explosive criminal maintenance practices occurred. Should Shugrue send a message to the U.S. Attorney in Brooklyn who was investigating the charges that he, Shugrue, was cleaning the maintenance side of the house by firing Leonard? Shugrue's gut reaction was that he should probably let Leonard go. However, upon further reflection, Shugrue decided to keep Leonard on board since, at that point, the indictment had not yet been issued. Furthermore, Shugrue needed Leonard's knowledge of the operation, at least until he could hire someone else with similar operational experience and strengths.

Within just a matter of weeks, Shugrue would wonder whether he made the right decision about Leonard.

Todd G. Cole, an elderly southern gentleman and a former chairman of CIT Financial Corporation, was Eastern's vice chairman and could have been relieved without any effect on the organization whatsoever. However, Shugrue wanted to keep Cole around to function as a sort of "elder statesman" with the creditors and the outside constituencies with whom Eastern and Shugrue had to deal on a daily basis. Cole was excellent in this regard.

Eastern's senior vice president of human resources, Thomas J. Mathews, was another Lorenzo holdover who Shugrue felt had to go. Other than perhaps Frank Lorenzo, Charlie Bryan hated no man in America more than Tom Mathews. It was Mathews who dealt with the unions in general and the IAM, and Bryan, in particular. As long as Mathews remained at Eastern, Shugrue knew that Bryan wouldn't even sit down at the bargaining table. In Mathews's place, Shugrue named Alan C. Gibson, formerly Eastern's vice president of labor relations. Gibson, a lot less controversial than Mathews, actually had a good working relationship with all of the unions. Even Bryan said, after Gibson's appointment, "Shugrue seems to be making all the right moves so far."

Shugrue stopped with Bakes and Mathews in terms of chopping heads. However, it soon became apparent that the ax should have cut a little deeper on the ninth floor.

Barry P. Simon, Eastern's general counsel, was another Texas Air holdover who, while he had a house in Miami, still kept his family and main homestead in Houston. Although Simon had done an excellent job at Eastern, it was in Shugrue's best interest, particularly in such a sensitive position as chief legal counsel, to get someone in whom Shugrue had the utmost confidence and faith. Simon's attentions, if not allegiances, were always directed toward Houston and Texas Air. Berl Bernhard, Shugrue's chief adviser, sensed this from the very beginning and therefore had Shugrue name a young lawyer from Bernhard's law firm, John J. Sicilian, as deputy general counsel. Within a matter of weeks, it was clear that Sicilian was making the legal calls at Eastern, and Simon, who coveted returning to Houston anyway so that he could be with his family, soon accepted the job of general counsel at Continental, which is headquartered in Houston.

The strongest tie to Eastern's management past was David B. Kunstler, an old-line executive who was senior vice president of planning. Kunstler knew the airline industry extremely well but could never come to realize that a new way of thinking was required, new faces, new ideas, to bring Eastern back from the brink. Kunstler, who ruled his minions in the various departments he controlled with an iron fist, always seemed to object to and stand in the way of new ideas and radical strategies. Shugrue asked Kunstler to take early retirement in December 1990 just before Eastern shut down. Kunstler then became senior vice president for marketing and planning at Midway Airlines until that airline shut down in November 1991. Given the drastic change in course that Shugrue needed Eastern to take upon his taking over, it was felt that Kunstler's presence inhibited such activity. Nonetheless, Shugrue kept Kunstler on.

The other two executives on the ninth floor, Rolf S. Andresen, the chief financial officer, and George J. Brennan, who would soon be elevated to senior vice president of marketing by Shugrue, both played instrumental roles in the turnaround effort. Brennan, now in charge of marketing for Carnival Cruise Lines in Miami, was particularly astute, always developing creative marketing strategies. Andresen, a low-key guy but the perfect CEO for a company in as bad a shape as Eastern, was able to project to the day what the company's cash position would be up to forty-five days in advance. After Eastern he became the CFO at Pan Am, which shut down in December 1991.

The immediate result of the executive shuffling was a sense of renewed vigor throughout the workforce. The prevailing feeling among the employees was "somebody is actually doing something." Within the first seventy-two hours of Shugrue taking over, he had recharged the workforce and gotten them to focus on the possibilities of the future. Shugrue would say later, "That was perhaps the most important thing I could have done that first week."

However, such reshuffling of executives was only the beginning. Shugrue had a five-point plan for Eastern that, albeit difficult, seemed attainable at the time. First, Eastern's financial condition and cash drain had to be stabilized. A successful reorganization of the carrier would be impossible if it continued to lose more than $1 million per day. Although preferable, it was not imperative that Shugrue turn a perennial money loser like Eastern into a profit machine overnight. All that was required was that the order of magnitude of the cash losses be reduced to a manageable level. Second, labor peace had to be restored. The IAM was still on strike, and ALPA and the TWU, though not on strike, were agitating because they had been effectively locked out of the property by the permanent replacement workers. Shugrue knew that as long as Eastern's labor problems continued to be splashed across the front pages of newspapers across America, Eastern would never regain any stability in the marketplace. Third, the confidence of the American public had to be restored in the airline. Although related to the labor problems, the public's lack of confidence in Eastern also stemmed from the carrier's deep financial problems and the impending criminal indictment for maintenance violations. Fourth, Shugrue had to inject a sense of pride somehow into the totally demoralized workforce. Through strikes, bankruptcy, pending sales that ultimately fell through and moves toward liquidation, Eastern's employees had been through the emotional ringer, and as a result were completely demoralized. This, in turn, affected the quality of service Eastern personnel provided to customers. If the employees are upset, then the service they provide is bound to be less than acceptable, which, in turn, drives away customers. Shugrue had to figure out a way to make Eastern's besieged workforce feel good about itself. Fifth, and finally, if Shugrue was successful on the other points, he had to propose a plan of reorganization that would allow Eastern to pay back creditors as much as possible and to emerge from bankruptcy as a, hopefully, healthy airline with a future.

Though each of these five points, on their own, was a tall order to satisfy, Shugrue felt that he could do it with his common-sense management style and a bit of luck. The big problem was that each prong of the plan was interrelated with the others, which made strategy implementation that much more difficult. For example, Eastern's financial problems were directly caused by the labor unrest and the lack of public confidence in the carrier, which itself flowed from the low morale of the employees. One problem could not be solved without solving the others simultaneously. This would require a herculean effort by all those involved.

Figuring out what needed to be done was easy. The problem was how to do it and do it quickly enough to be effective. Although Eastern's remaining executives were competent in their various fields of expertise, Shugrue wanted them to concentrate on running the day-to-day operations of the airline. Their job was to ensure that what infrastructure remained at Eastern did not deteriorate any further. As for strategy, the "how" of what needed to be done, Shugrue, within a matter of a week after taking over, began assembling his own team of trusted advisers to assist him in putting together a strategic plan that would save Eastern. Amazingly, the effort was successful in the beginning, until the creditors' advisers began thinking that they knew more about corporate strategy and running an airline than Shugrue.

5

THIS PLACE NEEDS SERIOUS HELP

Shugrue's five-point strategic plan for Eastern was worthless without talented people to implement it. Unfortunately, Eastern's existing executives, by and large, were not capable of such work. An outside stimulus was required. Shugrue knew exactly the types of people he wanted to assist him and realized that immediate action was required. Shugrue observed dryly within a couple of days after his appointment: "This place needs serious help."

Shugrue is an incredibly instinctive type of manager. Although lacking in formal management education, Shugrue is an excellent reader of people and what it takes to motivate them. He is also very good at conceptualizing generally about the strategic direction a business should take. What makes Shugrue such a good leader is that he understands his weaknesses and then places great amounts of trust in those people to whom he has delegated authority in those specific areas. For example, Shugrue's strongest areas of functional expertise are in general corporate strategy, marketing and human resources management. As such, he usually manages those areas with constant oversight, prying into even the smallest details so as to familiarize himself with the operational aspects of those functional areas. On the other hand, in areas where he is not as strong, such as in financial and legal matters, he usually delegates full and complete authority to his advisers, while maintaining oversight and ultimate management responsibility himself.

The result was that Shugrue's ability to be successful at Eastern rested squarely on the abilities of the people he vested with responsibility in key areas of the corporation.

Near the end of the first two weeks of his tenure at Eastern, Shugrue invited his core group of advisers down to Miami to begin the process of implementing the five-point plan. When he first arrived in Miami, Shugrue stayed at the Colonnade Hotel in Coral Gables, about a ten-minute drive from Miami International Airport. The Colonnade, one of the finest hotels in Miami, also became the hotel of all of Shugrue's top lieutenants.

The night before all of the advisers were to begin their work at Eastern, Shugrue hosted an informal get-together for them in one of the Colonnade's fine restaurants. I had just arrived on an Eastern flight from New York and, by the time I checked into the Colonnade, the dinner had already begun.

At one end of a long table sat Shugrue with Berl Bernhard, his chief adviser, at his side. At Bernhard's suggestion, Shugrue had decided that Bernhard's law firm, Verner Liipfert in Washington, would function as the de facto legal department for Eastern as long as the trustee was in charge. Although Verner Liipfert stood to, and in fact did, reap millions of dollars in legal fees from this arrangement, the strategy actually made sense for two key reasons. First, when a company is in bankruptcy, legal issues always come to the fore. Shugrue needed a competent law firm to oversee the airline's legal work not only in bankruptcy-related issues but with corporate, securities, labor, regulatory and legislative issues as well. Verner Liipfert was ideally suited for this task because, unlike most law firms, its expertise was extremely high in all of these areas. Secondly, both Weil Gotshal and Eastern's general counsel, Barry Simon, had been selected by Lorenzo. Shugrue felt more comfortable knowing that his, and Eastern's, flanks were being guarded by lawyers he knew personally and had worked with before, and in whom he thus had the utmost confidence. Soon Harvey Miller and Bernhard would be engaged in open warfare to determine which law firm, Weil Gotshal or Verner Liipfert, would be the dominant decision maker and influence peddler with Shugrue.

In addition to Bernhard, three other lawyers from Verner Liipfert would play a large role at Eastern. The chief labor lawyer who would be in charge of negotiating agreements with the Eastern unions was Ronald B. Natalie. Natalie had negotiated collective bargaining agreements at Pan Am and other airlines and is considered to be one of the best airline labor lawyers in America. The chief corporate lawyer was Douglas M. Steenland. Steenland, now a senior lawyer at Northwest, would be responsible for overseeing Verner Liipfert's work on all Eastern matters within the law firm itself. Finally, John J. Sicilian, an associate formerly of the firm's Houston office, would actually be placed inside Eastern and act as deputy general counsel. Although formerly reporting to Eastern's general counsel Barry Simon, Sicilian really reported directly to the trustee, bypassing Simon altogether. It was largely because of this arrangement that Simon, within several weeks after Shugrue's arrival, resigned from Eastern and went to work for Continental in Houston. Sicilian would soon prove himself to be, next to Shugrue, the most vital individual in the organization.

On the public relations side, Shugrue chose Tom Conway of the Washington-based public relations consulting firm of Conway and Company. Conway's job was to oversee the Eastern public relations apparatus with a view to devising a public relations campaign that would, first and foremost, restore the confidence of the American public in Eastern.

From a marketing perspective, Shugrue brought in Jim O'Donnell, the former senior vice president of marketing at Continental with whom I had worked during my tenure there. O'Donnell, who had left Continental and started his own marketing consulting firm in Houston, was charged with revitalizing and refocusing all of Eastern's marketing efforts. Ever since the Texas Air acquisition back in 1986, Eastern's marketing had become stale and largely ineffective. Shugrue told O'Donnell to "break the mold" on new marketing ideas. And he did.

Even before arriving at the dinner that evening at the Colonnade Hotel, I knew what Shugrue wanted me to do. Basically, I was to be Eastern's chief strategist. First, Eastern had no strategic or business plan. I needed to come up with one that made sense very quickly. Second, I was to review all key operating and financing plans and decisions, and particularly the processes by which those plans and decisions were developed, to test for reasonableness. This function would put me directly at odds with several of Eastern's senior officers, most of whom were almost twice my age. Third, Shugrue felt that in order to reorganize Eastern successfully he first had to settle the prepetition transactions with Texas Air. I had to devise a plan to do that. Fourth, Eastern couldn't reorganize and emerge from bankruptcy without a plan of reorganization. I was in charge of structuring a plan that would then be presented to the creditors. Fifth, and finally, Shugrue just wanted me to keep an eye generally on what was going on, particularly in the executive suite on the ninth floor. Shugrue had little faith in the management abilities of several senior Eastern executives, and he didn't want to get "blindsided" by someone under him doing something totally stupid. I was to apply some management quality control to the executive engine that powered Eastern.

Taking on all of these responsibilities at one time in an inherently unstable environment such as the one at Eastern is a pretty tall order for any executive, let alone one who was just approaching his thirtieth birthday. However, I was excited about having a hand in resurrecting a once-proud American carrier and, in addition, I knew I could do the job.

My first day at Eastern, in early May 1990, started with me as a strategic management consultant to the trustee earning $10,000 per month plus expenses. From my first meeting that day with David Kunstler, Eastern's planning chief, I knew that the sparks would soon start to fly.

Shugrue called Kunstler into his office, where I was already seated, and told him that from now on I would be involved in every decision that Eastern's planning department, and therefore Kunstler, made. Pricing, scheduling, market planning, marketing, even fleet planning would be subject to my review. Kunstler, who still seemed to be somewhat in a daze over Bakes's firing, was completely unprepared for the working relationship he would have with his new "partner." Although Kunstler was polite about the whole affair, he would soon do everything in his power, albeit unsuccessfuly, to attempt to thwart my effectiveness.

Of the several tasks assigned to me by Shugrue, my first priority at Eastern was to work on a strategic plan for the airline as well as attempt to structure a settlement of the prepetition transactions. The prepetition transactions were very important to the entire reorganization effort. So important, in fact, that Shugrue kept asking me on a daily basis what type of progress was being made in reaching a settlement.

Texas Air had a very sour taste in its mouth regarding the Shapiro report that Eastern's creditors could possibly make a case valued at up to $400 million with respect to the prepetition transactions. The press, and Eastern's creditors, had incorrectly taken the report as prima facie evidence that Texas Air was guilty of some wrongdoing. The entire issue had been inflamed to the point where even mentioning the word "prepetition" to Texas Air officials would result in an immediately shortened conversation. Furthermore, Texas Air, and Lorenzo in particular, was still upset that Shugrue had even been appointed trustee in the first place. A company that they had controlled completely for four years was all of a sudden snatched away from them in one flashing moment. This was understandably a very difficult pill for Texas Air officials to swallow. It was into this type of emotional atmosphere that I was thrust to craft a settlement where all prior attempts to do so had failed.

After reading the examiner's report on the prepetition transactions, the one thing that jumped out at me as the best opening regarding a potential settlement was the issue regarding Bar Harbor Airways, the east coast commuter airline for which I had devised a business plan back in January 1990.

I felt, and Shugrue agreed, that in the environment that existed so soon after the trustee's appointment, any attempt to negotiate a complete settlement of all the prepetition transactions at once would be a waste of time. The best bet was to negotiate a settlement of a single issue, which had the least relationship to all the others, and then, after that first issue was successfully put to bed and the parties were shown that in fact a settlement was possible, negotiate a blanket settlement of all the remaining issues. Of all the prepetition issues, Bar Harbor was definitely the foot in the door. It was also the only deal in the history of the Eastern bankruptcy where Eastern actually purchased an asset rather than sold it. And the icing on the cake was that Eastern got paid to make the purchase.

Bar Harbor Airways, started in Maine back in 1943, was the oldest commuter airline in the United States. Bar Harbor absorbed Provincetown-Boston Airlines (PBA), itself a large commuter airline that operated in the Northeast and Florida, in 1987 and was itself later acquired by Texas Air.

Bar Harbor, like most commuter airlines, was valuable to its major airline partner because it funneled passengers from smaller communities to the major carrier's hub. In particular, Bar Harbor's route system provided value to Continental in the Northeast by feeding passengers to Continental's Newark hub and added value to Eastern in Florida by providing the same type of feeder traffic to Eastern's Miami hub.

When Texas Air used Continental to acquire Bar Harbor, it forced Eastern to render financial assistance in the transaction since Eastern would benefit from Bar Harbor's feeder traffic in Florida. Based on the agreement between the two carriers as to the amount of financial assistance rendered in conjunction with the acquisition, Continental ended up owning 59 percent of the stock of Bar Harbor and Eastern owned the remaining 41 percent.

Although Bar Harbor provided a lot of feeder traffic to both Continental and Eastern, Bar Harbor itself was unprofitable. This was due primarily to the division of revenues between Bar Harbor on the one hand and Continental and Eastern on the other. This "prorate" agreement, as is the case with most commuter and major airline partnerships, was structured not so much to make the commuter airline profitable as much as it was intended to avoid diminishing the amount of revenue that would flow to the major carrier.

Under many prorate agreements between a commuter and a major airline, a "straight-rate" formula is used to apportion revenue. Because the commuter airline always ends up flying a connecting passenger a much shorter distance than the major airline, the commuter usually ends up with a miniscule amount of the total ticket price.

Say a passenger purchased a ticket from New York to Key West, Florida, on Eastern and paid $179 one way. The traveler flew an Eastern jet from New York to Miami and then connected in Miami with a Bar Harbor turboprop, which operated as Eastern Express, to continue on to Key West. The total mileage traveled on this trip was 1,221 miles: 1,097 miles between New York and Miami and 124 miles from Miami to Key West. Since the straight-rate formula apportions revenues based on mileage traveled, it's easy to see which airline received the bulk of the ticket price. Under the formula, since Eastern carried the passenger roughly 90 percent of the total mileage traveled, Eastern got 90 percent of the ticket price, or $161. Bar Harbor, on the other hand, which carried the passenger only 10 percent of the total mileage traveled got the remaining 10 percent of the ticket price or roughly $18. This same example applied to Bar Harbor's routes in the Northeast that connected to Continental's hub in Newark.

The absurdity of this type of prorate arrangement lies in the fact that, because of much shorter distances traveled, the commuter's seat-mile costs are always at least twice those of the major airline. Yet the major carrier, under this type of arrangement, walks away with the bulk of the ticket revenue. Largely because of this phenomenon, most commuters today have negotiated different prorate agreements with their major airline partners than just merely "straight-rate."

With Continental's low fares to and from Newark and Eastern's even lower fares to and from Florida, it's easy to see why Bar Harbor lost money under the prorate formula it had with both Eastern and Continental. In fact, Bar Harbor lost so much money that Eastern and Continental had to make loans to Bar Harbor each month just to sustain the commuter's operations. From the time Bar Harbor was acquired by Texas Air until the Eastern Chapter 11 filing in March 1989, Bar Harbor had received $43 million in loans: $18 million from Continental and $25 million from Eastern.

Herein lies the source of the allegation by the examiner, Shapiro, that Eastern somehow got shortchanged on the Bar Harbor deal. Continental owned 59 percent of Bar Harbor's stock but made only 42 percent of the $43 million in loans, whereas Eastern, which owned 41 percent of the stock, made 58 percent of the total loans. If Eastern had made loans to Bar Harbor in proportion to its equity ownership interest in it, Eastern would have loaned only $18 million instead of the $25 million it actually disbursed.

Shapiro's finding that Eastern could assert a claim against Continental for up to $12 million arose from this discrepancy as well as the fact that most of Bar Harbor's operations, and therefore losses, were attributable to the Northeast routes into Newark, which provided absolutely no value to Eastern whatsoever. Eastern was, in fact, subsidizing Bar Harbor well in excess of what it would have otherwise done if Eastern were an "arm's-length" 41 percent shareholder. However, Eastern obviously had no choice in the matter because it was controlled by Texas Air, which wanted to minimize Continental's cash drain at the expense of Eastern.

Although Texas Air officials publicly denounced all of the examiner's findings and did everything possible to distance themselves from the report, privately they realized that some of the prepetition transactions, such as those involving Bar Harbor, were obviously unfair to Eastern. A very senior Continental executive later told me, "Of all the prepetition transactions, your strongest case was Bar Harbor."

Once the strike hit and Eastern filed Chapter 11 in March 1989, Bar Harbor's routes were substantially curtailed in Florida because Eastern's hub in Miami was no longer as large as it was prior to the strike. Also, since the beginning of Eastern's bankruptcy, Continental had taken over funding all of Bar Harbor's losses because Eastern was prevented from making additional loans while in bankruptcy. Continental pumped an additional $40 million into Bar Harbor just in the fourteen months from March 1989 to May 1990. Continental, suffering from cash problems of its own, decided that it could no longer afford such high levels of funding and thus decided, in early May 1990, to completely dismantle Bar Harbor's remaining Florida operations.

This appeared to be the opening that was needed to somehow structure a settlement of the entire Bar Harbor issue, which would hopefully pave the way for a settlement of all the remaining prepetition transactions. By taking advantage of Continental's planned restructuring of Bar Harbor's Florida operation, it was thought that a way could be found to restructure the entire company as part of a settlement. After reviewing the plan with Shugrue, he gave me the green light to proceed.

Neal F. Meehan, president of Continental's commuter airline division (Continental Express), was formerly president of Chicago Airlines as well as president of Midway Airlines. While at Texas Air he did a great job in the late 1980s consolidating all of Texas Air's commuters. Earlier in 1990, Shugrue and I had negotiated a deal with Meehan to purchase the Florida operations of Bar Harbor as a standalone entity. Although the deal ultimately fell through, I was intimately familiar with the operations and financial structure of Bar Harbor because I had performed all of the due diligence and devised a business plan for Bar Harbor that allowed the commuter to survive in Florida without the support of a large airline hub, since Eastern's Miami hub by that time had been dismantled.

In early May 1990 I called Meehan, who is always interested in negotiating a deal, and suggested that we get together immediately to discuss the situation. Because Continental had already announced that they were shutting down Bar Harbor's Florida operation completely on June 10, 1990, only thirty days away, time was of the essence. I immediately flew to Houston and, within a matter of hours, reached an agreement with Meehan on the type of deal structure that would be involved.

The deal called for Bar Harbor's operations to be divided into two distinct parts: the Northeast operations that supported Continental and the Florida operations that supported Eastern. Because an airline needs various licenses to be able to fly and these licenses are issued by the Department of Transportation (DOT) and the Federal Aviation Administration (FAA), it was paramount that Eastern acquire Bar Harbor as a corporate entity since the DOT and FAA licenses would then be naturally included in the deal. Continental would sell its 59 percent equity stake in Bar Harbor to Eastern, which would then own substantially all of Bar Harbor's stock. Bar Harbor would retain its Florida operations and assets but sell its Northeast operations and assets to Continental. As payment for these asset transfers, both Continental and Eastern would classify the almost $90 million in loans that they both made to Bar Harbor as an equity contribution, thus wiping that debt from the company's balance sheet.

After the transaction was completed, Eastern would own substantially all of Bar Harbor's stock and Bar Harbor would be an exclusively Florida commuter with almost no debt. Continental would own all of Bar Harbor's Northeast assets, which would be acquired by a Continental commuter subsidiary called Britt Airways. In addition, and this was the kicker, Continental would pay Eastern an amount to be determined in cash as an "inducement fee" to consummate the transaction. It would be, to my knowledge, the first transaction in aviation history where the seller (Continental) paid the buyer (Eastern) cash to buy the airline.

On my way back from Houston and the meeting with Meehan, I began to think through the required next steps. We had to conduct a full due diligence review of the airline's operations and finances, reach an agreement with Meehan on the size of the inducement fee that Continental would pay to Eastern, negotiate a definitive agreement, obtain the support of Eastern's creditors for the deal, get bankruptcy court approval for the transaction and then finally close the deal. Also, during all of this, we had to build an infrastructure which would operate the routes that we were acquiring. However, the first step was to devise a business plan that would convince Eastern's senior executives, as well as Shugrue, that we should go forward with the deal in the first place.

From the very beginning, Eastern's planning chief, Kunstler, was dead set against the idea of Eastern acquiring a commuter airline in Florida when Eastern no longer had a hub in Miami. Joe Leonard, Eastern's chief operating officer, felt the same way. In all fairness to both of them, their view was, and still is, the conventional wisdom.

Just about every commuter airline success story since deregulation has involved a commuter feeding passengers to an established hub of a major airline. Without the major carrier's hub, it is generally believed, the commuter will not be able to generate sufficient traffic to be viable. Kunstler, Leonard and just about every other airline "expert" both within and outside of Eastern felt that this was the only way a commuter carrier could be successful. However, those who subscribe to this view lack understanding in two key areas: (1) they don't appreciate past successes in the industry, and (2) they fail to understand the underlying strategic drivers behind success in the commuter airline business.

PBA, an airline that most people who live on the East Coast still remember, grew to be a profitable commuter airline with over $100 million in annual revenues without a feeder arrangement with a major carrier. PBA's early success, the airline was ultimately sold due largely to safety problems, proved that a commuter need not exist solely as a feeder to be successful.

The other key reason why Bar Harbor could be successful as a nonfeeder commuter airline in Florida stemmed from the demographic and geographic characteristics of the Florida market, the real determinants of profitability for any commuter airline.

Commuter airlines compete more against the automobile and other forms of surface transportation than they do against other airlines. The relatively short distances that commuters fly, usually under 250 miles on average, make it difficult to convince travelers to get out of their cars and into a turboprop aircraft, which most people feel is inferior to a jet anyway.

Florida is unique in that it is a very long state with many large and growing population centers. For example, it is 950 miles from Tallahassee, the state capital, to Key West, which is similar to the distance between Boston, Massachusetts, and Savannah, Georgia. Also, the 1990 census found that of the twenty fastest growing metropolitan areas in the U.S., several were located in Florida. Finally, even though many key Florida cities are within 250 miles of each other, the extremely large number of tourist and other surface vehicles in Florida have so clogged the state's highways that drives which would normally take only a couple of hours are routinely turned into day-long nightmares. Anyone who has spent almost six hours driving the 124 miles from Miami to Key West on U.S. Route 1 can attest to this fact.

For all of these reasons, in addition to the fact that no existing airline at the time focused on serving the needs of the local Florida business traveler, our analysis showed that Bar Harbor could be viable if it was organized with the needs of the local traveler in mind. However, I first had to convince Eastern senior management that this was in fact the case.

The business plan for Bar Harbor, after taking into account start-up losses associated with the new venture, showed that Eastern needed roughly $1.5 million out of the deal to break even, assuming it decided to operate Bar Harbor as a going concern and not just liquidate the commuter after buying it. During several meetings with Kunstler and his direct reports, who had performed an analysis that attempted to prove me wrong, the real issue came down to the question of what were the advantages of the deal to the Eastern estate.

Assuming Continental agreed to pay Eastern an inducement fee of at least $1.5 million, the benefits of the deal to Eastern were substantial even if Bar Harbor proved not to be viable as a going concern. First, a final settlement of one of the prepetition transactions would be accomplished. The first such settlement to be reached that would then open the door for the rest of the issues to be settled. Second, Eastern would get hard cash out of the deal. Third, Eastern would be freed from having to assume many of Bar Harbor's liabilities if in fact the commuter were liquidated, which Continental was planning to do within weeks. Finally, having Bar Harbor's aircraft flying around Florida and the Bahamas in Eastern's livery would provide additional marketing synergy to Eastern. Florida business travelers who flew

Bar Harbor from, say, Tampa to Ft. Lauderdale would more likely fly Eastern on their next long-distance flight because of frequent-flyer benefits.

Although agreeing with all of the points in support of the deal, Shugrue focused on the amount of cash Eastern would get and the settlement of one of the prepetition transactions. Even Kunstler finally had to come around and agree that the deal made sense if Eastern got sufficient cash from Continental.

Another reason to do the deal was that by buying Bar Harbor, Eastern would be saving the jobs of over 250 Bar Harbor employees in Florida and the Bahamas. I was concerned that nobody other than Shugrue focused on this as a rationale to at least favorably review the transaction.

After receiving internal Eastern approval to negotiate an agreement with Continental, and after completing due diligence that included chartering a Cessna 402 and flying to all of Bar Harbor's Bahamas locations to inspect personally the operations and equipment located there, I put together a negotiation team that would go to Houston and attempt to strike a deal with Continental.

Eastern's bankruptcy law firm, Weil Gotshal, had at first tried to muscle in on the deal by claiming that any negotiations with Continental had to involve them. I did not want to use Weil Gotshal at all. My strong preference was to use lawyers from Verner Liipfert as I thought they were stronger corporate lawyers than Weil Gotshal, and they had already assisted with most of the legal due diligence on Bar Harbor anyway. Two young Verner Liipfert associates, J. Richard Hammett in Houston and Gene R. Schleppenbach in Washington, had already basically structured the deal. It would have been counterproductive and a waste of time to try and reeducate attorneys from Weil Gotshal as to the details of the deal structure. Time was a convenience we didn't have. Continental told us we had until June 3 to negotiate a transaction and we weren't able to begin discussions until the last week of May.

Shugrue's position on the issue was that although he preferred to use Verner Liipfert for the same reasons that I did, he didn't want to do anything that would distance himself from Weil Gotshal so early into his tenure at Eastern. Weil Gotshal still had tremendous influence with Judge Lifland, the U.S. Trustee Harold Jones and the examiner David Shapiro, the key power players in the Eastern bankruptcy. One negative whisper from Harvey Miller of Weil Gotshal into Shapiro's or Lifland's ear would likely have nixed the Bar Harbor deal before it even had a chance to get off the ground.

So, under direction from Shugrue, I began immediately to coordinate with Weil Gotshal and Verner Liipfert a dual role for the two firms to play in structuring the Bar Harbor transaction. By doing so, we unnecessarily doubled the total costs to the Eastern estate in terms of legal fees but, from a political perspective, Shugrue felt it was a necessity to get the deal done.

To assist in the negotiations, I enlisted the help of an Eastern in-house lawyer, Roland S. Moore. Moore, always a jovial and soft-spoken fellow, had been at Eastern for many years and seemed to know more about what was going on at the place than anybody else. We were comfortable with Moore because he was one of the few people in a position of authority at Eastern who John Sicilian, the former Verner Liipfert lawyer who was now running Eastern's legal department, and I felt would not try to sabotage the deal from within.

One day in late May, Moore and I flew from Miami to Houston to meet with Verner Liipfert lawyers Hammett and Schleppenbach to discuss strategy before beginning negotiations with Continental the next day. That evening, we were shocked to learn that Bernhard had decided suddenly that Verner Liipfert could not be involved in the Bar Harbor transaction at all because Bar Harbor was a prepetition issue that would pose a serious conflict of interest for the law firm if in fact it did get involved. Prior to Eastern's bankruptcy, Verner Liipfert had done work for Continental and Texas Air, and as such it was allowed to represent the Eastern trustee only on the condition that it would not work on any prepetition matters. Well, Bar Harbor was definitely a prepetition matter, which basically disqualified Verner Liipfert from participating. "Why didn't they tell me this two weeks ago?" I complained to Shugrue during a middle-of-the-night telephone call. Shugrue, who stated that he didn't "have a fucking clue," nonetheless said, "What is done is done" and ordered us to bring Weil Gotshal into the deal as lead counsel.

The next morning Moore and I walked into the Houston offices of Weil Gotshal, which happened to be directly across the street from Verner Liipfert's Houston offices, and met with Deryck Palmer and several other Weil Gotshal attorneys. We were sitting in the conference room that had already been set up for the meeting with Continental officials, which was to begin within the hour, when we were hit with an even bigger bombshell.

First, Texas Air's general counsel, Charlie Goolsbee, called and said that he was not going to allow Continental executives to come over and negotiate unless and until Weil Gotshal recused itself entirely from representing Eastern in the matter. Goolsbee's concern was that since Weil Gotshal had, up until April 19, represented Eastern on behalf of Texas Air, it could not now turn and represent Eastern against Texas Air.

This was a very valid point. I immediately said to Palmer, "You guys had to be aware of this potential conflict, why didn't you mention it to me sooner?" Without responding, Palmer and the other Weil Gotshal attorneys ran down the hall to have a conference call with Bruce Zirinsky, the lead Weil Gotshal lawyer in New York on the Eastern case. After about an hour of waiting, we were finally told by Palmer that Weil Gotshal was recusing itself from the matter not because of Goolsbee's accusations but because, since Bar Harbor was a prepetition matter, the "appearance of impropriety would be too strong to ignore."

Moore and I were shocked. Here we were ready to negotiate a deal and our lawyers were telling us, out of the blue and at the last minute, that they weren't going to participate. By blaming its recusal on the fact that Bar Harbor was a prepetition matter, Weil Gotshal was able to avoid backing out of the deal for the more embarrassing reason that it had represented Texas Air on the same matter previously. Had the firm represented Eastern on the Bar Harbor deal, such representation might give the appearance that Weil Gotshal had put itself in a position possibly to use information garnered from such representation against Texas Air. Certainly someone at Weil Gotshal had to know that Texas Air would object to such activity. This episode made me wonder whether Miller and Zirinksy were adequately overseeing the Eastern case within Weil Gotshal.

At any rate, it was now past noontime and we were sitting in downtown Houston without counsel. After listening to a barrage of expletives from Shugrue about how we were getting screwed by Weil Gotshal, I asked him if he knew of any lawyers in Houston who could handle the job. He said he wanted to confer with Bernhard and would get back to us. About forty-five minutes later, Shugrue called us back at Weil Gotshal and said he had talked to a friend of his, Frank Calhoun, who was a partner at the large Houston law firm of Liddell, Sapp, Zivley, Hill and LaBoon. Calhoun assured Shugrue that his firm had the resources and expertise to represent Eastern in the Bar Harbor transaction.

After finishing the lunch that Weil Gotshal had so graciously prepared for us, we took our leave of the firm and trudged across Milam Street to the Texas Commerce Tower where Liddell Sapp was located.

Shugrue had called ahead to Calhoun to notify him that Moore and I were the trustee's appointed agents on the scene and therefore to render any assistance that we might deem appropriate. After an initial meeting with both Calhoun and the firm's managing partner, Bruce LaBoon, Calhoun began to assemble his team of lawyers who would work on the transaction. By now it was midafternoon, Continental was demanding that negotiations begin immediately, and the

Liddell Sapp attorneys, who hadn't even heard of Bar Harbor thirty minutes before, were now being asked to represent Eastern in what would certainly be a very complicated and contentious negotiation. Despite these difficulties, the Liddell Sapp attorneys rose to the occasion.

Although Calhoun was the senior partner responsible for the firm's new Eastern account, the key attorney on the deal was Gene G. Lewis, a Harvard Law School graduate and newly minted partner at the firm. He was assisted by Michael Ruttledge, a tax specialist, and H. William Swanstrom, a young corporate associate. After we described in as much detail as we could the general structure of the transaction, Lewis suggested since the day was almost over, we notify Continental that negotiations would begin the next morning. We readily agreed since the extra twelve hours or so would give Lewis and the rest of the Liddell Sapp team more time to review the several bound volumes of due diligence material on Bar Harbor that Verner Liipfert had prepared just weeks before.

Later that evening, reflecting on the day's extraordinary events in my room at the Doubletree in downtown Houston, I concluded that Weil Gotshal's activities had almost resulted in substantial harm to the Eastern estate. The Bar Harbor transaction, the only flicker of hope on the horizon to settle the prepetition issues with Texas Air, had almost completely disintegrated. In fact, Texas Air general counsel Goolsbee was ready to throw in the towel on the deal entirely after learning of Weil Gotshal's activities. At that moment, it was only my past working relationship with Goolsbee that kept him from recommending to Lorenzo and Ferguson that all negotiations end completely.

This episode confirmed the reservations Bernhard, Shugrue, Eastern lawyer Sicilian and I had about Weil Gotshal. From this moment on, we would keep a close eye on our trusted bankruptcy counsel.

Negotiations with Continental finally began on the Thursday before the Memorial Day holiday weekend. After an all-night session, with Ferguson of Continental and us reaching agreement fairly quickly on most issues, by midafternoon on Friday all points except one had basically been agreed to. The final issue was the amount of the cash inducement fee that Continental would pay to Eastern. I had earlier told Shugrue that Eastern needed at least $1.5 million for the deal to make sense. However, as part of our negotiating strategy, we continued to demand of Continental that Eastern needed at least $3 million to make the deal work. After going back and forth with Ferguson, we had definitely reached an impasse. Continental didn't want to pay more than $1 million and Eastern didn't want to accept anything less than $3 million.

Around two o'clock on Friday, after checking with Shugrue, we notified Ferguson that $3 million was Eastern's final offer and that this offer expired at five o'clock that same day, Houston time. I then left Moore and the Liddell Sapp attorneys at their offices and drove out to the Galleria area in Houston and took in a movie. Promptly at five o'clock, I called Ferguson from the movie theater to inquire of Texas Air's response and he responded, "We reject your offer." I then notified Moore and our counsel of that decision, drove out to Houston's Intercontinental Airport and boarded a Continental flight to Newark and then on to Martha's Vineyard, where I was to spend the holiday weekend at my family's home.

It appeared that our efforts to structure a deal had failed. Continental Express sent out notices that day to all their Florida employees saying that the deal had died and they would be terminated as of June 7 as originally planned. We were so close that we could taste a deal happening, but Ferguson was resolute in not wanting to pay more than just a token amount of $1 million in cash. His reason was straightforward.

Since this deal was the first of the prepetition transactions to be potentially settled, Texas Air did not want to establish a precedent in terms of the percentage of claim actually paid out in cash. Shapiro's report found that Eastern could assert a claim against Continental of upwards of $9 million with regard to Bar Harbor. If Texas Air had agreed to pay Eastern $3 million in cash, or 33 percent of the total amount Shapiro claimed could be recovered, then Eastern's creditors could have reasonably demanded at least 33 percent payment in cash on the remaining $400 million in prepetition claims, or roughly $130 million in cash. Since this was far and away more than what Lorenzo would pay now that he had been kicked out of Eastern, Ferguson was concerned that Lorenzo would blame him if the Eastern creditors pointed to the Bar Harbor settlement and demanded $130 million in cash as a settlement of all the remaining prepetition issues.

From the very beginning of the negotiations, I had realized this phenomenon was at work. Ferguson really didn't care about the operational aspects of Bar Harbor or of the transaction per se. His real concern was not paying an amount in cash as a percentage of claim that could come back and haunt him later on. Recognizing this from the beginning, we decided to stick to the $3 million number because we knew that even if Ferguson ultimately rejected it, as he did, we had one last ace up our sleeve that we could play to salvage the deal: Shugrue.

Early Saturday morning I called Shugrue from Martha's Vineyard at his home in Houston. After reviewing the situation with him, and the impasse regarding the inducement fee, he agreed to call Neal Meehan, the president of Continental Express, and propose the following. Instead of Continental paying a lump sum to Eastern of $3 million, Eastern would accept $1 million up front and the remaining $2 million over a period of four months. That way, Ferguson could save face with Lorenzo by saying he only paid a token amount of cash up front and Shugrue could support the deal in front of Eastern's creditors by saying he got fully twice what he originally expected to receive, albeit over a short period of time.

It was suggested that Shugrue call Meehan because Meehan was indebted to Shugrue from Shugrue's days at Continental, and it didn't hurt that the two men got along well. Shugrue asked him,

"Neal, why are you killing this deal?" Meehan, who was soon convinced of the reasonableness of the new offer, then presented it to Ferguson. The gambit worked. By using Meehan as a go-between, we were able to get Ferguson to agree to the new financial structure. My Memorial Day holiday turned out not to be ruined after all.

The following Tuesday, I was back in Houston with Roland Moore, Gene Lewis and the other Liddell Sapp lawyers. With the financial details of the deal already agreed to, all that was left was the wording of the definitive agreement. This proved, however, to be more difficult than originally envisioned. First, Ferguson and Continental demanded that we all meet in a small cramped conference room at Continental's headquarters, as opposed to the spacious facilities at Liddell Sapp. This strategy of getting the other guy on your own turf, one of the oldest tricks in the book, had been taken to its most illogical extreme we thought. At any rate, we acceded to Ferguson's demands and labored to put together a definitive agreement.

Having reached an agreement with Continental, and after eating at what was reported to be President Bush's favorite barbeque joint, our attentions then shifted to the Eastern creditors. They would have to approve any deal that we ultimately reached with Continental. In the beginning we weren't too concerned. After all, why wouldn't the creditors jump at a deal that would pay them $3 million over four months in addition to releasing the Eastern estate from over $62 million in liabilities relating to Bar Harbor? Any reasonable person would go for such a clearly attractive deal, or so we thought. We soon found out how wrong we were.

Joel Zweibel and Adam Harris, the lawyers for the creditors' committee who by this time had switched to the law firm of O'Melveny and Myers, acted as though they were on some type of ego trip. Perhaps it arose from their recent victory over Harvey Miller and Weil Gotshal during the trustee hearings. As the months progressed, it appeared that Zweibel and Harris felt that the trustee actually owed them something for his having been appointed in the first place. This, more than anything else in my view, was the basis of all the trouble that Zweibel and Harris caused for Shugrue and Eastern as the case progressed.

And it didn't take me long to figure this out. After just one discussion with Harris, whom Zweibel had appointed as the lead contact for the creditors on the Bar Harbor deal, I discovered that Harris, who had relatively little business experience, wanted to run the deal himself. "Who authorized you to negotiate with Continental without my approval?" he screamed when first notified of the negotiations that were still continuing at the time. "Why wasn't I involved in the negotiations from the beginning?" he continued.

I found Harris's manner very strange. First of all, Shugrue was under no obligation to notify the creditors about the Continental negotiations. Under bankruptcy law, the trustee is vested with the authority to manage the estate and look out for its best interests. Correctly, Shugrue had determined that receiving $3 million in cash was in the best interests of the Eastern estate, and therefore its creditors. Only upon the signing of a definitive agreement was Shugrue required to notify the creditors of his intentions. Furthermore, if we had allowed either Zweibel or Harris to get involved in the negotiations with Texas Air at the beginning, there would have been no deal at all given the already acrimonious relations between Texas Air and the creditors. There is no doubt that the involvement of Harris or Zweibel in the Bar Harbor negotiations would have ensured their complete and total failure. In fact, Texas Air officials probably wouldn't have even agreed to meet with them.

After listening to Harris's continued complaints about his lack of involvement in the deal, I told him that since an agreement with Texas Air was imminent, we would not allow him to get involved until the deal had been signed. However, once the deal was executed, we promised to sit down with him and the rest of the creditors' advisers and outline the deal in detail as well as present them with a business plan for Bar Harbor.

At this moment I realized that we had put ourselves between a rock and a hard place. The negotiations with Texas Air were coming down to the final, tense hours. I knew from speaking to Texas Air executives that they did not want to negotiate with Zweibel or Harris. If Harris had been allowed to stick his neck in the deal at that time, the entire transaction would have blown up, and with it the chance for Eastern, and its creditors, to get $3 million in cash from Texas Air. On the other hand, by locking Harris out of the deal, we risked having him go out of his way to make the entire process from here on out as difficult for us as possible.

We executed a definitive agreement with Texas Air and Continental for the Bar Harbor transaction on June 13, 1990. However, as in all bankruptcy cases, the deal was subject to approval by Eastern's bankruptcy court. This meant that we would have to get the creditors to go along because if they objected to the deal, it was extremely unlikely that Judge Lifland would approve it over their objection. We also had to be concerned about the examiner, Shapiro, who time and again had advised the judge to accept the positions advanced by the creditors. Although Shapiro had no economic interest in the case, his influence with Lifland was so strong that if the creditors convinced him to oppose the deal, then Lifland would almost certainly not approve it.

Liddell Sapp had done an outstanding job in documenting an agreement that everyone could agree on so quickly. I was so impressed with the work of their attorneys, particularly that of the young partner Gene Lewis, that I suggested to Shugrue that he retain Liddell Sapp as special counsel to see the Bar Harbor deal through to the end. Shugrue, similarly impressed with the firm's work, quickly agreed because Liddell Sapp also had bankruptcy expertise. Their bankruptcy expert, Douglas Little, had participated in the negotiations with Texas Air and was now familiar with the issues to be presented in court.

Little, and his counterpart in Liddell Sapp's New York office,

David Kittay, immediately began to draft the motion and schedule a court date for Lifland to consider it. However, before we could even get that far, Shugrue received a stinging telephone call from Zirinsky, the Weil Gotshal lawyer. Zirinsky claimed that it was inappropriate for Liddell Sapp to take the Bar Harbor deal to Lifland because Weil Gotshal was official bankruptcy counsel for Eastern. "Wait a minute," Shugrue asked in amazement. "Didn't you guys already beg off of this deal?" Zirinsky held firm. Weil Gotshal, as official bankruptcy counsel, should file the motion on behalf of Eastern.

Upon learning of this change in events, Moore and I were flabbergasted. Just two weeks before, Weil Gotshal had left us high and dry on the Bar Harbor deal, refusing even to represent us in negotiations because of a serious conflict of interest problem. Now, after Liddell Sapp had done all of the dirty work, Weil Gotshal wanted to come back into the deal and present it to the court, as if they had handled the transaction from the very beginning.

I asked Zirinsky what had happened to the serious conflict of interest that just a couple of weeks before had sent the firm scurrying for cover. He said that the conflict of interest had disappeared now that the agreement with Texas Air had been signed. Texas Air was now in the same sphere of interest with Eastern, both wanted to see the deal get court approval. As such, Weil Gotshal was no longer conflicted and could proceed with the deal (and incidentally generate another $500,000 in legal fees).

More importantly, though, this gave Weil Gotshal an opportunity to consolidate its position with the trustee and ensure its continued representation of the Eastern estate altogether. By this time, Shugrue was thinking seriously about firing Weil Gotshal. Their actions during the Bar Harbor deal had angered him. The primary factor keeping Shugrue from firing Weil Gotshal was Bernhard's contention that Harvey Miller's close relationship with Lifland was too valuable to lose. Shugrue's mounting discontent had evidently gotten back to Weil Gotshal, which realized that it better protect its flank on the Bar Harbor deal or lose the entire Eastern case to another firm, perhaps Liddell Sapp.

As usual, in the end Bernhard's view prevailed, which meant that Weil Gotshal would have some involvement in the Bar Harbor transaction. However, I was able to get assurances from Shugrue that Moore and I would be in charge of running the deal and that, furthermore, we would have a definite say as to the extent and type of Weil Gotshal's involvement.

This latter issue was crucial to the deal's ultimate success. Both John Sicilian and I felt that the best chance of getting the transaction approved was to have Liddell Sapp take charge of the legal work. Liddell Sapp had no history in the Texas Air–Eastern–creditors imbroglio and didn't "give a bunch of cow chips," as one Liddell Sapp attorney put it, what anybody thought of their strategies so long as their client's interests were advanced.

This was clearly the type of representation that we needed to get the deal approved. Thus, Liddell Sapp was given the green light to proceed with drafting the motion and filing it with the bankruptcy court. The firm would be the counsel of record on all matters regarding the Bar Harbor deal. Weil Gotshal's role, we determined, would be limited to assisting us in our discussions with the creditors when the time came for them to approve the deal.

Figuring that the longer the deal hung out there without court approval, the more chances everyone would have to take shots at it, we instructed Doug Little of Liddell Sapp to file the motion immediately and get a court date as soon as possible. The same day, Little notified me that we were able to get on Lifland's calendar for the last week of June, about two weeks away.

While all of the legal maneuverings proceeded apace, back at Eastern an organizational infrastructure had to be built to operate Bar Harbor if in fact the deal was ultimately approved. Unlike most stock purchases of companies, where the corporate infrastructure comes with the deal, in the case of Bar Harbor the dual ownership of the company by Continental and Eastern meant that only assets would come with the purchase. Eastern needed to build an infrastructure to manage the Bar Harbor assets it would soon be acquiring.

The most important concern in setting up the Bar Harbor infrastructure was Eastern's ongoing labor situation. Although ALPA had called off its strike, the union was still effectively locked out of Eastern pending a resolution of the permanent replacement issue. However, the ALPA contract was still intact and that contract had a "scope clause" in it. The scope clause allowed ALPA to represent the pilots of any wholly owned subsidiary of Eastern. If the Bar Harbor deal was approved, and if it was a wholly owned subsidiary of Eastern, ALPA would have a right to represent the Bar Harbor pilots. This would have meant the death knell for the new Bar Harbor. Bar Harbor as constituted at this time, before the restructuring, was nonunion and still needed over $90 million in subsidies from its parents, Continental and Eastern, to keep flying. Layering on top of that ALPA pay scales and their restrictive work rules would have literally killed the commuter before it even had a chance to get off the ground.

In structuring the deal, we were fortunate in the existing stock ownership of Bar Harbor. Bar Harbor had two classes of common stock, Class A and Class B. The Class A shares held all of the voting rights whereas the Class B shares had no votes at all. Under the agreement with Continental, Eastern would be acquiring all of the Class A shares but only 80 percent of the Class B, nonvoting, shares. The remaining Class B shares were held by some retired Bar Harbor pilots living in Maine. They held those shares by virtue of a distribution from a dissolved employee stock-ownership plan. We referred to these pilots as the "Maine Hermits" because nobody could locate them. Frankly, nobody tried terribly hard either, since their ownership of some of the shares of Bar Harbor prevented Eastern's ALPA scope clause from taking effect. Bar Harbor technically would not be a wholly owned subsidiary of Eastern and it could continue to be a nonunion airline.

Rick Hammett, one of the labor lawyers at Verner Liipfert who was assisting us at Eastern, also suggested that Bar Harbor's infrastructure needed to be established totally separate from that of Eastern. Although Eastern would end up owning 99.5 percent of the stock (Class A and Class B) of Bar Harbor, Bar Harbor had to be a separate airline to avoid any "single carrier" issues that could also result in Eastern's union agreements applying to Bar Harbor. Thus, I enlisted the assistance of Terry D. Reimer, a former Eastern maintenance vice president, to assist me with setting up the Bar Harbor organization. Reimer had left Eastern but recently returned as a consultant to help Eastern sort through its existing maintenance problems.

In setting up the Bar Harbor organization, Reimer and I faced a huge problem. In order for us to be ready to take over Bar Harbor's operations sometime in early August, we had to go all-out starting in early June to hire pilots, mechanics and other employees as well as recertify the airline with the FAA and address other key issues. Yet, until we knew that the creditors would support the deal, and the deal actually received bankruptcy court approval, we had to tell everyone that they were a provisional hire until those approvals had been obtained. Notwithstanding the difficulty in trying to hire competent people in such an uncertain environment, we were tremendously successful at attracting the types of quality people that were necessary to get the airline flying correctly.

We were faced with two choices. We could play it safe, not hire anyone and wait until we received all of the final approvals for the transaction. However, we would not have been able to close the deal and take over Bar Harbor's operations until well into late fall. As it turned out, by then the creditors were publicly calling for Eastern's liquidation and Continental would have probably backed out of the deal, and Eastern wouldn't have received any money at all. Or, we could take our chances, start building an organization and work feverishly to make sure that the transaction was approved and the deal closed before the end of summer. Over the objections of many senior

Eastern executives who wanted to play it safe, I recommended to Shugrue that we had to take the bull by the horns and ramp up the organization immediately, even though we had no assurances that the deal would ultimately be approved.

I had many sleepless nights from this day forward until the deal was finally approved. After all, had we not received court approval, we would have been the biggest laughing stocks in the aviation world for spending all of this time and effort hiring hundreds of employees and not have a company for them to work for. Notwithstanding the riskiness of the decision, and knowing that prudence counseled in favor of waiting, we decided that Eastern could not afford not to have this deal close, which necessitated that we pursue the more aggressive, yet riskier, course.

After leaving Reimer with the responsibility of overseeing the day-to-day details of building the Bar Harbor infrastructure, I concentrated on convincing the creditors and their advisers that the Bar Harbor deal made sense for Eastern. We knew that Adam Harris, the creditors' lawyer who had given us such a hard time from the start, would be the biggest problem. Although the deal was beneficial to Eastern on its face (how else were the creditors going to get $3 million in cash from an insolvent commuter airline that was otherwise going to be liquidated?), we knew and expected that there would be trouble from Harris and others.

The real problem was that the appointment of the trustee had suddenly and substantially altered the balance of power within the Eastern bankruptcy. From the beginning of the case until the appointment of the trustee, Lorenzo and Texas Air had exercised almost unfettered control over Eastern's operations, asset sales, strategic direction and proposed plans of reorganization. Throughout this period the creditors and their advisers were nothing more than passive reactors to Lorenzo's policies and proposals. However, Shugrue's appointment changed all of that. Not only had the creditors beaten Lorenzo and Texas Air in getting a trustee appointed in the first place, but they used their newfound power to begin to take a proactive role in the management of the airline. The creditors actually felt, albeit incorrectly, that Shugrue was at Eastern as their "employee" whom they controlled and to whom he reported.

Indeed, their advisers, especially the lawyers and investment bankers, felt that no deal could happen at Eastern unless they had initiated it, negotiated it and passed upon it for the creditors. Because the creditors' advisers had not been involved in the Bar Harbor negotiations, they made it a point to do everything in their power to kill the deal, even though it would put $3 million in the pockets of their clients.

Although Liddell Sapp had obtained a date for the court hearing of the Bar Harbor motion in late June, we agreed to postpone the hearing until July third because Shugrue was presenting his first business plan on Eastern to the creditors' advisers the last week of June. Despite the objections of just about everyone involved in the Bar Harbor transaction, who must have had plans to start their Fourth of July holiday a bit early, we stuck with the July third hearing date. If we were going to get blown out of the water on the deal, we wanted to find out sooner rather than later in order to curtail the organizational buildup that was going on and minimize the attendant costs. It was also our hope that having a hearing the day before the holiday would also minimize the potential objections that we would get on the motion. Unfortunately, we were wrong on this latter point!

The day after the Eastern business plan was presented to the creditors' advisers, we gave a presentation to those same advisers on the overall structure of the Bar Harbor transaction as well as a strategic business plan for the airline once Eastern acquired it. The meeting was held at the offices of O'Melveny and Myers on East Fifty-third Street in Manhattan. On behalf of the creditors, Adam Harris of O'Melveny was present as well as William Murphy and Allen Holt of Ernst and Young, the creditors' accounting firm. Also present were representatives of David Shapiro, the examiner. R. Bruce Holcomb, an attorney from Shapiro's Washington law firm and Harry A. Kimbriel, Jr., Shapiro's airline consultant. On behalf of Eastern, in addition to myself were Roland Moore, the in-house lawyer, as well as a financial consultant, Bill Wooten, temporarily transferred from Eastern's treasury department to assist us on the deal. Also, Gene Lewis and Doug Little from Liddell Sapp were on hand as well as Deryck Palmer of Weil Gotshal.

Although we expected some resistance once we began our presentation, we were completely taken by surprise at the level of vitriol that was directed toward the entire Bar Harbor transaction. Here we were presenting the Eastern creditors with a deal that paid them $3 million in cash in addition to saving them from having to assume another $63 million in Bar Harbor liabilities if the airline was liquidated as Continental was planning to do, and all the advisers could do was ask us why they had not been involved in negotiating the deal from the start. I later learned, from an important member of the creditors' committee, that the real reason for their resistance was that the advisers were concerned about their own reputation with the committee once it was learned that such an attractive deal for the creditors had been negotiated by the trustee and his representatives, as opposed to the people whom the creditors had retained to look out for their best interests.

The meeting ended with Harris saying that "we'll get back to you" on the extent of their analysis. In the meantime, they ordered that we postpone yet again the hearing date for the motion from July third. "We won't have enough time to analyze the transaction and make a recommendation to the committee," Harris said. I responded, "Adam, time is of the essence in this transaction, the [Eastern] estate can't afford to wait any further to see if this transaction will ultimately be approved or not. We have to stick with the July third hearing date."

"If you refuse to postpone the hearing, then we will recommend to the committee at once that they oppose the transaction," Harris shot back. Everyone in the room on the Eastern side of the conference table was shocked.

Although I figured that Shugrue would probably agree with me that we could take on the advisers and have a good shot at winning, I also knew that Bernhard, who is extremely cautious, would counsel against such a direct confrontation between the trustee and the creditors' advisers so early in Shugrue's tenure. Further complicating matters was the examiner's position; Shapiro would no doubt side with the creditors given the opinion of his airline consultant, Kimbriel. Kimbriel, a former airline executive with an M.B.A. from Harvard, had run Air Atlanta up until its liquidation. His comments on the deal in the O'Melveny conference room were clearly negative. I wondered whether this was because he had not been asked to contribute to the Bar Harbor business plan.

Thus, faced with a likely recommendation from Bernhard to Shugrue to retreat, which would have killed the deal immediately, and with guaranteed strong opposition not only from the creditors but Shapiro as well, I decided that the overall interests of the Eastern estate in getting the transaction approved would be best served if we "tucked tail" on this one so we could live to fight another day.

"All right, Adam. We'll postpone the hearing until the end of July. But we just can't afford to wait any longer than that," I said. With that, the meeting adjourned.

Soon thereafter, Bernhard discovered through a confidential source, probably Shapiro, that the creditors' advisers might consider changing their minds on the Bar Harbor deal if they had a greater say in putting together the business plan for the airline. What did Harris, an attorney, or Goldman Sachs, an investment bank, know about the commuter airline business? Yet, the power play was definitely on to determine who would have ultimate control over the deal. Shugrue told me, "The only way to get this deal approved is to play ball with the creditors." I agreed and decided to have them work with us in putting together a business plan for Bar Harbor.

Although politically expedient, this type of strategizing by committee made absolutely no economic sense whatsoever. Kimbriel, the examiner's consultant, who at the beginning was against the deal, all of a sudden became a staunch advocate of the transaction when his suggestions of where Bar Harbor should fly and at what times of the day were adopted. Similarly, the investment bankers at Goldman suddenly became converts when their suggestions were incorporated into the business plan. Glenn Engel, Goldman's airline analyst, had little, if any, experience in the commuter airline business yet thought that his suggestions were worth their weight in gold. At a meeting at Goldman one day, I had to explain to Engel that a commuter airline's seat-mile costs are high relative to those of major carriers because of the short length of the trips flown by the commuter.

The net result of all these suggestions from the creditors' advisers was a business plan that I knew, on its face, would not result in a viable carrier. Basically, the advisers wanted Bar Harbor to focus on feeding Eastern at Miami. Well, that made absolutely no sense whatsoever because Eastern no longer had a hub in Miami. My plan was to establish a secondary hub at Tampa, Florida's second largest city after Miami, because no major carrier had yet established a hub there. The competition would be minimal and the large number of business travelers flying to and from Tampa would increase the yields Bar Harbor would receive. As it later turned out, Bar Harbor's Tampa hub did substantially better than its flights out of Miami in terms of both load factor and yield.

The business plan proposed by Kimbriel and the creditors' advisers presented an ethical dilemma. On the one hand, if we didn't agree with their business plan, they would certainly oppose the transaction, which would certainly kill the deal. On the other hand, if their business plan was implemented, Bar Harbor would die a quick and certain death as an airline. To be true to myself, I couldn't just turn my back to the obvious economic irrationality of their suggestions. Also, if Bar Harbor died under the weight of their business plan, Shugrue would end up taking the blame and not the creditors' advisers. In fact, they would be the ones most likely to throw the darts even though it was their plan that had caused the damage.

After discussing this issue internally at Eastern, we agreed on a compromise solution. In order to facilitate the approval of the transaction, we approved the creditors' business plan. However, we added the explicit qualifier that it was ultimately the trustee, through his representatives, who had sole management responsibility for Bar Harbor and that he reserved the right to make whatever changes to the airline's business plan that were required due to changes in marketplace conditions. After much haggling over what this qualifier meant, the creditors' advisers finally agreed that they would not issue a recommendation at all on the deal. In essence, they would let the full creditors' committee decide for itself.

It was disturbing that we were forced to jump through all of these hoops and yet, in the end, the creditors' advisers wouldn't even support their own business plan in front of their clients. We took this to mean that they did not truly believe in the viability of their own plan. Yet, at this juncture, only a couple of days before the hearing, a nonvote from the advisers was better than a no vote.

On the day before the hearing, there was a conference call with the full creditors' committee in which Shugrue outlined the transaction and described why it made sense for Eastern. In addition to the obvious financial benefits of the deal, Shugrue pointed out that the news that Eastern was actually acquiring an airline and was growing would help put an end to the talk of immediate liquidation that had followed the appointment of the trustee. Obviously, the news that Eastern was acquiring Bar Harbor would put travel agents and the traveling public more at ease with booking future travel on Eastern. After the conference call, the committee agreed to withdraw its previously filed objection to the deal.

On July 31, 1990, the court hearing to consider the Bar Harbor motion was held before Judge Lifland. The only objection to the deal came from the preferred stockholders' committee. By this time, the preferred stockholders realized that they were not likely to receive any payout in the Eastern case. In fact, the preferred stockholders objected to almost everything the trustee attempted to do throughout the Eastern bankruptcy. Lifland quickly brushed aside their objections and approved the transaction.

Unsecured creditors have priority in bankruptcy over preferred stockholders, which means that the preferred stockholders don't get a cent unless and until the unsecured creditors get repaid in full. Since it was clear by July 1990 that the Eastern unsecured creditors were going to take a serious "haircut" on the Eastern bankruptcy, it would have been much less expensive in terms of legal fees and much more efficient in terms of overall case administration if the preferred stockholders' committee had been disbanded at that time. Once it became clear that the unsecured creditors would not be paid in full, the preferred stockholders no longer had an economic interest in the case. Congress should look at modifying the Bankruptcy Code to allow for the mandatory withdrawal from a bankruptcy case of those classes of interest that no longer have an economic interest in the case. Eastern could have saved roughly $5 million in professional fees and a similar amount in aggravation had such a rule been applied to the preferred stockholders in the case.

After the hearing, Roland Moore, Doug Little from Liddell Sapp, one of his associates, Karen M. Zuckerman, and I had a celebratory dinner at Tavern on the Green in Central Park. Little said, "Congratulations," and I responded, "Thanks, but the storm clouds are definitely forming on the horizon." Within just a matter of weeks, my prognostication would come true.

We were extremely lucky on the Bar Harbor deal. The court hearing to approve the transaction occurred on July 31, 1990. Less than seventy-two hours later, Saddam Hussein's forces invaded

Kuwait, which drove fuel prices through the roof and passenger traffic through the floor. Had the hearing occurred after the invasion, the substantially changed circumstances in the marketplace would have likely forced even me to recommend to Shugrue that we not go forward with the deal. But, as they say, timing is everything! (For a more detailed description of what ultimately happened to Bar Harbor after the acquisition, please refer to the Postscript at the end of the book.)

6

WE'RE OFF TO A GREAT START

Immediately after assembling his key advisers in early May 1990, Shugrue began to implement his five-point strategic plan to turn Eastern around. There was so much to do and such little time in which to do it that Eastern was a frenzy of activity, at least among those who really were interested in being part of a successful turnaround. I was surprised that, with all the work that had to be done, most of Eastern's executives continued to act as if it were "business as usual."

For example, I never saw any senior Eastern executive in the office on any day of any weekend during the entire time that I was at Eastern. At the time I thought, "Here we are losing over $1 million a day, and these guys aren't even putting in extra effort." It soon became apparent that most of the Eastern senior executives had already given up hope and that the only thing they were concerned with was using up their accrued vacation time and negotiating a good severance deal. Because of this apathy on the part of senior management, Shugrue decided that if anything at all was going to get done, it would have to be accomplished by the "brain trust" that he had brought in to assist him in reorganizing the carrier.

Immediately after the appointment of the trustee, Eastern's level of advance passenger bookings dropped by almost 30 percent. Neither travel agents nor the traveling public were interested in booking flights on Eastern when everything they read and heard predicted the carrier's imminent demise. In this type of environment, it is extremely difficult to fill airplanes with paying passengers even if you substantially discount the fares. What Eastern needed was a complete image makeover. A new marketing and advertising campaign that would tell people that Eastern not only was still around but would continue to improve in the future. This would restore confidence among travelers and travel agents, and give a big boost to the demoralized Eastern workforce, which thought that their jobs would be taken from them at any moment.

Jim O'Donnell, the marketing guru whom Shugrue had brought in as part of the brain trust, immediately suggested that what was needed was a change in advertising agencies.

Eastern's incumbent ad agency was Lintas: New York, which was a very large and established agency. I was familiar with them because my former employer, MasterCard, was one of their clients. Even at MasterCard, I thought that Lintas's work, while attractive, did not adequately address the overall image of the product. MasterCard suffered a serious image problem against the likes of Visa and American Express, and yet the Lintas campaigns never really addressed the image problem. Eastern needed an image makeover and Lintas, it seemed, was not the agency for the task.

O'Donnell, after investigating who could do the best job, suggested Ogilvy and Mather, also of New York. Ogilvy seemed to be the right shop because it was responsible for giving American Express some of the best image advertising it had had in quite some time.

Both Shugrue and O'Donnell felt that if Ogilvy could be even half as successful with Eastern as they had been with American Express, then Eastern would be in pretty good shape.

Lintas was abruptly fired, which was a bitter pill for them to swallow because, in addition to being Eastern's long-time agency of record, Lintas was also one of the single largest unsecured creditors of the Eastern estate.

At about the same time that Shugrue and O'Donnell were changing ad agencies at Eastern, I had decided that it was important that Bar Harbor have its own agency to handle its advertising in Florida and the Bahamas. Historically, commuter airlines have merely relied on the advertising of the major carrier with whom they are affiliated. Usually this is sufficient, but because Eastern didn't have a hub in Miami, Bar Harbor would need an agency capable of devising a campaign that would give intrastate business travelers an incentive to get out of their cars and into Bar Harbor's planes.

I asked O'Donnell to come up with a short list of small agencies, preferably located in South Florida, that had travel or airline experience as well as a reputation for creative image advertising. After several interviews, we chose McFarland and Drier of Miami to handle the Bar Harbor account. McFarland and Drier, owned by William McFarland and William Drier, or the "Bills," had as clients the tourism account for the entire state of Florida as well as the acclaimed Carnival Cruise Line account. However, what really persuaded me to go with them was their account executive, Timothy M. Swies. Swies had worked on the New York Air and Eastern accounts back in the 1980s, so he was well versed in airline marketing strategy.

Ogilvy and Mather, within a couple of weeks after working closely with O'Donnell, came up with the idea for the "100 Days" campaign for Eastern. The idea behind it was that Eastern would get better as an airline each day over the first one hundred days of the trustee's tenure. The campaign was unique in that it was an external advertising campaign as well as an internal employee communications program. The TV and print media campaign supporting the program was so successful that after the 100 Days, which encompassed the August 1990 invasion of Kuwait, Eastern had substantially improved in terms of customer satisfaction, on-time performance, advance bookings and load factor. By most measurements, the campaign was considered a huge success.

However, the 100 Days campaign didn't do much to stem the flow of losses exceeding $1 million per day that Eastern continued to incur. Beginning in mid-May, Shugrue instructed Eastern's senior executives to begin preparing a business plan for Eastern that would be presented to the creditors. Although I was involved in the preparation of that plan, Shugrue had instructed me to conduct my own strategic analysis of what Eastern needed to do to become viable. The results of my personal analysis differed substantially from those incorporated in the plan that was ultimately presented to the creditors in early July.

The "official" Eastern business plan, devised and presented before the airline world was turned upside down on August 2, 1990, estimated that Eastern would lose roughly $350 million between June and the end of the year, but would approach break-even, after asset sales, in 1991. The structure of the airline in the plan was similar to that which existed in June when the plan was prepared. Eastern would continue to focus on its Atlanta hub in addition to heavy north-south flying along the East Coast, mostly the Northeast to Florida. This plan was presented to the creditors in July and was approved by their advisers soon thereafter. Of course, the August invasion of Kuwait, just two weeks after the business plan was presented, rendered those projections totally irrelevant.

However, my own analysis of the Eastern situation painted an entirely different picture from that embraced in the official plan, even without the harsh effect that would soon hit Eastern on August 2.

In short, my analysis showed that Eastern would not be viable as long as it retained the Atlanta hub. Delta was too large and too entrenched in Atlanta for Eastern ever to hope of making a dent, I concluded. Further, because the high-yield business traveler continued to avoid Eastern like the plague, the Atlanta hub actually became a substantial cash drain on Eastern. Eastern was routing passengers through the hub on connecting flights who paid extremely low leisure fares, resulting in an overall yield that was substantially below what was required to break even, not to mention turn a profit. The Atlanta hub, in my view, had to be blown away entirely if Eastern was ever going to have a chance of making it.

The implications of this suggestion, however, were dark indeed. If Eastern's Atlanta hub was dismantled, all that would be left would be north-south routes on the East Coast, mainly focusing on leisure traffic from the Northeast to Florida. Instead of 156 aircraft, Eastern would need no more than 20. Instead of 20,000 employees, Eastern would only need 2,000. In short, a radical restructuring and downsizing of the airline was required if Eastern was ever to have a shot at becoming profitable.

I estimated that the Atlanta hub could be sold as a turnkey operation to another airline for at least $300 million. This was the key attraction to the plan since, at the time, Eastern had few valuable assets left to sell. However, Shugrue was concerned that once word leaked out about the plan, even though he thought it made sense, it would be interpreted as a wholesale liquidation, which would cause the entire house of cards to fall even before we could get around to implementing the plan. Further, such a move would be politically unpopular because the unions, who sat on the creditors' committee, would likely fight the move. They were agitating to return to the property, but if the Atlanta hub was sold or dismantled, most of the potential jobs for them would evaporate as well.

More importantly, Shugrue also believed that the creditors' advisers would not go for the plan. Without the Atlanta hub, Eastern was absolutely worthless to another airline. Zweibel and Goldman

Sachs continued to pursue discussions with every airline trying to get somebody to buy Eastern as a going concern. Without the Atlanta hub, no airline in its right mind would even consider the idea. Shugrue didn't want to put himself in the position of advocating a sale of the Atlanta hub, having the creditors take that as a sign of liquidation and then fight the plan, with the result that it would look like Shugrue was attempting to liquidate the carrier slowly over the creditors' objections in contravention of all of his public statements to date that Eastern was a viable entity.

Shugrue's political instincts were shortly proven to be correct with respect to the motives of the creditors' advisers. Thus, my plan to dismantle or sell the Atlanta hub was put on the back shelf for the moment.

The Eastern legal department was in complete disarray when John Sicilian, the former Verner Liipfert lawyer, took over soon after Shugrue's appointment. Barry Simon, Eastern's general counsel, was on his way back to Continental and Weil Gotshal was acting almost as if it were the client.

Compounding the problem was that Eastern had over thirty different law firms doing work for it on various matters, and there wasn't anyone around who could succintly describe which firm was working on what matter. Sicilian immediately consolidated all of the major work in two firms: Weil Gotshal and Verner Liipfert. Weil Gotshal handled all of Eastern's matters in the bankruptcy court, and Verner Liipfert handled or oversaw matters pertaining to the rest: corporate, securities, labor, criminal, etc. Although firms with special expertise handled particular matters, there was always somebody from Verner Liipfert involved to oversee the matter generally. This was important because it allowed Sicilian, who was acting general counsel, to keep abreast of everything that was going on since the Verner Liipfert attorneys would obviously keep him closely informed.

Staying informed was not always easy, though. On several occasions I was in Sicilian's office when he would be frantically placing calls to Zirinsky and even Harvey Miller at Weil Gotshal in an attempt to get them to respond to calls placed days earlier. Sometimes it took an irate telephone call from Shugrue directly to Miller or Zirinsky to get Weil Gotshal to keep Sicilian informed of their activities.

The cause of this friction may have been Weil Gotshal's displeasure with Bernhard and Verner Liipfert's legal oversight of the Eastern bankruptcy. Until the appointment of the trustee, Weil Gotshal was the undisputed legal "King of the Hill" at Eastern, reporting directly to Lorenzo at Texas Air. Attorneys like Miller and Zirinsky were able to make key decisions on Eastern's behalf. This came to an abrupt end with the appointment of Shugrue because Shugrue vested Bernhard, and therefore Verner Liipfert, with overall legal responsibility. At any rate, Weil Gotshal must have become upset with having to answer to Bernhard and did everything to retain the power it had previously had in the case.

Nonetheless, Weil Gotshal soon got the message that Bernhard was the chief adviser to the trustee and that, therefore, Verner Liipfert was the chief law firm. Weil Gotshal, though undoubtedly upset with the new power arrangement, was not sufficiently upset to quit and forego the $1.5 million in monthly bills that it submitted for working on the Eastern case.

Soon after taking over, Shugrue received a telephone call from Harry Jones, the U.S. Trustee in New York. Jones asked Shugrue if a lawyer who used to work for Jones could have a job at Eastern. The lawyer's name, interesting enough, was Frank Sinatra. Shugrue, surprised that any lawyer from New York would want a job working at the struggling Eastern, which was located in Miami, nevertheless consented. We were fearful of placing Jones's handpicked candidate in a position where he could possibly obtain access to key confidential information. Thus, Sinatra was placed in the Eastern legal department where he reported to John Sicilian, who immediately put him to work overseeing the most mundane legal matters. Sinatra became so bored that, after only several weeks, he wanted to leave Eastern altogether. In fact, on several occasions Sinatra walked up to my office on the ninth floor from the legal department's fourth-floor offices and asked what I was working on and whether I needed any "specialized" legal help. Being an attorney myself, my usual response was, "Thanks, Frank, but I've got it covered."

Tom Conway, the public relations guru of the Shugrue brain trust, immediately took over Eastern's public relations department. Shugrue placed heavy emphasis on public relations because he believed that a strong public relations campaign would substantially improve Eastern's position with the traveling public as well as improve the morale of the airline's employees. Conway quickly consolidated his control of the Eastern public relations department such that no press release would go to Shugrue for approval unless Conway first approved it. This structure led Eastern's vice president of corporate communications, Robin Matell, within a matter of weeks after Conway's arrival to resign. In Matell's place, Conway suggested that Shugrue appoint Matell's long-time assistant, Karen Ceramsak. Ceramsak, a young woman with heavy political public relations experience, turned out to be an excellent choice as Eastern's official spokesperson.

Wertheim Schroeder and Company was chosen by Shugrue as Eastern's new financial adviser. However, after several weeks, many Eastern executives, including Shugrue, began to question the wisdom of that decision.

Under the Texas Air regime, Eastern's investment banker was Smith, Barney, Harris, Upham and Company, a large and reputable Wall Street firm with experience in transportation-related matters as well as complex reorganizations and restructurings. Smith Barney, though it billed Eastern almost $4 million in investment banking fees during the year that Eastern was in bankruptcy prior to the trustee's appointment, had done an excellent job in terms of its work on asset sales and the structuring of various reorganization proposals.

Wertheim, on the other hand, prior to the Eastern case had not had much experience in transportation matters in general, not to mention airlines. Wertheim's strength is in the media and publishing fields; airlines, not to mention complex restructurings of them, are not. In fact, it was Wertheim that represented America West Airlines in early 1989 when it attempted to outbid Donald Trump for the Eastern Shuttle. America West was eventually unsuccessful in acquiring the Shuttle because Wertheim was unable to raise the necessary financing. In the financial environment that existed during the first half of 1989, it was relatively easy to raise financing for any airline deal, as Checchi demonstrated with Northwest and Marvin Davis with United. Yet, Wertheim had struck out.

Shugrue came to Wertheim by way of one of its managing directors who had previously been a high-ranking government official in Washington. Bernhard and Shugrue felt that this person's Washington contacts would be helpful in the Eastern reorganization given the highly politicized nature of the carrier's bankruptcy proceedings.

Upon learning that Bernhard and Shugrue were seriously considering Wertheim, I became concerned. The prevailing view on Wall Street was that Wertheim's financing abilities in airlines were weak and that the firm had not had much experience in dealing with complex bankruptcies. My preference was to retain a firm such as Morgan Stanley and Company or Wasserstein, Perella and Company. These were Wall Street firms with sufficiently large staffs, big capital positions and sufficient airline and bankruptcy experience. In my view, Wertheim was just too small in terms of both resources and capital, not to mention its general unfamiliarity with airlines, to represent Eastern adequately in such a complex bankruptcy case.

The Wertheim team was led by one of their managing directors, Arnold Kroll, who also sits on the board of America West. Assisting him was Michael Grad, another managing director, as well as two associates: Craig Marshak and Renard Stroutman. That was basically the extent of the Eastern team at the firm.

In early July 1990, Shugrue asked me what I thought the real chances were of selling Eastern as a going concern with all or a large portion of its employees. I replied that the chances, in my opinion, were almost nonexistent for several reasons. First, the fact that Eastern was in bankruptcy necessarily complicated any deal in which a party, whether another airline or not, would buy it because any sale of the airline as a whole would likely have to be accomplished through a plan of reorganization. Putting together a plan, not to mention negotiating with the unsecured creditors, had to include an ultimate resolution of the prepetition transactions with Texas Air and a settlement of the contingent pension liabilities of almost $1 billion with the PBGC. These issues, while not insurmountable, guaranteed a very complicated negotiating process with respect to a reorganization plan. Second, Eastern was losing over $1 million each day. Thus, any offer for the airline would probably include only a token amount of cash, if any at all. It was questionable whether the creditors would accept a deal that didn't include a substantial cash consideration. Third, the labor problems had to be solved. No one was going to be interested in buying Eastern without a resolution of its union problems. That process would very likely require nasty court fights through the bankruptcy court, appellate federal courts and perhaps even the Supreme Court, which could take years. Fourth, even if all of the above problems could be solved and solved quickly enough to be of benefit to Eastern, the potential buyer had to believe that Eastern, after the acquisition, would be a viable airline. My previous confidential analysis had already convinced me that Eastern wasn't viable with an Atlanta hub. Yet, that was the most valuable asset left in the estate. Without it, Eastern would be so small that one could start an airline from scratch with less money and headache than buying Eastern. The only way to avoid this problem was to structure a transaction in which the Atlanta hub was so valuable to a buyer, such as an existing airline, that it was worth swallowing Eastern whole because that would be less expensive than investing hundreds of millions of dollars to build the Atlanta hub from scratch.

All of these issues, in my view, made an acquisition of Eastern as a going concern unlikely in the extreme, and I so represented to Shugrue. However, I also told him that "the only way this company can be sold as a going concern is if we can find someone with a deep enough pocket to fund the transaction and then present him with a business plan that gives him a viable operation afterwards." "You're right," he said. "We need to come up with a viable business plan that we can then shop to potential investors." After a collective pause of a few seconds, we both looked at each other and said, almost simultaneously, "Pan Am."

Very few people understood what ailed Pan Am, and how to fix it, better than Shugrue, largely in part because he had worked there for twenty years and had run its operations for almost half of that time. In fact, back in 1989 Shugrue and I had put together a business plan for an investor who was interested in a takeover of Pan Am. Pan Am and Eastern were excellent merger candidates because each offered what the other didn't have. In fact, at one time prior to deregulation, Pan Am attempted to merge with Eastern but was thwarted by the Civil Aeronautics Board (CAB). Before deregulation in 1978, the CAB had veto authority over airline mergers.

There was a host of reasons why a Pan Am–Eastern merger made strategic and financial sense but four factors stood out. First, Pan Am lacked the domestic route network that Eastern's Atlanta hub and other operations provided. The Atlanta hub could be structured to provide feed traffic to just about every Pan Am international route. Second, both Pan Am and Eastern had the same types of aircraft in their fleets, Airbus and Boeing, which would allow for minimal fleet integration costs. Third, since both airlines had huge maintenance and employee bases in Miami, substantial cost savings could be generated by dismantling one of the bases, probably Pan Am's. And fourth, Pan Am's low aircraft utilization would be substantially improved, resulting in higher revenues and lower average costs overall, due to flying more domestic routes over Eastern's system.

In short, a Pan Am–Eastern merger would save both airlines.

With an understanding of the strategic strengths underlying the attractiveness of such a merger, Shugrue instructed me to begin work immediately with Wertheim on a confidential memorandum and model outlining the transaction that we would then provide to potential investors. Because of the work that Shugrue and I had previously done on Pan Am, I had the computer model and most of the narrative already on computer diskette. Also, because of the advance work that I had already done, I thought that Wertheim would be able to put something together in a matter of days. I was mistaken.

First, it took Wertheim almost a week just to get the two associates assigned to Eastern focused on the project at hand. I then put together both the original computer model as well as the narrative for the descriptive memorandum. However, Wertheim wanted to make "substantial" changes to what I had done, so they spent another week or so debating what those changes would actually be. At the end of the second week, they determined that my work, after all, did not need to be "substantially changed." After another week of producing the documents, the descriptive memorandum was finally completed. Thus, after more than three weeks, the final Wertheim product (it had to go out under their name even though I wrote it) was ready to be distributed to potential investors. Since such matters are usually accomplished in a matter of a couple of days to a week, we clearly were not off to a propitious beginning. Even Shugrue was getting annoyed at the unnecessary delay and began to question his decision in hiring the firm.

The merger model showed that a deal could be structured for a relatively small investment of $400 million in equity. The deal would provide for a reorganization plan for Eastern that would result in Eastern's creditors receiving 50 cents on the dollar for what they were owed, a tender offer for all of Pan Am's outstanding common stock, and a merger of Eastern into Pan Am. The resulting merged company would have over $600 million in cash, would generate over $6 billion in revenues in the first full year of operations, and would be profitable by the end of the second year. The plan called for the merged carrier to operate under the Pan Am name and the retention of just about all of both airline's employees. Furthermore, the Eastern nonunion employees would be integrated into the Pan Am unionized workforce.

The difficult part of the project then began—finding potential investors. The major airlines were out. After all, why would, say, a Northwest raise millions of dollars to finance a Pan Am–Eastern merger resulting in a stronger unified competitor? Banks were out as well since this deal, if it was going to be done at all, had to be done solely with equity. Nobody in their right mind would finance this deal with even a penny of debt given the overleveraged state of Pan Am, not to mention Eastern's bankruptcy.

Our only option, it seemed, was to find well-heeled individual investors or foreign carriers that would see a strategic benefit to a Pan Am–Eastern merger and be able to act quickly. The Wertheim people and I then discussed those individuals who had shown an interest in airline deals before and who also had the financial resources necessary to consummate a transaction. Los Angeles billionaire Marvin Davis, who had made runs at both Northwest and United, was an obvious choice for a phone call. His son, John Davis, operates an independent movie studio in Los Angeles and reviews all of his father's deals. John, a Harvard Business School graduate, was an acquaintance of mine so I called him and asked if he would be interested in "the most important airline deal in history." John, a jovial and down-to-earth type of guy given his immense wealth, responded, "Sorry, but I just can't see how you can make one sick dog well, let alone two of them." A pretty astute investor in his own right, the younger Davis had put his finger on the key point. Although the business plan and financial model we put together for the merger showed a strong deal, the sales job necessary to disprove Pan Am and Eastern together as financial basket cases was going to be monumental.

It was decided that Wertheim would beat the bushes for investors as quickly as it could. However, since Shugrue was placing responsibility for the deal in my hands, I wasn't about to sit back and wait with crossed fingers for Wertheim to come up with a miracle investor. Given Wertheim's performance to date, I concluded that the only way we were even going to have a shot at this deal was if we found an investor on our own. Shugrue agreed and gave me the green light to contact those parties quietly whom I thought would be interested in investing $400 million in a Pan Am–Eastern merger.

The ideal candidate, it seemed, would be an individual or small group of investors who knew something about aviation, could act quickly and had the ability to write a check for $400 million without having to raise financing from third parties themselves. After racking my brain for several days over who would meet the criteria, I came across one individual. So as to protect his privacy, he is referred to herein simply as the "Investor."

The Investor had spent his entire life in aviation or aviation-related fields. He had built one of the country's largest aviation services companies from nothing to a billion dollars in revenue over a short period of time. He sold his stake when the company went private, making a huge amount of money. That, in addition to his many other business ventures, gave the Investor a personal net worth conservatively estimated at around $500 million. I had met the Investor a couple of times before and felt that if anyone would be interested in this deal, he would.

After broaching the subject over the telephone, I flew to Washington to present the proposal in detail to the Investor and his staff. The Investor responded that "this is the type of transaction my partners and I have been looking for." He was interested in the deal for two key reasons. First, as a native of a Latin American country, he always flew Pan Am to Latin America and was interested in its history as well as its continued viability. Second, the amount required to do the deal, $400 million, could easily be handled by him and a handful of his closest friends and fellow investors.

He promised to review the material and get back to me within seventy-two hours if he decided to pursue the deal further. With that, I immediately returned to Miami to brief Shugrue and Bernhard on the Investor's initial enthusiasm. I then checked in with Wertheim to see if they had uncovered any leads. As expected, they hadn't.

The Investor called back within seventy-two hours. To my delight, he said that he was interested in pursuing the transaction further. He requested a face-to-face meeting with Shugrue so that he could inquire in a more detailed fashion the structure of the deal and the business plan for the merged carrier going forward. However, the real reason the Investor wanted a direct meeting was so that he could look Shugrue in the eye to determine if Shugrue actually believed in the plan. I readily agreed to set up the meeting because I knew that Shugrue was strongly committed to the transaction. I also knew that Shugrue's salesmanship abilities would probably convince the Investor to go forward.

The meeting was set up to occur a few days later in New York with the Investor, Shugrue and Bernhard. Shugrue wanted an informal atmosphere so he suggested drinks at the Union League Club, located in the shadow of the Pan Am Building. Representatives from Wertheim Schroeder were not invited because Shugrue didn't want to bring in the investment bankers unless and until he had received a commitment from the Investor that he would proceed.

The meeting went extremely well, and the next day the Investor called me to say that he would probably go forward with the deal but that he wanted to confirm Pan Am's interest in the idea before making a final commitment. This was, no doubt, a fair request. Although I was enthusiastic that the Investor was predisposed to the merger, I was very concerned about the Pan Am piece of the puzzle.

About three weeks before Shugrue's meeting with the Investor, I set up a meeting at Pan Am with Pan Am's chairman and CEO Tom Plaskett to discuss the merger idea. The meeting included myself, Mike Grad from Wertheim and Wertheim's airline analyst. In addition to Plaskett, Pan Am's chief financial officer, Richard H. Francis, was also in attendance.

The purpose of the meeting was to alert Pan Am to our plan so we could possibly coordinate financing efforts. Our feeling was that since Plaskett had to know he was in the same boat as Eastern, he would be inclined to work with us to find a common solution to both airlines' problems. However, we were really not quite sure what Plaskett's total motivation would be since, although he was in the same boat as Eastern, his end of the boat at that time was still above the water line.

I began the meeting by outlining the strategic and financial advantages of a Pan Am–Eastern merger. Both Plaskett and Francis were in agreement that the plan made sense. After answering some operational questions about Eastern, I asked Plaskett, "What do we need to do to see this happen?" Plaskett replied that his biggest worry, aside from finding financing, was the union issue. I told him we were certain there wouldn't be a problem there. I knew there wouldn't be a labor problem because one of Verner Liipfert's labor lawyers, Joseph L. Manson, had already gone to the Pan Am unions and received their oral agreement to merge Eastern employees onto the bottom of the Pan Am union seniority lists. Since Eastern was nonunion due to the permanent replacements, the seniority integration would take place rather smoothly.

After answering this question for Plaskett, I sensed that there was something else on his mind that made him feel uneasy about the whole matter. I wouldn't find out what it was, though, until it was too late.

Thus, when the Investor told me he wanted to speak with Plaskett at Pan Am before making up his mind about funding the merger, the lingering concern about the meeting at Pan Am made me very uneasy when dealing with the Investor. How would Plaskett respond? What was the unspoken issue that seemed to captivate his thinking?

Having no choice but to accede to the very reasonable request of the Investor, I arranged for him to meet with Plaskett. The result of that meeting was devastating.

Within a matter of hours after his meeting at Pan Am, the Investor called me back almost irate. "Those bastards over there are only interested in who's going to run the merged company. They don't give a damn about cleaning up the mess they're already in," he yelled. Basically, the Investor told me that Plaskett kept peppering him about whom he was going to pick to run the merged carrier if the deal went through. The Investor, knowing he would choose Shugrue, nonetheless remained noncommittal with Plaskett. Yet Plaskett kept hammering away, trying to get the Investor to come out and say what the management team would look like. After forty-five minutes of this, the Investor gave up and ended the meeting, without even having a chance to discuss the deal on the merits.

In his parting words to me ending his involvement in the deal, the Investor said, "The problem at Pan Am is that the guys who have the responsibility [management] don't carry the risk, and the guys who carry the risk [shareholders] don't have the responsibility." I thought this to be a rather telling pronouncement, particularly given Pan Am's subsequent liquidation.

When Shugrue found out about the Investor's conversation with Plaskett, and the Investor's total disgust with the situation, Shugrue said, "Dammit, I knew those guys at Pan Am would screw up this deal."

At first, I thought Plaskett was just totally immersed in what his role would be in the merged carrier, which would explain his odd behavior with the Investor. However, I later learned, through a contact at Pan Am, that Plaskett may have intended to scare off the Investor hoping that Eastern, without the deal, would soon go down the tubes and leave Pan Am as the dominant north-south carrier on the East Coast. If true, it was a major strategic blunder on Plaskett's part because Pan Am's situation was so dire that the removal of Eastern from the marketplace would not fix Pan Am's problems. This, in fact, was proven correct. When Eastern shut down in January 1991, Pan Am had already filed for bankruptcy earlier in the month, and thereafter finally sold most of its assets to Delta. In September 1991, as a condition of the asset sale to Delta, Pan Am's creditors asked both Plaskett and Francis to resign, which they did. Of course, in December 1991, Pan Am shut down and was liquidated.

Plaskett had a chance, just by saying yes to the deal, to do something that would have resulted in both carriers becoming viable, flying collectively under the Pan Am name. Instead, both carriers have been reduced to ashes.

After coming so close with the Investor only to fail at the last minute, I checked in with Wertheim Schroeder to see if they had found any potential investors. I wasn't at all surprised when they told me that they hadn't even gotten a nibble.

In late September, Wertheim finally made some progress. Through a contact in their Tokyo office, who worked with a friend of Shugrue's in Tokyo, discussions with Japan Air Lines (JAL) began over a deal in which JAL would invest $400 million in a Pan Am–Eastern merger and then take a 20 percent equity stake in the merged carrier. The deal made sense for JAL because a merged Pan Am–Eastern would provide JAL with substantial feed traffic for JAL's Pacific routes to and from the United States. This would help JAL compete against the leader in the Pacific, United Airlines.

Unfortunately, by the time JAL got interested in financing a Pan Am–Eastern merger, the invasion of Kuwait had already occurred, which sent a chill through every airline on earth. Even JAL was scared of the fallout from the substantially increased oil prices, global recession and evaporation of airline traffic that the spectre of war produced. Notwithstanding their concerns, JAL actually was very interested in the deal. Particularly so since one of their senior executives was a close friend of Shugrue's.

Throughout all of October 1990, seeing that the creditors were probably going to start calling soon for Eastern's liquidation, I bombarded JAL officials with faxes and personally delivered messages from Shugrue's Tokyo contact: "If you're going to move, please move quickly. Time is of the essence." Although the Japanese are known for their slow and very deliberate processes when evaluating deals, by mid-October Eastern didn't have the luxury of waiting for the normal time frames to run their course. We were grasping at straws just to keep the airline alive for the next several weeks.

In the end, the prospect of war in the Persian Gulf, in addition to the required quickness with which they had to act if they so decided, forced JAL finally to back out of the deal. Even a last-minute Tokyo trip by Shugrue to try and convince JAL otherwise, as well as enlisting DOT Secretary Skinner to opine that such a transaction would be in the best interests of American aviation were, ultimately, unsuccessful.

During the discussions with the Investor and JAL to try to put together a deal in which Eastern would merge as a going concern with Pan Am, we also had to consider simultaneously the option that Eastern would be liquidated. If so, how could the airline's most valuable asset, the Atlanta hub, be used to maximize value to the Eastern estate and therefore its creditors?

Al Checchi, the chairman of Northwest, is probably the smartest airline chieftain in the industry today. A 1973 Harvard M.B.A. and a former financial hero at Marriott during the 1980s, Checchi pulled off the unlikely in the summer of 1989 when he outbid Marvin Davis and Pan Am and consummated the $3.65 billion leveraged buyout of Northwest, one of the last big LBOs of the decade. As soon as he did the Northwest deal, just about everyone in the industry predicted that he would fail when the first recession rolled around and he tried to meet his huge debt payments.

So far, Checchi has proven them all wrong. His ingenious use of sale leasebacks and the outright sale of nonstrategic assets allowed him to pay down a large part of his LBO debt even before the recession kicked in during the second half of 1990. Thus, by the time Eastern was scrambling for merger partners or investors, Checchi was in a great position to pounce, which he did.

In July, Checchi sent a proposal to Shugrue that basically called for Eastern's orderly liquidation. Checchi proposed that Northwest would take over Eastern's Atlanta hub, hire roughly 5,000 of Eastern's 20,000 employees, acquire a handful of Eastern aircraft and the Miami maintenance base and sell off the rest of the airline in liquidation and split the sales proceeds with the creditors. The creditors would get a small amount of cash up front, approximately $150 million, would receive an estimated $250 million from the sale of the rest of Eastern's assets and would also receive 10 percent of the profits that the Atlanta hub generated for Northwest over the ensuing ten years.

After reviewing the Northwest proposal at Shugrue's request, my first inclination was to jump up and down for joy. Here was a deal that, albeit calling for Eastern's liquidation, at least put to productive use the only key asset left in the estate as well as preserving 5,000 jobs and providing for some economic benefit to the creditors. After I relayed to Shugrue my generally positive feelings on the offer, he agreed that, if no other deal to buy Eastern as a going concern came along, this was probably the best way to go.

The creditors asked for a meeting with Checchi to discuss in more detail the offer and its implications. Within a week or two a meeting was scheduled in New York at the offices of Northwest's law firm. Checchi's chief strategist and a former McKinsey and Company consultant, Laura Levinson, an intelligent and attractive woman, was also present. In addition was Ben Hirst, Northwest's general counsel, who had just left the same position at Continental. On behalf of Eastern, in addition to myself, were Shugrue, Arnold Kroll and Mike Grad from Wertheim Schroeder, and Rolf Andresen, Eastern's CFO. Art Newman and one of his associates from Chemical Bank represented the creditors.

Everyone waited in the conference room for Shugrue to arrive. Shugrue was delayed because he was in another room on the telephone trying to negotiate a plea bargain on behalf of Eastern with Andrew J. Maloney, the Brooklyn U.S. Attorney who by this time had indicted Eastern and several employees for maintenance violations. While we were waiting for Shugrue, Hirst and I reminisced about our hectic days at Continental back in the mid-1980s. I then found out that Checchi grew up in Somerville, Massachusetts, not far from my home in Boston and where I had attended school in Cambridge.

When Shugrue arrived, but before Checchi began, Shugrue walked over to me and whispered, "Make sure you write down everything he says."

Checchi started the meeting by outlining the benefits of the transaction to Eastern and its creditors. He also offered to consider increasing the cash consideration after the completion of due diligence. Although I was impressed with the offer, I really don't believe that either Newman or Shugrue were. For one thing, Shugrue had all along stated that he would sell Eastern only as a going concern. The Checchi deal obviously called for a liquidation that, if enacted, would force Shugrue to backpedal from his earlier public stand. More damaging, however, was the sense I got that Checchi's manner might have put Newman off. Although probably not done intentionally, the manner in which Checchi made his presentation could easily have left one with the impression that he felt that he was there to do Eastern and its creditors a favor. Although in reality his position was very strong, I believe it may have hurt Checchi's ability to deal with the creditors, and Newman, in the future.

The meeting ended with an agreement that Northwest would finish conducting its due diligence and would submit a formal proposal as soon as possible. After Checchi and his colleagues left the room, Newman told us that he didn't think that the offer was high enough. Given the environment that we were then facing, I thought the offer was both fair and reasonable. However, I didn't make my feelings known to Newman at that time.

What followed was another couple of months of haggling back and forth between Eastern's creditors and Checchi over the real value of the deal to the Eastern estate. Newman and the rest of the creditors' advisers demanded that they take charge of the Checchi negotiations, so Shugrue graciously let them. The result was a completely bungled negotiation that ended up with the creditors getting absolutely nothing.

Although I believed that the Checchi deal was fair, and Wertheim Schroeder had completed a valuation analysis that supported that finding, the creditors continued to push Checchi to increase the value of his bid. By October, it had become crystal clear that Eastern was not long for the world, and yet facing a forced liquidation, the creditors continued to play hardball with Checchi.

One day I told Shugrue that if the creditors didn't hurry up and jump at the deal, Checchi would walk. After continued intransigence on the part of the creditors, Checchi did just that and soon withdrew his offer altogether.

When Eastern shut down in January 1991, the Atlanta hub, at one time Eastern's most valuable asset, automatically became immediately worthless. This is because no airline was going to spend hundreds of millions of dollars to restart the hub's operations in the face of having to fight tooth and nail with financially strong and market-entrenched Delta in Atlanta. The creditors' advisers delayed and overplayed their hand to the point where the only credible bid on the table was withdrawn. As soon as Eastern shut down, all that remained of the Atlanta hub were leases on gate space which Eastern didn't even own, meaning that the terminals were eventually turned back to the city of Atlanta without the Eastern estate getting any material value for doing so.

The creditors have only themselves and their own advisers to blame for this fiasco. Checchi was ready, willing and able to do a deal immediately. The creditors would have received fair value for the Atlanta hub and other assets and at least five thousand Eastern employees would have retained their jobs. Instead, the advisers' bungling resulted in the creditors getting absolutely nothing.

In October Carl Icahn, chairman of TWA, approached Eastern about acquiring the Atlanta hub as well. Icahn's motivation was a bit different from Checchi's. Unlike Northwest, TWA really needed Atlanta because it suffered from similar problems as Pan Am. Although TWA had a large domestic hub in St. Louis, its overall feeder network was smaller than what was necessary to provide value to TWA's international routes.

Icahn is known as a smart investor who hardly ever overpays and thinks long and hard before he jumps. Although we analyzed Icahn's proposal in detail, we didn't think that Icahn would go through with the deal for two major reasons. TWA already had a large domestic hub in St. Louis, which meant that if he acquired the Atlanta hub, given the relatively close proximity of the two cities, one hub would be superfluous. Additionally, Icahn was running into liquidity problems of his own at TWA, which cast doubt on his willingness to close a deal. I believe that the real reason he was interested was to get a close look at Eastern's books through due diligence so that he could estimate for himself how much air Eastern had left under its wings. Once he completed his due diligence, he became less than excited about the deal, probably figuring that Eastern had only a couple of months left, which would help TWA on its Florida routes during the winter season.

During the hectic days of October 1990, when we were pulling out all the stops to try and find a way to put together some deal for Eastern, it seemed that just about everyone on the planet had access to Eastern's "confidential" financial information. In this regard we were between a rock and a hard place. On the one hand, since we were desperately shopping Eastern, we had to provide various parties with confidential information. On the other hand, if we didn't provide the information, the parties who were interested wouldn't be able to act, let alone act within the two-to-three-week time frame that was required given Eastern's dire condition.

In the end, no airline evidenced a serious interest in acquiring Eastern as a going concern. This wasn't surprising. By the fall of 1990 war was on the horizon, we were in a recession, airline traffic had dried up and fuel prices were still more than twice what they had been before August 2, 1990. Given the environment in late 1990, when the industry as a whole would report its worst financial results in history, it is understandable that no other airline seriously considered acquiring Eastern.

The closest we came to such a deal was with the investor who was going to finance a Pan Am–Eastern merger. Yet even that opportunity, in the end, disintegrated. After the creditors' advisers scared away Checchi, we were left trying to find some opportunity to salvage value for the creditors, even if it meant liquidation.

During those final days of looking for a deal, all types of ideas were flying around that, whether they made sense or not, required effort to investigate given the frenzied environment. One proposal involved Jay Pritzker, the Hyatt Hotel magnate, in which he would pay a small sum, $25 million, for some key operating assets of Eastern, fly a scaled-down airline along the East Coast, put all of the other assets in a liquidating trust and split the difference with the creditors on the resulting asset sale proceeds. Basically, the same type of deal that he had done with Braniff in the mid-1980s.

Given the only alternative left by this time—total liquidation—Pritzker's deal was actually somewhat attractive. However, before we could get him moving seriously toward doing a deal, the creditors began calling for Eastern's liquidation, which obviously put an end to any potential deals.

Other than Pan Am, of all the deals that showed themselves, the creditors would have maximized their position if they had agreed to the Checchi offer. However, their continued delaying tactics and a total misreading of their negotiating position by their advisers resulted in scaring even that deal away. The only vestige the creditors have of that transaction, and all the other botched transactions, are the bills for legal, accounting and investment banking fees totaling millions of dollars for work that resulted ultimately in the scuttling of the very deals that would have provided some financial relief to them.

After the invasion of Kuwait, Eastern's losses doubled to a little over $2 million per day. Shugrue used to joke that, after the invasion of Kuwait, Weil Gotshal's legal bills also doubled to roughly $2 million per month. I told him, not entirely in jest, that the relationship between Eastern's losses and the huge professional fees it was paying was more than just "spurious correlation."

In an average month, Eastern paid almost $5 million in "professional fees," which included legal, investment banking, accounting and consulting fees. In other large and complex bankruptcies it's the same story, a large portion of a debtor's cash flow goes to pay lawyers, investment bankers and accountants.

The bankruptcy law, as presently written, actually encourages such excesses. Under the law, professional fees must be paid as incurred, and they are given priority status in payment, even over the prepetition claims of unsecured creditors, as "administrative expenses" of the estate. Congress presumed that companies entering bankruptcy would have difficulty getting professional help if the providers of those services had doubts about ultimately getting paid. As with most well-meaning legislation, the practical effect has been exactly the opposite. In fact, many small and medium-sized businesses end up being liquidated outside of bankruptcy because of their fears that they will be sucked dry by professional fees if they file Chapter 11. In such cases, the purpose of the bankruptcy law, to help companies reorganize and keep them alive, is subverted because these companies go out of business rather than risk paying exorbitant sums while in bankruptcy.

The intemperances with large and complex bankruptcy cases, such as Eastern's, are even more shameful. Under the law, the estate of the debtor must pay all administrative expenses. Thus, there is no incentive for the professionals who represent parties other than the debtor to keep their fees and costs to a minimum. In fact, the exact opposite holds. There is a big incentive for professionals to charge more than what is necessary to get the job done since, in the end, the estate pays the tab. The result is that the party paying the bill (the estate) has little or no control over the party providing the service (the professional), resulting in financial irresponsibility of the highest order.

In addition to the sixteen parties that made up the Official Committee of Unsecured Creditors, or creditors' committee, Eastern also had over one million other creditors. Of course, most of these parties retained their own advisers and, since Eastern ultimately paid the bill for those services, there was no incentive for anyone to "watch the clock." Even among the key players in the Eastern bankruptcy case, the list of advisers who advised the advisers cascaded into a valley of financial excess.

What follows is a breakdown of just the key players in the Eastern case (there were several hundred different advisers in total involved) and their advisers. All fees charged by all of the advisers were ultimately paid by Eastern. Also, keep in mind that behind each law firm, investment bank, consulting firm or accounting firm listed below stood an army of associates, analysts and other staffers whose work was billed and added to the total amount Eastern had to pay on a monthly basis.

*Denotes representation exclusive to the period prior to the appointment of the trustee.

Examiner (title later changed to Special Adviser)
David I. Shapiro
Dickstein, Shapiro & Morin
Washington

Examiner's Counsel
Stanley J. Samorajczyk
Hazel, Thomas, Fiske, Beckhorn & Hanes
Washington

Examiner's Airline Consultant
Harry A. Kimbriel, Jr.
Kimbriel & Associates
Southport, Conn.

Special Counsel for Eastern
Berl Bernhard
Verner, Liipfert, Bernhard, McPherson and Hand
Washington

Frank Calhoun
Liddell, Sapp, Zivley, Hill & LaBoon
Houston

Bankruptcy Counsel for Eastern
Harvey R. Miller
Weil, Gotshal & Manges
New York

SEC Counsel for Eastern
Michael L. Jamieson
Holland & Knight
Tampa

Labor Counsel for Eastern*
John J. Gallagher
Akin, Gump, Strauss, Hauer & Feld
Washington

Corporate Counsel for Eastern*
James W. Giddens
Hughes, Hubbard & Reed
New York

Special Litigation Counsel for Eastern*
Mary Boies
Mary Boies and Associates
Bedford, N.Y.

Parker C. Folse III
Susman, Godfrey & McGowan
Houston

Criminal Counsel for Eastern
Jane W. Parver
Kaye, Scholer, Fierman, Hays & Handler
New York

Financial Adviser to Eastern*
Nicholas J. Sakellariadis
Smith, Barney, Harris, Upham & Co.
New York

Financial Adviser to Eastern
Arnold Kroll
Wertheim, Schroeder & Co.
New York

Airline Consultant to Eastern
Daniel Kasper
Harbridge House
Boston

Accountant to Eastern*
Arthur Andersen
New York

Accountant to Eastern
Price Waterhouse
Miami

Official Committee of Unsecured Creditors

Member	*Counsel*
Chair: Alan Boyd Airbus Industrie Washington	Lillian Kraemer Simpson, Thatcher & Bartlett New York
John Bavis Air Line Pilots Association Washington	Bruce Simon Cohen, Weiss & Simon New York
Bruce Lewis American National Bank and Trust Co. of Chicago Chicago	Harold L. Kaplan Mayer, Brown & Platt Chicago

Member	*Counsel*
Bonnie Jean Peter AT&T Basking Ridge, N.J.	Richard Lieb Kronish, Lieb, Weiner & Hellman New York
Scott Scherer Boeing Company Renton, Wash.	Henry L. Goodman Zalkin, Rodin & Goodman New York and Graham H. Fernald Perkins Coie Seattle
Thomas Boyle Citicorp New York	Mary Rose Brusewitz Shearman & Sterling New York
Mary Grace Shore Eastern Noncontract Employees Charles City, Va.	None
Thomas H. Flood General Electric Cincinnati	Richard Epling Sidley & Austin New York
Mark Manski IBJ Schroeder Bank & Trust New York	Richard S. Miller Rogers & Wells New York
John Peterpaul International Association of Machinists Washington	Joseph Guerrieri Guerrieri, Edmonds & James Washington

Member	*Counsel*
William A. Overlock Lintas: New York New York	Leo Egan Lintas: New York New York
Tom Statas Cater Air International (a division of Marriott) Potomoc, Md.	None
Ronald O. Kelley Rolls-Royce Greenwich, Conn.	H. Barry Vasios Gilbert, Segall & Young New York
Mary Jane Barry Transport Workers Union Miami	Malcolm A. Goldstein O'Donnell & Schwartz New York
Thomas B. Zakrzewski United States Trust New York	James Gadsen Carter, Ledyard & Milburn New York
Thomas A. Ansaldi United Technologies Hartford	George Weisz Cleary, Gottlieb, Steen & Hamilton New York

Counsel to Creditors' Committee

Joel B. Zweibel
O'Melveny & Myers
New York

Investment Banker to Creditors' Committee

Donald R. Gant
Goldman, Sachs & Co.
New York

Financial Adviser to Creditors' Committee
Arthur Newman
Chemical Bank
New York

Accountants to Creditors' Committee
Ernst & Young
New York

Airline Consultant to Creditors' Committee
Jack B. Fier
Jack B. Fier & Associates
Huntington, N.Y.

Official Committee of Preferred Stockholders
Robert J. Dwyer
IAM Trust
Washington

Mr. Charles Silvers
Miami

Mr. & Mrs. Rhett G. Cooper
Columbia, S.C.

Mr. Frank Sobchak
Fort Lauderdale

Counsel for Preferred Stockholders' Committee
David A. Strumwasser
Berlack, Israels & Liberman
New York

Investment Banker for Preferred Stockholders' Committee
Wilbur L. Ross
Rothschild, Inc.
New York

Selected Miscellaneous Counsel
Cadwalader, Wickersham & Taft (N.Y.)
Cravath, Swaine & Moore (N.Y.)
Crummy, Del Dio, Dolan, Griffinger & Vecchione (Newark)
Davis Polk & Wardwell (N.Y.)
Dow, Lohnes & Albertson (N.Y.)
Dreyer & Traub (N.Y.)
Duker & Barrett (N.Y.)
Marshall S. Filler, P.C. (Washington)
Fordham & Starrett (Boston)
Gardere & Wynne (Dallas)
Gendel, Raskoff, Shapiro & Quittner (Los Angeles)
Gibson, Dunn & Crutcher (N.Y.)
Greenberg, Traurig, Hoffman, Lipoff, Rosen & Quintel (Miami)
Hill & Barlow (Boston)
Jones, Day, Reavis & Pogue (N.Y.)
McCarter & English (Newark)
Mudge, Rose, Guthrie, Alexander & Ferdon (N.Y.)
Ogletree, Deakins, Nash, Smoak & Stewart (Washington)
Pepper, Hamilton & Scheetz (Philadelphia)
Riker, Danzig, Scherer & Hyland (Morristown, N.J.)
Schoeman, Marsh & Updike (N.Y.)
Shea & Gould (N.Y.)
Siff, Rosen & Parker (N.Y.)
Smith, Gambrell & Russell (Atlanta)
Stroock & Stroock & Lavan (N.Y.)
Sullivan & Cromwell (N.Y.)
Vladek, Waldman, Elias & Engelhard (N.Y.)
Webster & Sheffield (N.Y.)
Willkie, Farr & Gallagher (N.Y.)
Wilmer, Cutler & Pickering (Washington)
Winston & Strawn (Chicago)

The number of advisers in the Eastern case was exceeded only by the amount of the fees that they charged. During the last months of Eastern's life, of the roughly $5 million in monthly professional fees that Eastern paid on average, 80 percent was spent on the top seven fee producers:

Weil, Gotshal & Manges	$2,000,000
Verner Liipfert	750,000
O'Melveny & Myers	500,000
Dickstein, Shapiro & Morin	350,000
Wertheim, Schroeder & Co.	150,000
Goldman Sachs & Co.	150,000
Chemical Bank	100,000
Top 7 Total	$4,000,000

In some months, the total was substantially higher. Furthermore, the average figures that are shown above do not include fees paid for special projects. For example, Shapiro spent an entire year investigating and then reporting on the prepetition transactions. His firm submitted its bill for that work and the numbers were simply staggering:

Fees:	$4,073,660
Expenses:	742,555
Total:	$4,816,215

Included in the expense total was $82,138 in secretarial overtime and $25,271 for meals.

Ironically, had Texas Air settled the prepetition transactions just by reimbursing the Eastern estate for Shapiro's legal bill incurred in investigating them, the creditors would have received more in value than they ultimately ever did from Texas Air on the prepetition transactions themselves.

The nimiety of advisers and their respective legions in this case, not to mention their exorbitant fees, played a large role in killing Eastern. First, it is difficult to imagine the huge amount of senior management time and effort, on a daily basis that was diverted from focusing on fixing Eastern's problems to responding to requests for information from all the advisers in the case. Shugrue himself often complained that he thought that the job of trustee really was as a "provider of information." Second, the amount of money that went out the door each month in paying for professional fees, roughly $5 million during the latter stages, could obviously have been spent much more productively in a revenue-generating capacity. For example, had only half of what went to professional fees on a monthly basis been spent instead on advertising, Eastern's advertising budget would have almost doubled with a positive impact on load factors and revenues. Finally, the decision to shut Eastern down in January 1991 was driven largely by Shugrue's concern that, ultimately, Eastern would not even have enough money left to be able to pay its administrative expenses, which consisted mostly of professional fees. Were a different system in place for the payment of professional fees in bankruptcy, it is quite possible that Eastern could still be flying today!

During a speech given to the American Bar Association in the summer of 1991, Vice President Dan Quayle, chairman of the White House Council on Competitiveness, suggested that the nation's legal system needed to be overhauled if American industry was ever to become truly competitive on a global scale. Such an overhaul should definitely include the Bankruptcy Code. The vast majority of companies that enter the abyss of bankruptcy never make it out. In fact, a 1991 survey of all Chapter 11 filings found that only 17 percent resulted in court-approved reorganization plans. It's a good bet that the remaining 83 percent that ended up in liquidation did so largely because of the professional fee payment structure inherent in the Bankruptcy Code.

As of the end of 1991, the LTV Corporation had spent over $150 million, roughly 10 percent of the corporation's net worth, on professional fees during its five-year bankruptcy odyssey, which will likely continue for several more years. By the time Eastern's case is officially closed, more than $100 million in professional fees will have been incurred, just as in the Drexel Burnham Lambert and Federated Department Stores bankruptcy cases. What is needed is an immediate and substantial overhaul of the Bankruptcy Code to reduce both the length and cost of bankruptcy proceedings. Any overhaul should focus on eliminating pointless litigation, reducing the number of committees and curtailing the number of professionals and their respective costs.

I can't help but imagine that American competitiveness would benefit substantially if the bankruptcy laws were changed to make it more likely, rather than less likely, that American businesses could emerge from bankruptcy as healthy global competitors.

7

THEY'LL NEVER BE ABLE TO MATCH

Throughout the summer of 1990, it was apparent that Shugrue's five-point strategic plan was having a positive and immediate impact on Eastern. Eastern's load factor, or percentage of seats filled, increased substantially through the summer months above and beyond the normal summer seasonal peak levels. Eastern improved from being near the bottom of the major airlines in on-time performance before Shugrue's arrival to being number two overall. Passenger surveys showed that people who hadn't even dreamed of flying Eastern in the spring were coming back during the summer, largely because of the aggressive image advertising campaign that had appeared on national television, on radio and in newspapers and magazines across the country. Even employee surveys reflected a sea change in the level of employee morale at Eastern. All of these advances occurred within a matter of ninety days.

Notwithstanding all of these important improvements over such a short period of time, Eastern continued to lose money. Lots of it. Over $1 million a day.

The problem was simple. Eastern's costs were in line with what they needed to be; however, Eastern's revenues were falling far short of the mark. In other words, Eastern had a serious yield problem.

Prior to the strike and bankruptcy filing, Eastern continually had yields in the 12 to 14 cent range. This meant that the fares Eastern was able to charge generated, on average, revenue of between 12 and 14 cents per passenger per mile flown. Unfortunately, Eastern was never profitable in those days because its costs to fly its passengers who paid from 12 to 14 cents per mile were, on average, around 11 cents per mile. This meant that Eastern had to fill at least 79 percent of its seats on every flight just to break even, which was an almost impossible task. An airline that fills 65 percent of its seats in an average month is considered to be doing extremely well. Eastern had trouble during many months just breaking 60 percent.

During bankruptcy, because of the strike and the new nonunion workforce, Eastern's costs per seat-mile had dropped to around 8 cents. However, all of the negative publicity caused by the labor and safety problems that the airline faced had completely scared off the business traveler who pays the highest fares. This resulted in mostly leisure travelers flying Eastern, which caused the airline's yields to drop to around 10 cents per mile. The net result was that lower costs were met with lower yields and, therefore, Eastern's breakeven load factor continued to hover around 80 percent. Even if Eastern quadrupled its advertising expense, it was never going to come close to filling 80 percent of its seats.

Thus, the way to return Eastern to profitability was to figure out how to get the yields back up to the 12 to 14 cent range that existed prebankruptcy. Even if Eastern only made it back up to 12 cents, with costs of only 8 cents, the airline's breakeven load factor would drop to 67 percent, something that was definitely in the ball park!

Eastern's yield problem was not unlike the yield problem that

Continental faced in 1987 after the Big Bang and its attendant service problems. Whenever consistently bad publicity engulfs an airline, it is normally the business traveler, whose travel costs are usually reimbursed by his employer, who stops flying the airline. The cure for the problem at Continental, though it took almost three years to reap its full benefits, was the *YONEPASS* program that was initiated in late 1987.

"We need to do something like *YONEPASS* at Eastern," I said one evening over drinks to Jim O'Donnell, the marketing guru whom Shugrue had brought in as part of the Eastern brain trust. O'Donnell knew exactly what I meant because he had been directly involved in structuring the *YONEPASS* program at Continental.

Realizing that Eastern's situation was desperate, more so than that of Continental's in 1987, O'Donnell saw that something more than just a *YONEPASS* kind of idea would be required. "Let's not just give them a first-class seat for the price of coach," he said one day. "Let's also give them a hell of a lot more first-class seats at that same low price." From this stroke of marketing wizardry came one of the most revolutionary concepts in the history of airline marketing, Eastern's First Class Program.

Although the idea was revolutionary, the program itself was very simple. An average Boeing 727 in Eastern's fleet had 12 first-class seats up front. By moving the partition between coach and first-class back just a couple of rows, up to an additional 12 seats could be placed in first-class, for a total of 24. Of course, on Eastern's larger aircraft such as the Airbus A300 and Boeing 757, one could fit up to 48 seats in the new first-class configuration. Then, instead of just regular seats with cloth fabric, brand new leather seats would be provided, which were also wider and had more legroom. Finally, the entire first-class in-flight service product would be redesigned. New china and tableware, fine wines and meals would be served, regardless of trip length. Even new uniforms and training for the flight attendants. And all for the price of a regular coach ticket. The end result would be a first-class makeover the likes of which the airline industry had never before seen.

O'Donnell, the Eastern marketing staff and the advertising agency had a field day with creating the new advertising and marketing campaign for the first-class roll-out. The commercials, which aired on national TV immediately after Labor Day, featured Shugrue walking down the aisle of the new expanded first-class section of an airplane talking to customers about the leather seats, greater legroom, etc. However, my enthusiasm for the program was focused on the additional revenue-generating capability of an Eastern airplane and how quickly it could get the airline back up to 12-cent yields and a chance at breaking even.

By almost doubling the number of seats that would potentially be filled with passengers paying full coach fares, and given the fact that before the program began only an average of two passengers per flight were paying such fares, if Eastern filled only 50 percent of the new first-class seats, the airline would increase substantially the number of full coach passengers it carried on an average flight. Such an increase would immediately allow Eastern to break even. The sensitivity analyses showed that Eastern could get by with only five additional passengers who paid full coach fares per flight, *ceteris paribus* (a term economists use to mean "everything else remaining constant"). This meant that as long as Eastern kept the back of the airplane filled with the same number of low-fare travelers that it was carrying before the program began, all Eastern needed to break even systemwide was an additional five passengers per flight under the new first-class program.

The implementation plan called for every single one of Eastern's 156 jet aircraft to be taken out of service, refitted with the new first-class cabin and put back into service by early October. The project involved every department of Eastern to such an extent that Shugrue used it as a convenient opportunity for a complete corporate image makeover. One that would get employees to focus on providing the best customer service possible.

The cost to implement the program was estimated at roughly $16 million. Of course, a one-time expenditure of such magnitude had to be approved by the creditors because the $16 million would necessarily come from the special escrow account set aside to pay them. After a detailed presentation to the creditors' committee given by Shugrue and just about all of Eastern's senior executives, Goldman Sachs determined that the program would not work. Goldman believed that Delta, Eastern's main competitor in Atlanta and the one airline likely to be harmed the most from the program, was going to be able to render the program ineffective merely by adopting a similar first-class program of its own.

This argument was incorrect for several reasons. First, Delta had never during the Eastern bankruptcy lowered its fares to match Eastern's. In fact, Eastern continued to have fares averaging 25 percent less than Delta's out of Atlanta, and Delta continued to handle more traffic out of Atlanta than Eastern, largely due to public doubt about Eastern's viability. Why all of a sudden would Delta lower its fares, and dilute its own revenues, merely to match the fares of its already-decimated competitor where that competitor had never before been a threat? Second, it was physically impossible for Delta to expand its first-class cabins as Eastern planned to do without suffering substantial revenue and operational problems. It was estimated that it would take Delta eighteen months to reconfigure its entire fleet, which was twice the size of Eastern's, to match the new Eastern first-class configuration. Even Harry Kimbriel, Shapiro's airline consultant, believed that not only would the first-class program be unmatchable by Delta, or anyone else for that matter, but that the expectation of generating five additional first-class passengers per flight was reasonable.

The creditors finally agreed to the idea. The program began on

October first, and the results were nothing less than extraordinary. Full-fare bookings, which averaged less than 1,500 per day before the start of the program, ballooned to 18,000 per day within just a matter of weeks. Advance booking and revenue estimates were being greatly exceeded. There was a huge increase in full-fare passengers in only one month and at 30 percent higher yields. Advance bookings for the month of November were at their highest level in five years, and five years before this, Eastern was an airline two-and-one-half times larger in size.

Unfortunately, before the program had even a full month of existence, the creditors' public calls for Eastern's liquidation in November completely destroyed the value that had been so painstakingly built into the product. After all, no business traveler was going to book a trip on Eastern if the ability of the airline to fulfill that trip was in doubt, regardless of how wide a first-class seat may have been offered. The first-class experiment, which was working beyond expectations, died before it really had a chance to be effective.

After Midway Airlines filed for bankruptcy in 1991, it adopted a similar program for its aircraft. David Kunstler, Midway's planning chief and former senior vice president of planning at Eastern, had seen the benefits of the first-class program at Eastern and attempted to transport the same results to Midway. Unfortunately, because of Midway's other problems, the program was largely ineffective and Midway was forced to shut down and liquidate in November 1991.

Besides the first-class program, Eastern's marketing strategy was to attempt to position Shugrue as a type of Lee Iacocca of the Nineties, as one account executive from the ad agency Ogilvy and Mather put it. Just about all airline advertising focuses on the product offered. For example, where you can fly and how much it's going to cost you. Eastern's advertising tried to change the focus of the advertising to a story, or image, of an airline fighting back with quality service, caring employees and a vision for the future, all personified by an individual who was appointed by the court to try and mount a turnaround. The great advertising that was actually put together was directly related to the change in focus that the marketing strategy provided.

Perhaps the most famous of all of Eastern's postbankruptcy promotions was the advertisement in which Shugrue is standing in front of an Eastern 757 in a Miami maintenance hangar holding a question-and-answer session with hundreds of Eastern employees assembled in front of, behind and above him. The advertisement became so popular that David Letterman, the television comedian on NBC, performed a skit in which he pretends to be an Eastern employee asking questions during one of the Q&A sessions in the hangar. Letterman's skit was so funny that Shugrue contemplated, but in the end decided against, showing a video of it as part of his presentation at a creditors' committee meeting. "You never know how those guys will react to humor," Shugrue joked during an officer staff meeting.

Working at Eastern during that period was not a normal endeavor. In fact, it was far from normal. So much was going on that it was difficult even for Shugrue to keep a handle on all of the various activities. He relied on his brain trust to keep the Eastern beast in check and to flag any potential trouble spots. The most valuable person in this regard was Sicilian, the chief in-house lawyer. It was amazing that Sicilian could keep track of so many different issues, any one of which would be enough to cripple the airline if allowed to fester out of control. Although much of his time was spent riding herd on Weil Gotshal and, to a lesser extent, Verner Liipfert, Sicilian's most important job was to protect Shugrue's flank from the many broadsides directed toward the trustee. At this, Sicilian excelled.

Perhaps one of the most important areas that Sicilian kept his eye on was the labor issue. Obviously, one key component of Shugrue's five-point strategic plan to resurrect Eastern was to negotiate a settlement of the union issues that had decimated the carrier and, in fact, led to its bankruptcy filing. Given his long-time reputation in the industry as being fair with labor, Shugrue entered the Eastern situation with the deep-felt belief that he could structure a settlement that would be satisfactory to all parties.

When Shugrue arrived at Eastern in April 1990, both ALPA (pilots) and the TWU (flight attendants) had already called off their sympathy strikes in favor of the IAM. However, although no longer technically on strike, ALPA and the TWU were effectively locked out of Eastern because Eastern had hired replacement pilots and flight attendants to get the airline up and flying again. Both ALPA and the TWU were looking for ways to get their members back on the Eastern payroll, because they had made very little progress, if any, in this regard with Eastern President Bakes and with Lorenzo. Also, since a good portion of ALPA and TWU members had either crossed the IAM picket lines during the strike or returned to work voluntarily after it, some ALPA and TWU leaders were concerned that the unions themselves might be completely broken unless a settlement was reached quickly with Eastern. Thus, both ALPA and the TWU considered Shugrue's appointment as a unique opportunity not only to settle the replacement worker issue but also, in the final analysis, to save the union locals themselves.

Charlie Bryan and the IAM, however, were still on strike with no settlement on the horizon when Shugrue was appointed. Bryan, since the beginning of the strike, had filed numerous lawsuits against Eastern and Texas Air attempting to force Eastern to rehire his strikers but to no avail. Unlike ALPA and the TWU, many of whose members had crossed picket lines or had otherwise returned to Eastern voluntarily, very few IAM members had crossed the picket lines. Thus, the IAM had a limited number of "eyes and ears" inside Eastern, which could keep Bryan and the IAM leadership informed as to what was going on inside Eastern on a daily basis. The resulting isolation that Bryan and the IAM felt was amplified by the fact that Bakes and Lorenzo, during the entire bankruptcy, made no serious effort to negotiate with Bryan.

Thus, although a key player in the course of Eastern events prior to the bankruptcy filing, Bryan was relegated to the sidelines with no key role whatsoever postbankruptcy. For a union leader with as much reliance on public relations as Bryan, this must have been unbearable. Shugrue's appointment was the first ray of hope that Bryan had seen since March 1989 to interject himself back into the spotlight at Eastern.

Since ALPA and the TWU had by the time of Shugrue's appointment already called off their sympathy strikes, the issue with them was the rights of the permanent replacement pilots and flight attendants at Eastern versus the rights of the ALPA pilots and TWU flight attendants. ALPA and TWU claimed that because they had called off their strikes, their members were legally entitled to return to work at the same rates of pay and under the same work rules that existed before the strike. In their view, the replacement workers now at Eastern were there as temporary replacements only until ALPA and the TWU called off their strikes and their members returned to their old jobs.

Of course, Eastern's position on this issue was very different. Immediately after the strike when the airline was grounded, Eastern put out a desperate call to potential replacement workers to help get the airline flying again. The replacements, many of whom had to endure both verbal and physical harassment from IAM picketers, were promised that they would have permanent jobs at Eastern no matter what the ultimate resolution of the union situation turned out to be.

Upon his arrival at Eastern, Shugrue stated, "My highest priority as trustee is to resolve the long-standing labor disputes at Eastern because that is essential in order to reestablish Eastern as a viable carrier." However, he also added the proviso that "we will not sacrifice the well-being of the permanent replacement workers."

Thus, for any settlement at all to be reached, a way had to be found to appease both ALPA and the TWU without offering up the permanent replacements as sacrificial lambs.

Shugrue and Sicilian put Ron Natalie, Verner Liipfert's labor lawyer, in charge of the Eastern labor negotiating team. Natalie's strategy was to negotiate a settlement with ALPA first, because it was expected that the TWU would follow along. Working closely with Al Gibson, Eastern's senior vice president of human resources, Natalie delivered to the Eastern ALPA leadership a simple but straightforward message from Shugrue: "We'll do whatever we reasonably can to settle except fire the permanent replacements."

Notwithstanding this reasonable position, ALPA was resolute. Eastern had to fire the permanent replacement workers before the union would formally agree to allow its members to be recalled. This position on the part of ALPA is difficult to understand because the Supreme Court, in an earlier case involving a similar issue with TWA and its flight attendants, had ruled that TWA's permanent replacement workers were protected against possible displacement caused by the recall of formerly striking union members.

Faced with the unpleasant option of going back on his promise to the replacement pilots, who by this time had formed their own in-house union called the Eastern Pilots Association (EPA) to protect themselves against possible displacement by ALPA members, Shugrue decided that ALPA's negotiating stance gave him no choice but to stand firmly behind his promise to the EPA pilots. Thus, after several weeks of ultimately unsuccessful negotiations with ALPA, Eastern filed a motion in the bankruptcy court to throw out the ALPA contract altogether. Also, in early August, the pilots' contract had come up for amendment, and the union officially had joined the IAM on the picket line again. This new ALPA strike, however, was completely ineffective since the permanent replacements continued to work at the airline.

Because of the changes to the Bankruptcy Code made in 1984 after Lorenzo had unilaterally thrown out Continental's labor agreements in 1983, the new code section, Section 1113, provides that a debtor may reject a collective bargaining agreement only if there has been a good faith effort to negotiate with the union, the union has rejected the proposal and the "balance of the equities" clearly favors rejection. Basically, Section 1113 provides for a judge, rather than a debtor or trustee, to make the ultimate determination whether a labor agreement can be rejected.

In mid-August, Judge Lifland agreed with Shugrue that the permanent replacement pilots of Eastern should be protected, and agreed to the Section 1113 relief sought by the trustee. Lifland's order allowed the permanent replacement pilots to continue flying at Eastern, and ALPA members would be recalled only if there was room for them below the replacement pilots, which at the time there was not.

At about the same time that Lifland issued his ruling in favor of Eastern, a federal district court in Miami, in another suit filed by ALPA on a similar issue regarding the permanent replacements, ruled in favor of ALPA. Immediately after the IAM strike began in March 1989, all but 200 or so of the 3,600 Eastern ALPA pilots walked off the job in sympathy with the IAM. After ALPA ended its sympathy strike in November 1989, fewer than 50 ALPA pilots had been recalled. This was largely because, by November 1989, many of the replacement pilots were in the process of being trained and, after that training, Eastern would have no need for the returning ALPA members. ALPA, if it couldn't get all the replacements thrown out, settled for arguing that its members should be recalled prior to those replacement pilots who were in training at the time ALPA called off its strike. ALPA filed suit on this matter in the United States District Court for the Southern District of Florida to get a restraining order against Eastern's hiring any of the replacement pilots who were in training at the time ALPA called off its strike until all of ALPA's members had been recalled. Since Eastern had already hired over 2,000 replacement pilots, including those in training, the practical effect of such a restraining order would be the ultimate firing of all the replacements and forced recall of the ALPA pilots.

Evidently, ALPA's strategy of filing the lawsuit in Miami, where it could be assured of a warm judicial reception, paid off because the court ruled in their favor. Eastern immediately appealed this ruling to the United States Court of Appeals for the Eleventh Circuit, which is located in Atlanta, but lost there as well. In late December 1990, the Eleventh Circuit stated that "the District Court properly concluded that the Railway Labor Act requires Eastern to reinstate returning strikers prior to awarding pilot positions to new hires in training."

After toying with the idea of appealing the issue to the Supreme Court, Eastern decided to abide by the Eleventh Circuit ruling and began recalling ALPA members. In early January 1991, Eastern agreed to recall sixty former striking ALPA pilots. However, by that time, the move was largely symbolic since just two weeks later Eastern shut down for good.

ALPA's decision to fight the issue all the way was actually a smart strategic move. Although Shugrue offered the union an olive branch back in the late spring of 1990, had ALPA accepted anything less than the firing of the permanent replacements, ALPA's members would have still been on the street. Eastern wasn't growing much after the trustee was appointed, which meant that opportunities for the recall of ALPA members were slim anyway. ALPA was a lot better off going for broke trying to get all the replacements fired in one fell swoop rather than waiting for the obviously dying Eastern to grow large enough for ALPA members to be recalled as part of an ongoing fleet expansion. Unfortunately for ALPA, their gambit didn't pay off because Eastern didn't last long enough for them to reap the fruits of their court victory.

After Eastern shut down in January 1991, ALPA's national president, Captain J. Randolph Babbitt, said, "Shugrue completely ignored the fundamental labor problems that had to be resolved if the airline was ever to have even a prayer for recovery." What Babbitt didn't say was that the ALPA negotiating position left Shugrue no choice in the matter.

While Natalie negotiated with ALPA, Shugrue kept busy attempting to figure out how he would handle Charlie Bryan and the IAM. Unlike ALPA, the IAM contract had expired and, in fact, had already gone through the required Railway Labor Act dispute resolution process with the National Mediation Board. Thus, the only way the IAM could get back on the property was to negotiate a completely new agreement with the trustee. Shugrue knew that this would be difficult for a couple of reasons. First, after the strike Eastern had hired new nonunion mechanics off the street starting at $9.50 per hour. This was substantially below the $16.50 per hour starting wage for which the old IAM contract provided. Given Bryan's past history regarding wage demands, Shugrue reasonably expected that Bryan would not budge much, if at all, from the old wage scale, notwithstanding Eastern's horrible financial condition. Second, and more importantly, it is possible that Bryan may not have desired to reach an agreement with Eastern anyway. Bryan may have seen that Eastern was dying and that it would be only a matter of time before the end arrived. He thus could have felt that he and the IAM were better off from a national perspective if he pushed Eastern over the edge. Eastern's destruction could then be used as a warning to other airlines by the IAM as an example of what could happen if the IAM is pushed too far. If this were true, then Shugrue obviously wanted to be careful about putting too many detailed proposals on the negotiating table.

This made the negotiating environment with the IAM extremely difficult and sensitive. Although there was not the level of personal animosity in the negotiations with Shugrue as there had been with Lorenzo, Shugrue became suspicious that Bryan himself did not want to reach an agreement.

The IAM talks ended before they really even got started, and the IAM, as well as the rest of the Eastern unions, spent the time during the last months of Eastern's life doing everything possible to hammer the final nail in the carrier's coffin.

Without a doubt, the most serious union broadside after

Shugrue's arrival occurred in early September, after all three unions saw that labor settlements were, for whatever reasons, not going to happen. The unions began a smear campaign against Eastern consisting of union members, particularly ALPA pilots, showing up at large travel agencies in Miami and Atlanta bad-mouthing Eastern in general and raising questions about the carrier's safety and financial viability. Such acts were particularly destructive because of the general concern that Eastern was unsafe even during the time that the trustee was in charge. ALPA played upon those lingering doubts in the minds of travel agents, and the result was that the agents began steering large numbers of bookings Eastern would have received otherwise toward Delta.

Eastern's real cause for concern over the smear campaign was that the unions were using their positions as members of the creditors' committee to acquire confidential information about Eastern and then divulging it in a way designed to damage Eastern. It got so bad at one point that Eastern's financial results would be printed on the front pages of the *Miami Herald, Atlanta Constitution* and *Wall Street Journal* almost as quickly as Eastern's middle managers learned what they were.

In an effort to stop both the leaks and the very damaging smear campaign, Eastern filed motions in bankruptcy court both for the removal of the unions from the creditors' committee altogether as well as for an injunction against the smear campaign. By the time either of these motions could have a practical effect, they were rendered moot in late October by the public outcry for liquidation by the creditors.

Indeed by late July 1990, Shugrue's five-point plan for Eastern was actually beginning to show tangible positive results. Even Eastern's financial condition had improved somewhat by this time. Although Eastern continued to lose, in terms of net-income, over $1 million per day, the carrier's negative cash-flow from operations had decreased somewhat. Since Eastern was in bankruptcy, reported net-income figures were really irrelevant. The key was how much cash Eastern ate up on a daily basis over and above that which it generated in revenue. From a strictly cash-flow standpoint, Eastern had made and was continuing to show improvement. This was the result of the overall progress that had been made in addition to a surgical cost-reduction program that had been put in place. Even discussions with several parties, such as Northwest's Checchi, to purchase some or all of Eastern's assets were, at the time, showing substantial progress.

By late July, Shugrue could honestly look back on his first hundred days as trustee and conclude that he had done an excellent job of not only keeping Eastern afloat but actually getting the airline to start turning the corner on its myriad problems.

Well before dawn hit the early morning sky above Miami on August 2, 1990, I was up working on some papers in my suite at the Colonnade Hotel in Coral Gables. I decided to take a break and turned on the television. As soon as I turned the channel to CNN, I was shocked to see a film clip showing Iraqi tanks streaking across the desert toward Kuwait City. Although I did not fully appreciate the seriousness of what was soon to transpire, operations Desert Shield and Desert Storm for example, I did have an uneasy feeling in the pit of my stomach that Eastern's fragile financial position would somehow immediately change for the worse.

On August 1, 1990, Eastern was paying 56.5 cents per gallon for Jet A fuel. By the end of that same week, Eastern's average price for Jet A had exploded to almost $1.20 per gallon, an increase of 112 percent. Obviously, the immediate effect on Eastern was devastating. Eastern's second biggest expense, fuel, had more than doubled overnight without any increase in the airline's revenues. As a result, Eastern lost double the amount each day than it had prior to the oil shock. Instead of losing $1 million per day during the month of July, Eastern lost $2 million per day during the month of August. And this was the best month of the year for airline travel! What would happen during the slow months of September and October, when load factors normally drop twenty percentage points from their August peak?

All of the progress that had been made during the prior three months was automatically and suddenly rendered moot. After all, everyone knew that no amount of advertising would increase revenues enough to counter a doubling of the airline's second largest expense. A change in the attitude of Eastern managers after August second was obvious and immediately detectable. The "jump" in everyone's step, the enthusiasm that Eastern was making headway, were no longer present. Many executives began leaving for jobs either at other airlines or in other industries. At one point the outflow of Eastern managers became so bad that I remarked to Sicilian, "The ship's sinking so fast that even the rats are starting to jump overboard."

Shugrue, in an effort to stem the loss of Eastern management talent, quickly had Verner Liipfert devise a program that would act as "golden handcuffs" to provide a strong incentive for Eastern managers to ride it out. The program was called the Key Employee Retention Program, or KERP. In mid-August, KERP was adopted for full-time key employees to protect them in case Eastern shut down and to prevent a brain drain during such a crucial period for the company.

KERP had two components. The first was a retention/incentive component that encouraged 168 designated key management and operational employees to remain with Eastern and rewarded them for reaching certain benchmark calendar days in Eastern's employ or for Eastern reaching certain financial milestones such as a sale of all or substantially all of its assets. The second was a separation component that encouraged the 168 key employees to remain at Eastern by providing a reasonable level of financial security for continuing in Eastern's employ during the pendency of its Chapter 11 case. A key employee could receive a benefit under one of the components but not both.

KERP had a total cost to the Eastern estate of almost $25 million. The separation part of the program called for corporate officers to receive up to eight months' salary. Nonmanagement employees would receive up to four weeks' pay.

The impact of August second was felt directly in other areas as well. Rolf Andresen, Eastern's CFO, immediately began to track Eastern's cash flow on a daily basis. Each day, he would get a report from James P. McGuinness, Eastern's treasurer, on how much cash Eastern had in its operating bank accounts as of the close of business and how much money in checks was outstanding. This amount would then be projected over a thirty-day period based on revenues estimated to be received. The result was that Andresen was able to give Shugrue a day-by-day estimate of Eastern's cash position and, finally, a time frame for when the cash would eventually run out. The fact that a company with over $2 billion in annual revenues would have to track its cash flow on a daily basis is an example of one of the serious problems that the Iraqi invasion caused for Eastern.

Of course, a direct result of the invasion was an added kick to the recession, which manifested itself in the early fall with a substantial reduction in the volume of airline passenger traffic both in the U.S. and abroad. Thus, although Eastern's fuel costs remained at roughly double what they were preinvasion, revenues were actually dropping significantly, as no amount of discounting could get enough people to travel during the fall to make up the difference. Although the entire industry was experiencing this phenomenon, Eastern was hurt the most because its cash position was so tenuous.

The Iraqi invasion, and the resultant cost increases and revenue evaporation that it caused, in and of itself was enough to accelerate Eastern's demise. However, when combined with the effects of a major criminal indictment for maintenance violations, the result was just too much for Eastern to bear.

On July 25, 1990, following an extensive federal investigation into illegal maintenance practices at Eastern from July 1985 through May 1989, Andrew J. Maloney, the United States Attorney in Brooklyn, unsealed a sixty-count criminal indictment issued by a federal grand jury. The indictment named as defendants Eastern as well as ten current and former employees, including Edward F. Upton, Eastern's former vice president of maintenance and engineering. The indictment charged that the defendants conspired to defraud the federal government through their interference with Federal Aviation Administration (FAA) and Department of Transportation (DOT) safety procedures. The illegal acts included falsifying aircraft maintenance records and failing to make certain required maintenance and corrective repairs at Eastern's maintenance bases located at John F. Kennedy International, LaGuardia and Atlanta Hartsfield airports. The defendants were also charged with concealing from, and rendering false testimony to, the FAA.

Anthony P. Valenti, an investigator in the case, stated in his affidavit: "My investigation has revealed that Eastern management employees routinely falsified FAA required maintenance records to make it appear that required maintenance and corrective repairs had been completed on aircraft when, in reality, either the work had not been accomplished or the purported corrective actions taken were not designed to correct the problems."

In the world of aviation, there are no more serious charges than those included in the Eastern indictment. In fact, this was the first time in U.S. aviation history that an airline had been indicted for deliberately and purposefully putting passengers at risk by failing to maintain its aircraft adequately.

One of the most serious violations charged was one known as "pencil whipping." Under FAA regulations, Eastern maintenance personnel had to sign aircraft log books every time a maintenance procedure was performed on an airplane or engine. The log books are crucial because they also keep track of all the procedures that are performed during an aircraft's lifetime. Most maintenance procedures have to be performed after a certain number of flight hours. Pencil whipping occurs when someone signs a log book saying that a particular procedure was performed when in fact it was not performed. Since just about every maintenance procedure on an airplane or engine is performed based on the number of flight hours since the last procedure, pencil whipping results in maintenance that is overdue and not performed until the next cycle, which could be months after the actual time required. During that period when maintenance procedures that should have been performed are not, tragedy can strike.

Some of the individual Eastern defendants were charged with signing their names to log books when they themselves did not do the work. Others were charged with forging others' names or, even worse, signing fictitious names and entering false employee numbers. The government charged that these reprehensible practices occurred largely because maintenance managers were under extreme pressure from senior management to cut corners on maintenance procedures to keep the airplanes in the air as long as possible, thus maximizing revenue and minimizing maintenance costs. The indictment stated that the violations occurred "as a result of unreasonable demands, pressure and intimidation put on [maintenance personnel] by Eastern's upper management to keep the aircraft in flight at all costs.... "

Airline pilots are more sensitive about maintenance than anyone since they put their lives in the hands of mechanics every time they step into the cockpit. As a former pilot himself, Shugrue was deeply troubled by the indictment because the charges, if true, meant that Eastern's maintenance infrastructure constituted a public menace that had to be completely eradicated. In fact, Shugrue said many times after his appointment as trustee, both publicly and privately, that if he ever found any evidence of ongoing maintenance violations at Eastern, he would immediately shut down the entire airline and fire everyone in the maintenance organization from top to bottom. And he meant it. There was simply no excuse for an airline to condone practices in which its passengers were put at grave risk due to a lack of management control over the purposefully illegal acts of its employees.

The implications of the indictment were nothing short of catastrophic. Passengers, already fearful of flying Eastern because of its shaky financial condition, were in the summer of 1990 given another, more substantial reason to stay away from the airline: safety concerns. Although the indictment covered an earlier time frame than that encompassing the trustee's tenure, serious damage had been done to Eastern's image. Unlike with most airline safety issues, when an airline simply pays an FAA fine and the news blows over fairly quickly, this was different. Eastern never really recovered from the sting of the indictment.

But lost passengers and a tarnished image were only the tip of the iceberg. Since the acts described in the indictment occurred prior to Shugrue's appointment, and since changes in Eastern's maintenance organization had been made after the acts occurred, Shugrue was content to settle the issue immediately by pleading out the indictment as far as Eastern as a corporate entity was concerned. However, the U.S. Attorney, Maloney, evidently believed that wrongdoing extended all the way up Eastern's chain of command and therefore wanted Eastern as a corporate entity to plead guilty to conspiracy.

This posed a big problem. First, Shugrue had no evidence that would prove either the violations were isolated events by some irresponsible mechanics and middle managers or they had been sanctioned, either directly or indirectly, by Eastern senior operations executives. Without direct proof of senior management involvement, Shugrue felt that he could not reasonably plead the corporation to conspiracy. If he did, then numerous Eastern officers could conceivably be accused of being unindicted co-conspirators, whether they actually had knowledge of what was going on or not. Corporate criminal liability is a rather murky area of the law. It is unclear to what extent higher-up corporate officers can be held individually criminally liable for the acts of subordinate employees.

Another reason why Shugrue didn't want to take the chance with a corporate conspiracy plea at that time was that the public and regulatory backlash would have been much worse than it otherwise ended up being due to a plea with respect to the wrongful acts of individuals. For example, if Eastern had pleaded to conspiracy, a federal felony, then the corporation itself would have become a convicted felony conspirator, which could have resulted in the DOT finding that Eastern was no longer fit to operate as an air carrier, resulting in the airline's forced shutdown. A similar fate met E.F. Hutton after it pleaded guilty to two thousand counts of check kiting and wire fraud in the late-1980s; the firm was unable to conduct business in several states thereafter. In fact, a conspiracy plea by Eastern could possibly have even exposed Texas Air officials to liability for the wrongful felonious acts of its wholly-owned subsidiary.

For these and other reasons, Shugrue held his ground with Maloney. He would not plead to corporate conspiracy and call into question the validity and effectiveness of the entire maintenance organization of the airline. Maloney, on the other hand, was equally adamant that Eastern had to plead to conspiracy in order to settle the charges. Since Shugrue and Maloney could not come to terms, Maloney set into motion the preparations for a criminal trial, and began to flex his considerable muscle as a federal prosecutor.

On Saturday, December 1, 1990, several FBI agents stormed into Eastern's Building 16 headquarters in Miami with a search warrant. An Eastern staff member working that day said that the FBI agents came in with their guns drawn. After searching through a multitude of documents, they left. However, the impression had been made. In cases of corporate, or white collar, criminality, federal prosecutors use such tactics to send the message to the target of the investigation that the U.S. Attorney's office is willing to play hardball. Manhattan federal prosecutors had in mind the same thing when they arrested several Wall Street executives in their offices during the insider trading scandals of the 1980s. As far as Eastern was concerned, Maloney's ploy was effective. After the FBI raid, there was a discernible change in the way in which Eastern viewed the maintenance investigation. It suddenly became a matter of the utmost importance. There was also a change in the way in which Shugrue viewed his top operations executives.

Joseph B. Leonard was Eastern's executive vice president and chief operating officer. As such, he was the person with overall responsibility for the maintenance organization. Leonard joined Eastern in April 1984 and worked his way up the operations organization of the airline to become acting CEO in July 1986, just before the Texas Air acquisition was officially consummated. Leonard left Eastern the day before the FBI raid and is now a senior executive at Northwest.

Prior to February 1990, reporting to Leonard was Edward F. Upton, Eastern's vice president of maintenance and engineeering. Upton was directly in charge of maintenance from April 1986 until he resigned in February 1990. Prior to joining Eastern, he was a director of line maintenance at Northwest. Upton resigned after it became clear that he was a target of the criminal investigation. After Upton's resignation, D. Roger Ferguson took his place and was vice president of maintenance and engineering through the trustee's tenure. Reporting to Ferguson and Leonard was Phil Anson, staff vice president of aircraft maintenance.

After the indictment was announced, Shugrue began to focus more attention on the maintenance operation that Leonard, Ferguson and Anson were running. In fact, almost immediately after the indictment was unsealed, Shugrue commissioned a secret audit by an outside consultant to determine if there were any ongoing maintenance irregularities. Although none were found, several of Shugrue's advisers suggested that Shugrue fire Leonard because of all the controversy stemming from events that happened on his watch. They also suggested that Leonard's firing would send a message to Maloney that Shugrue was cracking down on the maintenance organization. Although somewhat swayed by the argument, Shugrue was concerned that if Leonard was fired, Maloney might misread the action as an implicit admission of guilt. Thus, Shugrue kept his own counsel and kept Leonard on board.

Although the damage to Eastern's image had already been done by the announcement of the indictment, more trouble occurred in early November when Valenti, the federal investigator, claimed that he believed similar maintenance violations were occurring on an ongoing basis. If true, this meant that Leonard's representations to Shugrue that the maintenance organization had been fixed were untrue. More importantly, it would also put Shugrue in a very difficult position because he had guaranteed to the FAA and the traveling public that since his arrival Eastern was a safe airline. The primary reason why Valenti's serious accusations (which because of Eastern's liquidation have not been resolved) did not get more exposure in the media was due to the imbroglio surrounding the creditors' call for the airline's liquidation in November.

Leonard's resignation occurred around the same time that Valenti's accusations were made. Although there is no evidence that Shugrue asked Leonard to resign solely because of such accusations, it is certainly within the realm of reason to believe that was the case. Soon after Leonard's departure, Shugrue appointed a longtime Pan Am colleague of his, Robert L. Gould, as Eastern's president and chief operating officer. Gould, a Yale graduate, was an aviator in the Marine Corps during the early part of the Vietnam War. He is also a very strong operations executive and someone on whom Shugrue could rely to ride herd on the maintenance organization. Gould's ability to do that, however, was constrained by Eastern's shutdown several weeks after his appointment.

In July and October, two of the individual Eastern indictees pleaded guilty to conspiracy and agreed to cooperate with the government's continued investigation. One of those who pled guilty, Elia Dragone, worked at the JFK maintenance base and said that the fraud that he committed had been orchestrated by his superiors.

In March 1991, after Eastern shut down, Shugrue decided that continuing to contest the conspiracy charges would no longer be cost-effective to the Eastern estate. As a result, Eastern pleaded guilty to seven of the sixty counts in the indictment, including the count which charged that Eastern, as a corporate entity, conspired with others to prevent the FAA from determining if the airline's employees falsified maintenance records. As part of its plea, Eastern also agreed to pay $3.5 million in criminal fines.

Although the plea bargain has ended the case for Eastern, the charges against the individuals who have not yet pled guilty will continue. The U.S. Attorney decided that he would reindict fourteen former Eastern maintenance employees as part of a new and more encompassing indictment. At this point it is unclear how far up the Eastern chain of command the accusations will travel. However, what is certain is that some of those directly responsible for maintenance at Eastern during the time period alleged in the indictment allowed a criminal conspiracy to fester that potentially endangered the lives of millions of passengers.

The indictments also lend support to the unions' charges that Eastern management, after the Texas Air takeover, cut corners with safety to keep costs down. When the union complaints first surfaced in 1987–88, they were dismissed mostly by Eastern and Texas Air officials as mere union harassment. Now, however, it appears that the union charges might have had merit. If passengers were indeed put at risk merely so that Eastern could save money on maintenance, that is completely inexcusable and reprehensible. The perpetrators should be sought out and punished to the fullest extent that the law allows.

The combination of the Persian Gulf War and the maintenance

violations dealt a devastating blow to Eastern's reorganization effort. The progress that had been made under Shugrue from the time of his appointment in mid-April until the end of July had been nothing short of miraculous. Then, within a matter of one week, Eastern was hit by the double bombshell of the indictment on July 25 and the Iraqi invasion of Kuwait on August 2. By mid-August, it was clear that Eastern would definitely not survive and that it was only a matter of time before the creditors would get tired of funding an obvious lost cause.

One transaction that Shugrue felt would go a long way in helping Eastern's liquidity position was that involving System One Holdings Inc., normally referred to as System One. The System One transaction, if consummated, would be of great benefit to Eastern not only because it would involve the settlement of the prepetition transactions, but also because it would substantially decrease the costs for Eastern's computer reservations system (CRS).

As is the case with all the other major airlines, the vast majority of the tickets for travel on Eastern were sold by travel agents. Travel agents receive commissions, averaging 10 percent of the total price of the ticket, from the airlines (as well as hotels and car rental firms, albeit with different commission schedules). Approximately 95 percent of all travel agencies in the United States have acquired a CRS, which provides travel agents with flight availability and other information relating to, among other things, flights, fares, hotels, car rentals, currency exchange rates and tourist information. The two largest CRS's are owned by affiliates of American (Sabre) and United (Apollo). As of 1990, System One operated the third largest CRS in the country.

CRS's are important to airlines because many studies have shown that an airline gains a competitve advantage in bookings if a travel agent uses the CRS provided by that airline. This advantage, usually referred to in the industry as "display bias," allows airlines that own the largest systems to exert the most market power in the distribution channel, travel agencies. Although there are some prohibitions on display bias, there are many ways in which a CRS can get around them.

For example, if you call your travel agent and request a flight from New York to Aspen, your agent will tell you that there are no nonstop flights in that market and that your best bet is to fly from New York to Denver and then connect in Denver for your flight to Aspen. The dominant carriers in the New York–Denver–Aspen market are United and Continental, both of which have flights that leave basically at the same times. If your travel agent is using an Apollo screen, then the chances are extremely high that she will book you on a United flight even if a Continental flight is scheduled to get you to Aspen earlier than the United flight.

These preferential schedule displays, when combined with the widely varying user fees charged other airlines and travel agencies, give the owners of the CRS a substantial competitive advantage over those airlines without a CRS. Certain rules of the DOT were intended to eliminate these allegedly unfair practices, but these rules did not achieve the intended result. For these and other reasons, the battle for CRS market share among airlines is tantamount to the battle for survival.

Prior to the Texas Air takeover, Eastern had a CRS called System One Direct Access (SODA). Continental did not have such a system, and Lorenzo knew that he would never be able to transform Continental into a megacarrier without one. Thus, almost immediately after the Eastern takeover in March 1987, a new Texas Air subsidiary called System One Holdings bought SODA and a related software unit called EAL Automation Systems Inc. These units collectively became known as System One.

The System One deal was one of the prepetition transactions in which Shapiro had claimed that Eastern got shortchanged, largely because Texas Air gave Eastern a note for $100 million for SODA when the unions' financial advisers, as well as those for Eastern (Merrill Lynch), claimed that the system was worth anywhere from $250 million to $300 million.

United and TWA have entered into agreements with other carriers providing for the shared ownership and joint marketing of each carrier's CRS. United has entered into an agreement with USAir and certain European carriers, and TWA has entered into an agreement with Northwest. In early 1990, TWA, Delta and Northwest merged their CRS's. Sensing the consolidation of CRS's in the industry, and that eventually System One would be left out, Texas Air began looking for a major partner for System One not only to increase its competitive position but also to provide additional funding to fuel its growth.

In February 1990, Texas Air, System One and Electronic Data Systems (EDS) entered into a preliminary agreement providing for the acquisition by EDS of substantially all of the assets of System One as well as the formation by System One and EDS of a CRS partnership that would market CRS services to Eastern, Continental, other airlines, travel agencies and other travel companies. The partnership would be owned 50 percent by EDS and 25 percent each by Eastern and Continental. EDS agreed to pay Texas Air $250 million, of which $170 million would be in cash, and both Eastern and Continental each agreed to give EDS a ten-year computer services contract. As a result of the deal, Eastern would shave roughly $5 million from its annual computer-services costs.

Eastern's reasons for wanting to close the EDS transaction were to achieve significant savings on Eastern's data processing and telecommunications costs, to obtain substantial and immediate operational benefits over Eastern's existing contract for data processing and telecommunications services with System One, to obtain an equity stake in a CRS which it didn't have, and to terminate the existing contract with System One with no liability to Eastern.

The negotiations over this deal had dragged on for almost a year and, because of the continually changing environment at Eastern, never were able to come to fruition. By October 1990, an agreement had been reached but there was a snag. At first, when Texas Air negotiated the agreement with EDS, a key condition of the deal was that Shapiro, the examiner, approve the transaction as it related to the contested prepetition transaction relating to System One. However, after the appointment of the trustee, Texas Air no longer wanted the deal limited to a settlement of just one of the prepetition issues but all of them. Thus, by the time Eastern finally reached an agreement with Texas Air and EDS in October 1990, a condition for the closing was that all the prepetition transactions had to be settled, save for Bar Harbor, which by this time had already been settled.

Doug Steenland, a Verner Liipfert lawyer who handled the negotiations with EDS, gave a briefing on the structure of the transaction to all Eastern officers in early October. The deal was extremely complicated and Steenland had done an excellent job in structuring and negotiating it. However, when he said that a settlement of all the remaining prepetition transactions was a condition to the deal, I immediately sensed that a deal probably would not happen. Making it more difficult was that EDS had placed a deadline of November 1 for all the conditions to be satisfied, including obtaining bankruptcy court approval. Since I had already been down this path regarding the settlement of the prepetition transactions with the Bar Harbor deal, it was easy for me to understand why meeting that condition would be so difficult.

As expected, the deal disintegrated near the deadline because the creditors refused to go along with the proposed settlement of the prepetition transactions. They thought that they could get more than what was on the table and, in the end, they received nothing. November first came and went, along with EDS, and the entire transaction dissolved.

EDS, on the other hand, was extremely lucky that it didn't go through with the deal as structured. As it turned out, Eastern shut down before the deal, had it been approved, would have actually closed. This would have resulted in the new CRS partnership generating revenues at least 40 percent below those EDS had counted on when it agreed to pay $250 million. Also, in early December 1990, Continental filed for bankruptcy, which resulted in an even further reduction in the CRS revenues that EDS had counted on receiving. Had EDS gone through with the deal, as originally structured, they would have looked foolish paying $250 million for an asset that, by January 1991, had decreased in value to less than $100 million.

The EDS transaction expired on November 1, 1990, and was another disappointment to Shugrue in his turnaround effort, which, by that time, had soured anyway. The Persian Gulf situation, the criminal indictment and the collapse of the EDS deal left the creditors with no choice other than to end the whole ball game. Within a matter of days, they moved to do just that.

8

A COMPLETE WASTE OF MONEY

By November 1990, Eastern was like the *Titanic* with only its smokestacks visible above water. In addition to all of Eastern's other problems, the creditors had lost any hope of selling Eastern as a going concern, or even a part of it. By this time Northwest, like every other carrier, was experiencing serious cash flow problems, which made an acquisition of a substantial portion of Eastern's assets prohibitive. There was just no way that Checchi could afford to sink up to $400 million in acquiring and then building up the Atlanta hub without endangering his entire Northwest empire. The creditors had delayed on the Checchi deal to such an extent that by the time they really needed somebody to write a check for Eastern assets, the opportunity had passed them by.

Once Checchi pulled back, and there were no other credible offers on the table for a substantial amount of Eastern assets, the creditors finally began to think seriously about liquidation. Although an argument could have been made at the time that they were several months too late in reaching this conclusion, by early November it was apparent to just about everyone that Eastern was a goner.

Several things occurred that put the creditors in a good position to push for Eastern's liquidation, besides the horrendous losses that were being incurred by the airline on a daily basis. The most important of these was a settlement of Eastern's pension liabilities with the PBGC.

The exact amount of underfunding in Eastern's pension plans was a matter of dispute. However, what was certain was that, depending on the actuarial assumptions one employed, the amount of the liability ranged from $850 million all the way up to $1.3 billion. With the PBGC standing out there with upwards of a $1.3 billion claim against the Eastern estate, a plan of reorganization or liquidation was impossible unless and until that huge contingent liability was somehow defined and settled. Texas Air and Continental had an interest in settling Eastern's pension plan liabilities as well because, under the law, if Eastern was unable to cover the shortfall, and it was obvious that it could not, then the PBGC could look to the assets of Texas Air, Continental and all of its affiliates to make up the difference. Such an occurrence would potentially force the entire Texas Air empire into liquidation, or at least bankruptcy. So, the Eastern creditors, before they could come up with a liquidation plan for Eastern, had to reach an agreement with the PBGC on the final disposition of Eastern's pension liabilities.

The lead negotiator for the PBGC was Diane Burkley, its deputy executive director. At the time, Burkley was involved with many other large pension negotiations with companies either in bankruptcy or close to it. These companies, such as LTV and Pan Am, had underfunded pension liabilities in the billions of dollars as well. Burkley was determined to structure a settlement in the Eastern case that could be used as a blueprint for future "mega-settlements" so as to avoid sticking the American taxpayer with the ultimate liability.

After months of complex negotiations between and among representatives of Eastern, Texas Air (which by this time had changed its name to Continental Airlines Holdings Inc. [CAHI] to reflect Eastern's absence from the group), the unions (for whose benefit the plans were established in the first place) and the PBGC, an agreement was reached on a settlement in mid-September. Basically, the parties agreed to settle and compromise the pension claims, terminate Eastern's pension plans and designate CAHI as the party that would bear the financial responsibility of ultimately covering the costs of termination.

The settlement called for Eastern to pay $30 million to the pension plans, the termination of the plans on October 15, 1990, and the PBGC taking a $565 million unsecured claim against the Eastern estate. Since, at the time, the Eastern creditors were looking at receiving less than five cents on the dollar from an Eastern liquidation, the PBGC realized that it would ultimately have to write off almost all of the $565 million claim. The settlement further provided that the PBGC would continue to pay pension benefits to all individual participants under the plans.

For its part of the settlement, CAHI agreed to assume responsibility to fund the Eastern pension obligations over a period of twelve years. CAHI would make an $81 million cash contribution up front, due May 15, 1991, plus it would pay $500 million over twelve years, roughly $42 million per year. This payment was secured by valuable CAHI assets such as many of Continental's lucrative international route authorities.

The financial settlement was excellent from Eastern's standpoint because it allowed all of Eastern's remaining unsecured creditors, for only $30 million, to erase roughly half of the potential $1.3 billion in additional PBGC claims against the Eastern estate. From the PBGC's standpoint, the settlement was pretty good since it only had to write off roughly half of its potential claim. The results for CAHI, though, were disastrous. On the one hand, CAHI really didn't have a choice because the only alternative was to have the PBGC file a lien against all of the corporation's assets. On the other hand, the result of the settlement was that CAHI would likely have to file for bankruptcy in the event that the specific collateral for the twelve-year payment obligation could not be agreed upon by the PBGC-imposed deadline of December 1, 1990.

In the end, CAHI actually did file for bankruptcy precisely because of the problems involved with determining which collateral would be pledged to the PBGC. Continental, by this time in a cash squeeze of its own, wanted to sell its prized Seattle-Tokyo route to American. However, this was one of the routes that had been pledged as collateral to the PBGC as part of the settlement. If Hollis Harris, then Continental's CEO, had gone ahead and sold the route, then the entire agreement with the PBGC would have unraveled and the agency would have slapped a lien on all of CAHI's and Continental's assets. If Harris didn't sell that route, and other assets, then Continental would likely run out of cash during the lean winter months. Faced with this dilemma, Harris did the only thing he could do. He put CAHI and all of its affiliates, including Continental, into bankruptcy with the hope of restructuring the previously agreed deal with the PBGC during CAHI's reorganization.

At any rate, CAHI's bankruptcy was CAHI's problem to be worked out with the PBGC. As far as Eastern and its creditors were concerned, that was of no consequence to them since Judge Lifland had approved the PBGC settlement in early October. This settlement of Eastern's single largest contingent claim paved the way for a plan of liquidation for the airline.

The PBGC has recently assumed a more active role in bankruptcies because of the numerous underfunded pension plans throughout corporate America. In fact, Congress is considering a bill that would give the PBGC priority over unsecured creditors in bankruptcy. Passing such a measure would be a big mistake. Unlike general unsecured creditors, the PBGC provides no capital to American businesses. If the sources of capital for business in America were placed in a subordinate position to a government agency, the "credit crunch" that the country is now facing would become even more severe.

Shugrue had been asked by the creditors to begin putting together a shutdown plan, or plan of liquidation, in mid-September. After having been refined and modified, it was presented to the creditors' advisers in late October. The plan outlined how Eastern would go about ceasing its flight operations, firing substantially all of its employees, protecting assets such as aircraft, spare parts and facilities, and then selling as many assets as quickly as possible to maximize payout to the creditors.

Simultaneously with Eastern's plan of liquidation, the creditors' financial advisers, Goldman Sachs, Ernst and Young and Art Newman of Chemical Bank, put together their own liquidation analysis. The advisers' analysis showed that Eastern's losses would not abate, would in fact continue to get much worse and that it was better to liquidate and sell everything immediately rather than continue to pump more money into the black hole that Eastern had by this time become. One of the advisers, when asked what the results of the analysis showed, said that Eastern's continued existence was "a complete waste of money."

The creditors' advisers had a lot of evidence to support their push for immediate liquidation of the airline. In August 1990, although Eastern reported a small net profit of $7 million due to $55 million in asset sales, the carrier suffered a net operating loss of roughly $40 million. By September, after the effects of the fuel hike and recession had a chance to really hit, Eastern incurred a net operating loss of $71 million, almost double the previous month's loss. Also in September, because passenger traffic had by then all but dried up, Eastern had an extremely low load factor of 51 percent which drove its breakeven load factor up to almost 82 percent. There was absolutely no way that Eastern would come close to approaching a 65 percent load factor, let alone 82 percent, even during the airline's historically heavy winter travel season.

But, as the advisers pointed out, Eastern's historically strong winter travel season was not likely to materialize in the winter of 1990–91. It was clear by November 1990 that the recession would substantially reduce the number of passengers flying to Florida and the Caribbean, Eastern's strongest markets, during the winter. In addition, the very real prospect of war in the gulf meant that if hostilities broke out, there wouldn't be anyone traveling at all. The creditors' financial advisers, led by Newman of Chemical Bank, therefore concluded that no matter how well the first-class program and other marketing initiatives worked, Eastern was on track to lose, on a cash basis, potentially $100 million per month during the winter. In fact, even with the first-class program, Eastern came up short on its October revenue projections by almost $10 million.

When the Eastern bankruptcy case began in 1989, Judge Lifland established special escrow accounts to hold the proceeds of asset sales for ultimate payout to the creditors of the estate. The first proceeds from asset sales went into an escrow account set aside for the secured creditors, those creditors who had liens on Eastern's assets, such as aircraft and engines. The amount of cash in the escrow account for the secured creditors was, as of September 1990, roughly $700 million. Although this was not an amount sufficient to pay back the secured creditors one hundred cents on the dollar of what they were owed, their ability to take possession of their collateral and sell it plus the $700 million in escrow was believed to be sufficient to provide the secured creditors with "adequate protection" for their collateral in case Eastern was ultimately liquidated.

Another escrow account was established for the benefit of the unsecured creditors, those creditors who didn't have liens against assets in the estate. These are the creditors who receive priority in bankruptcy and among whose seven largest usually constitute the creditors' committee. Most of the proceeds from any and all asset sales over and above the $700 million that was set aside for the secured creditors went into the escrow account established for the unsecured creditors. Though at one time during the Eastern bankruptcy the unsecured escrow account had almost $1 billion in it, by November 1990 that amount had dwindled to roughly $300 million. This is because Eastern's immense operating losses while in bankruptcy were subsidized almost totally by the unsecured creditors in the form of withdrawals from the unsecured escrow account.

For the thirteen months that Eastern was in bankruptcy prior to the appointment of the trustee, from March 1989 until mid-April 1990, Eastern suffered a net loss of $1.2 billion. Its operating loss during that same period, a more accurate picture of the cash drain, was almost $900 million. Also during this period, Judge Lifland had, with the creditors' approval, allowed $320 million to be withdrawn from the unsecured escrow account to help cover these substantial cash shortfalls.

The reasoning behind the approval of the first $320 million in escrow withdrawals was simple. Without such financial assistance, Eastern would have gone into immediate liquidation since Texas Air, the common stockholder, wasn't going to pump any more cash into the carrier. Eastern was being kept alive, in essence, for the sole benefit of the unsecured creditors. Since it was clear that the unsecured creditors were not going to receive one hundred cents on the dollar for what they were owed, the preferred stockholders weren't going to receive anything, not to mention Texas Air as the common stockholder. Thus, the $320 million in withdrawals was considered to be an insurance policy for the unsecured creditors so that they could keep Eastern alive until it was sold or a plan of reorganization was approved.

By the time the trustee was appointed in mid-April 1990, Eastern's prognosis had changed substantially for the worse. However, the airline still needed to be kept alive as a going concern on the chance that a deal could be struck to sell it, or at least most of its assets. This goes to explain why, in conjunction with the trustee's appointment in April, the creditors authorized an $80 million escrow drawdown.

However, unlike prior to the trustee's tenure when Eastern had at least a decent shot at being sold whole, after the trustee's arrival those chances were so exceedingly slim that the creditors reviewed every subsequent request for additional escrow drawdowns with heightened scrutiny.

After Eastern received $80 million from escrow in conjunction with the trustee's appointment in mid-April, the drawdowns continued unabated because of Eastern's deteriorating financial condition. Eastern withdrew an additional $50 million on June 28, another $50 million on August 14 and another $50 million on September 27 (which request was lowered from $75 million). By November, after only six months under the direction of the trustee, Eastern had siphoned off an additional $230 million from the unsecured escrow account. When combined with the $320 million that was used pretrustee, the unsecured creditors had seen $550 million of the money set aside to pay them go right down the drain with no tangible benefit whatsoever, other than Eastern's continued existence.

In late June 1990, when Eastern completed its business plan that was presented to the creditors in July, Eastern estimated that its net operating loss for all of 1990 would be around $300 million. By the end of October, Eastern had already lost $370 million. Although not even the creditors blamed Shugrue for failing to predict the Iraqi invasion of Kuwait in August, they were still concerned that the underlying structural quality of Eastern's operations had completely disintegrated. This is particularly so since Eastern missed its October revenue projections by such a wide margin.

As if all of this weren't enough, the creditors were also being told by Eastern that the estimated loss for November and December combined was going to be $123 million. This would bring the total 1990 estimated loss to $480 million, or roughly $180 million over the amount projected in the June business plan. Even if the additional loss was totally attributable to the events in the gulf, and therefore unpredictable, the creditors were looking at having to subsidize Eastern with additional funds from the unsecured escrow account. And that assumed that Eastern's projections were correct, which up to that point they never had been. According to the creditors' financial advisers, it was quite possible that Eastern could lose $100 million per month in November and December, requiring an additional $200 million from the unsecured escrow account. Not only would that break the bank for the unsecured creditors, leaving them with almost nothing in their escrow account, but it would also require dipping into the escrow account set aside to pay the secured creditors, something that the secured creditors had been promised from the very beginning of the case would never happen.

Faced with all of these factors, in addition to the fact that by November the unsecured escrow account had dwindled to less than $260 million, the creditors' financial advisers correctly concluded that they had better put an end to the phlebotomy before it got even worse. Thus, they recommended to the full creditors' committee in early November 1990 that Eastern shut down and be liquidated immediately.

Judge Lifland had, from the very beginning of the Eastern bankruptcy, assumed an activist role in the proceedings. In fact, few observers could remember a case in which a bankruptcy judge had applied his own views as to what should happen to a debtor as much as Lifland had with Eastern.

Immediately after the strike and the bankruptcy filing, Lifland decided that he was going to get Eastern up and flying again as soon as possible. And at all costs. "I want to see planes flying," he ordained during one court hearing soon after the bankruptcy began. For some reason, Lifland determined that it was in the "public interest" to have Eastern remain in service. One must only assume that the source of such a conclusion, since no economic or airline industry experts rendered any testimony that Eastern was in fact vital to the nation's air transportation system, came from some misguided view of the world that Lifland had internalized as his own. The nation's airline industry was actually better off without Eastern since there was so much overcapacity in the system anyway.

This explains why Lifland jumped at the Ueberroth deal. Although the structure of the deal made no economic sense for the seller, Texas Air, Lifland practically ordered the parties in the case, including the examiner Shapiro, to negotiate a deal. In the end that deal failed because, as in every other failed deal, all parties were not satisfied. Lifland should have learned then, after the Ueberroth fiasco, that he couldn't overrule the laws of economics simply by issuing a judicial decree from the bench. Unfortunately for Eastern's creditors, Lifland didn't get the message.

In March 1990, after it became clear that the creditors and Texas Air were not going to be able to agree on the terms of a reorganization plan for Eastern, the creditors wanted to liquidate the airline. However, because of Lifland's strong and vocal opposition to liquidation at all costs, Zweibel, the creditors' lawyer, knew that his motion for a trustee wouldn't have a chance with Lifland if it included a call for liquidation. Because of this, Zweibel's motion instead called for a trustee who would pursue a sale or move to "enhance the value of the estate." The creditors, in essence, were forced to accept a trustee who would operate the airline rather than liquidate it solely because Lifland's own personal position made it clear to everyone that he was not about to liquidate Eastern at that time. Unfortunately for the creditors, the only ones in the case with an economic interest, Lifland decided that his own view of what should happen took precedence over the views of the parties whom the Bankruptcy Code was designed to protect.

Thus, by November 1990, Lifland had proven himself to be a force of and unto himself. His views about Eastern, its operations, how it should be reorganized, to whom it should be sold, would carry as much weight, if not more, than the views of those who held an economic interest in the case. Although Lifland had already shown himself to be "foot loose and fancy free," as one member of the creditors' committee put it, with the creditors' money, nothing he had done previously would prepare the creditors for the extraordinary decisions Lifland would make, regarding their money, in the next several weeks.

By November, Shugrue was faced with a substantial dilemma. As an officer of the court, it was his job to look out for and protect the best interests of the Eastern estate, which theoretically coincided with those of the creditors. He had been notified that the creditors would oppose any more escrow withdrawals and would therefore push for liquidation. What was he to do? On the other hand, he had put a lot of effort into Eastern and hated to see it go down the tubes. Also, he was bolstered by the great progress that the first-class program was making. Based on projections provided to him by Kunstler, Eastern's planning executive, Eastern could conceivably break even on an operating basis before the end of the winter. In fact, as of November, fuel prices had already begun to drop a bit as the gulf situation cooled. Perhaps, Shugrue thought, there won't be a war, Eastern will meet its revenue projections, the recession won't be as bad as everyone thinks and a reorganization plan for Eastern can be filed by the end of the first quarter in 1991.

Obviously, actual events proved Shugrue wrong. The lull in oil prices was temporary, and soon thereafter the United Nations passed resolutions authorizing the use of force in Kuwait, which resulted in Operation Desert Storm in mid January 1991. The result was the worst quarterly loss for the airline industry in history as passenger traffic completely dried up, even to the sun destinations that Eastern had been counting on. Also, the recession got worse and fuel prices remained at their inflated levels. As it turned out, Eastern would not have made it through the first quarter of 1991 even if the unsecured creditors had given it all that remained in the unsecured escrow account. But Shugrue did not have the benefit of this knowledge back in November when the difficult decision had to be made to agree with the creditors and liquidate immediately or oppose them and beg Lifland for more time to enact a turnaround.

Under the Bankruptcy Code, a bankruptcy trustee is entitled to no more than 3 percent of the total amounts disbursed or turned over in the case to parties in interest. As of the end of October 1990, Eastern had total disbursements of approximately $1.6 billion. Thus, Shugrue's potential take at that time could have been as high as $48 million. Shugrue also received a monthly draw of $35,000, increased to $50,000 in December 1990, as ongoing salary. However, Shugrue's compensation in the Eastern case did not depend on whether Eastern actually continued to operate. Even if Eastern shut down, as long as the case continued through liquidation and Shugrue remained as trustee, Shugrue would continue to receive his monthly draw as part of the ultimate statutory percentage of disbursements. This meant that Shugrue had no monetary incentive to keep Eastern flying, he would continue to get paid regardless.

The real motivation behind Shugrue's decision to request additional escrow funds over the objection of the creditors, I believe, was his intense belief that Eastern still actually had a shot at making it. Although subsequent events made such a belief improbable at best, based on the information available to him as of early November 1990, Shugrue honestly felt that he had a chance and didn't want to admit defeat when he was potentially so close to victory. Shugrue is not the type of executive who would waste time, or money, pursuing a course of action that didn't make any sense. Had he really believed that Eastern was truly dead in November, he would have pulled the plug then.

By November, the mood around Eastern was just as bad as it was immediately before Shugrue's appointment. Everyone knew that Eastern would soon have to go back to Lifland for more money, and if it wasn't forthcoming, that would be the end of Eastern. Speculation in the press was rampant that Lifland would bar any further escrow withdrawals which would lead to immediate liquidation. Although the planning horizon at Eastern had previously been sixty days out into the future, in early November it was literally a day-to-day existence. In fact, throughout the month of October Eastern had to play complex cash-management tricks with its many bank accounts just to meet its payroll every two weeks.

Rolf Andresen, Eastern's CFO, told Shugrue that Eastern was going to run out of cash on November 15, when the first November payroll was due, unless additional funds were drawn down from the escrow account. Shugrue then instructed Kunstler to come up with his most realistic revenue forecast, by week, for the months of November and December. Based on this forecast, Shugrue was advised that Eastern needed at least another $30 million to tide it over through the middle of December.

This estimate, however, was far short of the actual cash requirements of the airline and was actually quite unreasonable. Since the trustee's appointment, Eastern had never drawn down less than $50 million at a time from the escrow account. Furthermore, each of Eastern's escrow withdrawals had lasted the airline, on average, only forty-five days. Thus, the recommendation that Eastern needed only $30 million for the last forty-five days of the year assumed that Eastern's revenues would be higher, roughly $20 million higher, than they had ever been during any forty-five-day period since April when the trustee arrived. Although the first-class program was working extremely well, and in fact bookings for November were the highest they had been for a November in five years, the substantially lower levels of traffic that Eastern was carrying due to the recession and war fears meant that revenues would be substantially lower than the bookings actually showed.

In short, there was very little chance that Eastern's revenue-generating capability over the last forty-five days of the year would be $20 million higher than it had been over any prior forty-five-day period since the trustee's appointment. Although the heavy Thanksgiving travel season was included in this time frame, also included were the first two weeks of December, which are normally the slowest two weeks of the year for air travel, because they are sandwiched between two holidays. A more reasonable estimate of Eastern's real cash needs for the last forty-five days of the year was at least $50 million, and probably closer to $75 million.

However, Shugrue had a problem with going to the creditors and asking for $75 million in the next drawdown for several reasons. First, during his tenure, they had never agreed to more than $50 million. Second, by early November Shugrue had received warnings that the creditors were extremely displeased with the idea of additional funding and he didn't want to push them too hard by asking for more than they had ever granted before. Third, he had already asked for a $75 million withdrawal on September 27 but had been forced, over loud objection, to scale back the request to $50 million. Given these factors, even though Shugrue had a good feeling that the estimates he was receiving from his managers were on the low side, he decided to stick with the request for only $30 million.

On November 8, 1990, Shugrue formally filed his request with the court and the creditors to withdraw an additional $30 million from the unsecured escrow account. For the first time in the history of the Eastern bankruptcy, the unsecured creditors formally objected to any further withdrawals. The stage had thus been set. Either Shugrue would prevail, and keep Eastern alive for a short while longer, or the creditors would prevail, which would force Eastern to shut down at midnight on November 15. A hearing on the issue was scheduled for the day before Eastern's cash was scheduled to run out, November 14.

The press trumpeted the fight between the creditors and Shugrue, rightly so, as the battle between Eastern's survival and immediate liquidation. This was the first time in history that the immediate fate of such a large company would be played out and decided in a courtroom and carried, almost live, to millions of viewers around the country and the world. In fact, on the day of the hearing, there were television cameras set up just outside the front entrance to the bankruptcy court at Bowling Green. Just about everyone who entered the door was filmed and asked questions by reporters as to what their position was on the Eastern case. When Zweibel showed up, he was asked what he was looking for from Judge Lifland and he responded: "The immediate liquidation of Eastern Air Lines."

The public stance of Zweibel relative to what the creditors' committee wanted out of the hearing was puzzling. In fact, about a week prior to the hearing someone among the creditors' advisers had actually leaked to the media that the committee would be seeking the immediate liquidation of Eastern at the November fourteenth hearing.

This was a big mistake. Obviously, the minute that news of the creditors' intentions was distributed, Eastern's advance bookings fell straight through the floor. After all, who in their right mind would make travel arrangements on Eastern, particularly during the hectic holiday season, when the odds were strong against Eastern's even being around at Thanksgiving?

The real damage by the creditors' advisers taking such a public stand on their desire to liquidate was that the downside risk of the strategy wasn't taken into account. What if they lost and Lifland kept Eastern alive for another couple of months? Obviously, the damage to Eastern's expected revenue stream by that time had been so acute that, in the end, even more creditors' funds would be needed to breach the shortfall caused by all of the negative publicity. The result was that the leak actually cost the creditors more money, as it turned out at least another $135 million more, by resulting in a public clamor for Eastern's liquidation in early November.

When the hearing began on November fourteenth for the additional $30 million, Lifland heard testimony from several key witnesses that provided estimates on Eastern's chances of succeeding as a stand-alone airline. Obviously, the creditors' financial advisers testified in favor of liquidation and Eastern's testified in favor of continued viability. However, the most surprising testimony, and probably the testimony to which Lifland accorded the most weight, came from Harry Kimbriel, the examiner's airline consultant. Kimbriel supported Shugrue's request for the additional $30 million because he said that "it's possible through the sale of assets to develop a stabilized cash flow plan that will support a plan of reorganization."

This testimony appeared, at least to many of the informed and objective observers in the courtroom, to be somewhat incredulous. Kimbriel, who at the beginning of the trustee's tenure had been hostile to most of the trustee's efforts, now had become Shugrue's and Eastern's best friend. The reason for that is Shugrue had instructed Kunstler to involve Kimbriel heavily in the formation of the most recent Eastern business plan. Shugrue's strategy, which worked, was that if Kimbriel felt that he had some ownership in the plan that would ostensibly save Eastern, he would have to support it.

Nonetheless, the contention that Eastern would be at least cash-flow neutral, if not cash-flow positive as Kimbriel was intimating, if it was allowed to live during the heavy holiday travel period, bordered on the absurd. Even if the 1990–91 winter travel season turned out to be the best ever, and all available data in November pointed toward it actually being one of the worst, which it was, Eastern was still on track to continue to lose at least $1 million per day, if not more. As for Kimbriel's contention that asset sales would ease the cash drain and provide the basis for a viable plan of reorganization, Eastern had been unable to consummate any material sales of assets since the summer. Why was it expected that Eastern would all of a sudden be able to sell enough assets in the winter to place itself in a position to propose a plan? Even some of the most ardent supporters of Eastern's continued existence, who were sitting in the courtroom during Kimbriel's testimony, were skeptical.

Kimbriel's testimony, however, was exactly what Lifland had been looking for. Lifland, who was searching for any possible way to keep Eastern alive and approve the $30 million request, needed a crutch on which he could support his decision. The Kimbriel testimony provided that crutch. Lifland could always point to the "objective expert testimony" that had been given if he was taken to task for unnecessarily wasting $30 million of the creditors' funds.

Zweibel, the creditors' lawyer, objected strenuously to the Kimbriel testimony, as well as that proffered by Shugrue and others supporting Eastern's position. However, in the end, he was unsuccessful. Lifland decided to grant the request for the $30 million withdrawal.

Because of the virulent objections by the creditors, and perhaps also due to the heavy national media coverage of the hearing, Lifland offered a "carrot" to the creditors as part of his order. Eastern would have immediate access to only half of what was requested, or $15 million, so that it could meet the payroll and other expenses that were due the next day. However, the remaining $15 million would be made available at the end of November, within two weeks, only if Eastern met its revenue projections that had been provided to the court as part of its most recent business plan. But Lifland's order also expressly provided that Eastern could modify its projections to take into account the effect of adverse publicity generated as a result of the hearing and the extensive media coverage. Here Lifland was being extremely clever because the effect of this condition was that, no matter what happened, Eastern would end up getting the additional $15 million.

Eastern submitted its most recent revenue projections and business plan to the creditors during the first week of November. As soon as they received the business plan, the creditors went public with their calls for liquidation. Almost immediately thereafter, as can be expected, Eastern's advance passenger bookings for the next two months fell precipitously. Thus, by the time of the hearing on November 14, it was already a foregone conclusion that Eastern would miss its revenue projections found in the November business plan, and by a wide margin! All Eastern had to do, therefore, was amend its earlier projections to cover what was actually expected to happen given the substantially decreased advance bookings. Under such leniency, it would be virtually impossible for Eastern not to receive the other $15 million.

Late in the evening of November 14, Shugrue emerged triumphantly from the bankruptcy court and announced, in front of many television cameras and reporters, "The judge has agreed with our request to keep Eastern flying."

Although the creditors had "lost" this one, overall it wasn't a major problem; because it was, after all, potentially only a $30 million issue. A key member of the creditors' committee said, "Even though we got blown out on the $30 million, we knew that even $30 million wouldn't last Eastern another month and that they'd certainly be back for more very soon. When that time came, we certainly expected that even Lifland would see the light and rule in our favor."

Within just a couple of days after prevailing on the $30 million request, which was shaved down to $15 million, Shugrue saw that the negative publicity had hurt Eastern more than expected. In the first week after the November fourteenth hearing, Eastern missed its revenue projections by almost $4 million. The outlook for the next several weeks was even more ominous. Shugrue was advised that if the trend continued, the additional $15 million would run out by the first week of December. By the third week of November, Eastern was sputtering on fumes, and the fumes were scheduled to evaporate within a matter of fourteen days. The only option, as Shugrue saw it, was to go back to Lifland immediately for more money.

Shugrue was boxed into a corner. Although he probably had a good feeling that Eastern was dead by mid-November, he couldn't very well admit it so soon after fighting the creditors tooth and nail for $15 million just a week before. If he did, the obvious question would have been, "Why was $15 million spent just to keep the airline flying for another two weeks?" On the other hand, if Shugrue decided to continue fighting to keep Eastern alive, he certainly needed much more than the up to $30 million that had already been allocated. In fact, he needed so much more that he decided to go for broke.

By the third week of November, two things were crystal clear. First, Eastern needed substantially more money than originally envisioned to stay alive through the end of the year. Second, the media circus surrounding each drawdown request made managing the airline efficiently on a daily basis almost impossible. Every time Eastern's trek into court for more money was splashed across every television screen and on the front page of every major newspaper in America, a major reduction in advance bookings resulted. Shugrue decided that Eastern would be better off if it didn't have to keep going back to Lifland, hat in hand, every two weeks asking for more money to keep flying.

Thus, during the third week of November, Shugrue dropped his bombshell. As a result of the negative publicity from the November fourteenth hearing, Shugrue said that Eastern's cash needs had exploded by a whopping $70 million. Shugrue was filing another request with the court, but this time he was asking for $135 million in one shot to keep Eastern alive through the first quarter of 1991. Shugrue filed his motion with the court, and a hearing was scheduled in front of Lifland for November 29.

When the creditors heard of this, they exploded. Although this was more money than Eastern had ever requested at one time, the creditors had already stated publicly that they wanted the airline shut down immediately in order to save what little money remained in escrow. In fact, if Lifland granted the request for the $135 million, there would be only $115 million left in the unsecured escrow account. However, of that amount about $20 million was already earmarked for a payment to the PBGC and another $50 million had to be set aside under a ticket-refund protection program that Eastern had established. Thus, only roughly $45 million would be left to pay unsecured creditors' claims of $1 billion. Surely, the creditors thought, not even Lifland would go this far!

Shugrue's reasons in support of the $135 million request focused on the small likelihood of the creditors' maximizing their ultimate payout if Eastern were liquidated in November. Shugrue's strategy was to keep Eastern alive through the first quarter of 1991, hopefully by riding the coattails of a good winter travel season and a quick resolution of the gulf situation. If that worked out, perhaps an airline would be willing to buy most or all of Eastern's assets, or, if liquidation was inevitable, at least the market would be more attractive at that time in which to auction off assets.

Shugrue's request was supported by the fact that the negative publicity from the earlier hearing had increased Eastern's immediate cash needs by an estimated $70 million: $40 million for lost revenues and expenses for additional advertising to restore Eastern's revenue base; $20 million to satisfy recent demands from key suppliers for prepayment; and $10 million for unconditional demands by credit card companies for additional deposits in order to continue processing credit card charge slips for travel on Eastern.

Interestingly, for one of the few times since Shugrue was appointed, the preferred stockholders' committee actually supported the trustee. In their motion supporting the $135 million request, the preferred stockholders stated, "There appears to be a real possibility that Eastern will break even on a cash flow basis within the first two months of 1991.... Therefore, it would be unwise to cut off Eastern's lifeline at this point in time." Such sophistry had not been seen in the halls of the bankruptcy court for some time. The only reasons the preferred stockholders supported the withdrawal were that it wasn't their money anyway, and as long as Eastern stayed alive, the preferred stockholders had at least some hope, albeit very little, of eventually getting something out of a reorganization rather than a liquidation.

The contention that Eastern would turn a $2 million daily loss into a break-even within a period of forty-five days was nothing short of nonsense. The preferred stockholders knew this, but used the idea as a weapon in their last-gasp effort to salvage something for themselves in the Eastern bankruptcy.

Shugrue's arguments in favor of the additional $135 million, although by no means clearly persuasive, were sufficiently credible to force the creditors to file a detailed response memorandum with the court.

In his response memorandum, Zweibel went straight for the jugular. "The Trustee seeks withdrawal of $135 million. However, at the hearing on November 14th the Trustee projected no further cash needs beyond the $30 million then in issue until the latter part of December (hedging only as to the alleged effects of the negative publicity). Since the Trustee admits that his estimate of the current revenue impact of the publicity is $55 million, assuming that estimate is correct the Trustee now should be seeking only $70 million (the $15 million not granted on November 14 plus $55 million), not the $135 million sought today. The Trustee clearly is using the publicity issue as an excuse for an unwarranted preemptive strike on the escrow account."

Zweibel also seriously questioned the structural validity of Eastern's November business plan. "Even before negative publicity from the November 14 hearing, Eastern missed its revenue projections for November 1–7 by $875,000. In the second week of November (8–14), Eastern missed its revenue projections by $2.43 million. Since the publicity attributable to the November 14 hearing did not surface until the day of that hearing, it is clear that the bulk of the revenue shortfall in the second week of November was attributable to other factors (such as the current fare war) and not publicity. In fact, [David] Kunstler said that the fall off in the second week attributable to the first-class program was only $500,000. Thus, the remainder of the $1.9 million was attributable to structural failures of the business plan."

Here Zweibel was only partially correct. The negative publicity actually started about a week before the November fourteenth hearing as word got out that the creditors would be opposing Shugrue's motion for further escrow withdrawals. Although the vast majority of the negative publicity certainly did not occur until after the hearing, Eastern did suffer some material negative-revenue impact before November fourteenth.

Nonetheless, Zweibel's position seemed pretty strong. By November both the travel and airline industries were in a deep recession. Also, because of the lower passenger traffic, Eastern's healthier competition (Delta) began drastic fare wars in Atlanta, ostensibly to stimulate traffic, but in reality to help push Eastern over the edge. Also, oil prices continued well in excess of $30 per barrel (which meant that Jet A prices continued above $1 per gallon), the level Eastern said was its plan maximum, and the news in late November about Operation Desert Shield was not at all favorable toward peace.

Zweibel made several additional points in his response. First, since the equity of Eastern was worthless, the creditors held the only remaining economic interest in the case and therefore their wishes should be heeded. "The creditors are the owners of the airline and firmly believe it should be closed.... The Trustee, as a matter of law and equity, should be required to abide by their wishes."

Also noted by Zweibel was the fact that the $135 million request would dissipate the bulk of the liquid assets of the estate, leaving hardly any funds to pay creditors. "Creditors should not be compelled to subsidize a gamble by a Trustee who has no economic interest at risk."

Finally, Zweibel reminded Lifland that there were no credible third-party offers either for Eastern as a going concern or for any of its assets. The Northwest proposal, which contemplated the shutdown of Eastern, had been withdrawn by Checchi, largely because of foot-dragging by Zweibel and the creditors' other advisers. Also, according to Zweibel, Carl Icahn's interest in the Atlanta hub for TWA was "inadequate and rejected."

Zweibel summarized his position very persuasively. "The Committee reiterates its views (a) that Eastern is not and cannot be a viable stand-alone airline; (b) that the Trustee's projection that unsecured creditors will receive a *de minimus* recovery of 2 cents is an admission that this estate is administratively borderline insolvent; and (c) that a further withdrawal of the magnitude now requested throws into doubt the ability of the estate to conduct an orderly liquidation. A liquidation of Eastern is inevitable. It should begin now before further funds are wasted and while Christmas holiday travelers have several weeks to rearrange their plans."

The stage had been set for one last dramatic showdown in Lifland's courtroom. A story had broken in the *Miami Herald*, written by its Eastern beat reporter Ted Reed, a few days before the November twenty-ninth hearing that had exposed Shugrue's plan to request $135 million in one shot. Thus, by the time of the hearing, emotions were extremely high on all sides. Eastern had one last chance at survival, the creditors had one last chance to protect their money and Lifland had one last chance to show the nation that he was a rational and fair bankruptcy judge.

9

THAT'S ALL, FOLKS!

By the last week of November 1990, all available signs pointed to the winter of 1990–91 as being one of the worst, if not the worst, on record for the travel and tourism industries. Oil prices continued to hover above $30 per barrel, which resulted in Jet A prices well above $1 per gallon, because of fears that the Persian Gulf situation would explode at any time. According to all of the basic economic statistics, the economy was slipping deeper into recession. The airline industry as a whole was well on its way to losing almost $4 billion in 1990, an all-time record. Drastic fare wars had erupted throughout the industry as several desperate carriers tried to stimulate traffic, with no success. Delta had really put the pressure on Eastern in Atlanta, not only by matching Eastern's already noncompensatory fare levels but also by lowering its first-class fares in an attempt to neutralize the effect of Eastern's first-class program. By this time, however, the first-class program had disintegrated because of the negative publicity surrounding Eastern.

All in all, the environment Eastern faced in late November 1990 was clearly the most hostile in which to attempt a turnaround. In fact, several executives from other airlines stated publicly that Eastern's artifical support in the marketplace, propped up by Lifland's continued approvals of funding requests, imperiled the entire industry by forcing otherwise healthy carriers to match the kamikaze pricing structure that Eastern maintained.

Given all of this, any reasonable observer would have to conclude, or so it seemed, that Eastern should be laid to rest without further delay. As one member of the creditors' committee put it, "Even my twelve-year-old daughter asked me why Eastern was still flying!"

When Judge Lifland called to order the hearing on November 29, the issue before him was simple. Does Eastern live or die? Or, rather, should it live or die? All the available evidence pointed to pulling the plug immediately and saving what little money remained for the creditors. They had already lost $15 million just during the prior two weeks, and Eastern was now losing more money than before. The only way that the $135 million request could be granted, many thought, was if there was an extremely likely possibility that the money would allow Eastern to keep flying long enough to break even on its own. If so, then a plan of reorganization might have a chance of being confirmed. If not, then there was no doubt that Eastern should be shut down. Otherwise, nothing would be accomplished other than throwing good money after bad.

The hearing drew as much, if not more, media coverage and publicity than the one just two weeks before. The key difference was that just about everyone thought that surely the creditors would prevail this time. Common sense just seemed to cry out for such a result.

Lifland astonished even some of his most ardent supporters when he announced that he was approving the trustee's request for an additional $135 million withdrawal from the escrow account. Alan

Boyd, the chairman of the creditors' committee who had testified at the hearing, was visibly shaken when Lifland announced his ruling. Although Lifland made some veiled reference to the sharp drop-off in bookings due to the negative publicity, a primary reason behind his ruling was that he did not want Eastern to shut down before the expected heavy Christmas travel period and have hundreds of thousands of passengers see their trips disrupted. The creditors paid $135 million for Lifland's concern.

When word swept across the country that Lifland had agreed to the $135 million request, just about everyone was dismayed. Upon hearing of the decision, a very senior Continental executive said, "We were just floored." A member of the creditors' committee said, "I couldn't believe it. I felt as though Lifland had just reached in our pockets and stolen $135 million of our money." Even some senior Eastern officials were taken totally by surprise. One said, "This is unbelievable. Shugrue definitely gets the salesman of the year award."

After Lifland's ruling, Charlie Bryan was quoted as saying, "I think it's just prolonging the agony. It's like a death watch going on." E. J. Breen, an ALPA official, added, "My feeling is that the body is still twitching but the plug has been pulled and Judge Lifland was not in the mood to sign a death certificate last night."

Lifland could make no public comment on the matter. Doing so would be frowned upon. However, as could be expected, the rumors flew fast and furious as to why he had approved the request. One of the more humorous rumors, totally without foundation, was that Lifland had purchased a nonrefundable ticket on Eastern to Florida for the Christmas holidays and didn't want to upset his own travel plans.

Lifland's decision was generally considered not only extrajudicial by many commentators but also just plain wrong. In the face of the marketplace telling him that Eastern was no longer a viable entity, Lifland decided to pursue his own personal goals of keeping Eastern flying at the expense of those whose interests, as a bankruptcy judge, he was supposed to protect. Certainly the bankruptcy laws were not adopted by Congress with such an intent. Although the goal of bankruptcy is to help financially strained companies reorganize and emerge healthy, when it is obvious that they are unable to do so, the goal of bankruptcy law should be to protect as best as possible the interests of those who have advanced credit to the estate. When the law is such that the creditors, the only ones with an economic interest in the case, are powerless to protect that interest, then something is definitely wrong with the process.

After the hearing, Shugrue returned to Miami as a hero having miraculously prevailed to keep the airline flying. However, by the end of the first week of December, even Shugrue had to wonder whether the approval of the $135 million was warranted. Advance bookings for the period December 15–31, the bulk of the key Christmas travel season that Eastern had been counting on, were abysmal, not just for Eastern but the entire industry. The double effects of recession and war fears were too much even for the normally heavy holiday season to overcome. Traffic was so bad that Eastern lost about $2.5 million per day during the month of December. This was more than it had lost on a daily basis in any other month since the beginning of the trustee's tenure. In fact, for the entire year of 1990, Eastern incurred a net loss of $1.1 billion.

By the beginning of January 1991, only four weeks after receiving the $135 million, Eastern had run through about half of it. Shugrue then came to the conclusion that the game was definitely over and Eastern had to be shut down immediately. Upon hearing of his plans, the creditors, although relieved that their wishes had finally been met, were still more than slightly perturbed that it took an extra $150 million of their money to make the point.

Eastern's shutdown plan was refined during the first couple of weeks of January. A few days before the shutdown was scheduled to occur, Shugrue, Shapiro, Zweibel and their most senior advisers walked into Lifland's chambers on the sixth floor of the bankruptcy court and announced the decision to shut the airline down and described the liquidation procedure. During this meeting, Lifland had to question the rationale for his decisions. In November, Lifland had approved $150 million for Eastern to use to keep operating for what turned out to be an additional eight weeks. Because the escrow account had dwindled so quickly, the creditors saw their potential payoff cut by more than 50 percent just during those two months.

As soon as Shugrue returned to Miami after the meeting with Lifland, word went out to Eastern's managers to prepare for a shutdown of the airline at close of business Friday, January 18, 1991, which was only two days away. The Eastern employee grapevine, already primed because of the delicacy of the situation, immediately picked up the news, so that by Thursday the press was predicting the airline would shut down the next day.

Late Friday, Eastern announced that it had ceased all flight operations and would begin immediately to liquidate its remaining assets. Although Eastern still had roughly half of the $135 million that Lifland had granted, Eastern needed to use those funds for an orderly liquidation, including paying professional fees. Thus, as far as funds available for operations were concerned, the well had run dry.

Almost immediately after the shutdown, Eastern began to receive bids from several airlines such as United, Northwest, Delta and Continental for such assets as gates, slots, terminals and aircraft. Eastern received so many different types of bids for various assets that it decided to hold an auction. In early February, representatives from just about every major airline appeared at a midtown Manhattan hotel to bid on just about everything of value that Eastern offered for sale.

After a court hearing to approve the bids, some of the spoils were distributed. Delta acquired an entire concourse of terminal space at Atlanta. Since Eastern had shut down, the Atlanta hub was no more. All that remained was terminal space, which Delta quickly swiped so that no other airline could come in and establish a large hub to compete with Delta at its Atlanta home. United got Eastern's gates and slots at Chicago's O'Hare Airport, which it used to consolidate its position there against American. American, looking to expand in Florida, purchased Eastern's attractive Orlando gate and terminal facilities. Northwest, in the biggest asset play, acquired all of Eastern's gates and slots at Washington's National Airport. Northwest outbid United for those choice assets and now has a large presence at National. Even Continental, by the time of the auction in bankruptcy itself, acquired all of Eastern's gates and slots at New York's LaGuardia Airport.

The auction resulted in about $260 million for Eastern's creditors, a good take for one day. However, this fell far short of the nearly $1 billion that the unsecured creditors were owed. In fact, a substantial portion of the auction proceeds had to be used to pay secured creditors, those who had liens on the aircraft and gates that were sold. Thus, the unsecured creditors ended up with far less than the full $260 million.

Unfortunately for the creditors, the liquidation of Eastern's remaining assets turned out to be an unmitigated disaster. At first, it was thought that Northwest would come in and buy all of the remaining Atlanta facilities such as the gates which Delta didn't buy as well as a large maintenance facility. That deal ultimately fell through, and the Atlanta facilities were eventually returned to the city of Atlanta at no substantial gain to the Eastern estate. Eastern's only remaining assets were about one hundred old and noisy aircraft, such as Boeing 727s and Douglas DC-9s, aircraft that fail to meet FAA noise regulations and which won't be able to fly in the U.S. by the end of the decade anyway. Given the continued depressed state of the used-aircraft market, Eastern's remaining aircraft will likely be sold, if at all, to foreign carriers at fire-sale prices. Finally, Eastern's Miami maintenance and office facilities, as well as its gates at the Miami International Airport, were turned back to the Dade County Aviation Department without any material benefit to Eastern's creditors.

Eastern's liquidation is a textbook case of how not to liquidate an airline, or any business for that matter. The creditors' best chance for a deal that would have paid them a substantial sum, the Checchi deal for the Atlanta hub and other assets, was allowed to fall by the wayside. Then the creditors found themselves in a position where they couldn't control the funds they had in the estate, and ended up losing $150 million of such funds within a matter of eight weeks. Finally, left with no choice, the creditors held a fire-sale auction of Eastern's assets after the airline had already shut down.

An orderly liquidation of Eastern, had it begun back in the fall, would have resulted in the creditors getting a decent return on their claims.

Eastern is now but a faded memory. Its assets substantially sold, its offices and facilities shuttered, its aircraft mothballed in the desert. The many instances of incompetence, greed, animosity, vanity and even criminal conduct certainly all contributed to the airline's ultimate demise.

There were many losers in the Eastern debacle. By far the biggest losers were the unsecured creditors, who ended up receiving, on average, *less than one cent for each dollar they were owed.* In fact, even many of Eastern's secured creditors ended up receiving less than 100 percent of what they were owed because the value of the collateral that secured their claims had dissipated with Eastern's shutdown. The Eastern creditors have the dubious distinction of receiving one of the lowest payouts in the history of American bankruptcies.

The preferred stockholders, who purchased over $200 million of Eastern preferred stock during the 1980s, ended up with shares that can be used henceforth only as wallpaper. Although it is usual for common stockholders to get wiped out in bankruptcy, preferred stockholders usually end up with at least something. Not in the Eastern case.

Eastern's common stockholder, Texas Air (which later changed its name to Continental Airlines Holdings Inc.), actually faired well in the Eastern deal. True, its 73 million shares of Eastern common stock were rendered totally worthless. But prior to the Eastern bankruptcy, it was able to acquire assets of Eastern at attractive prices and put those assets to more productive use at lower-cost Continental. It also was able to vault to the top of the pack in airlines in terms of size for a brief period in the late 1980s. The key disadvantages of the Eastern deal, from Continental's standpoint, stem from its having to assume over $500 million of Eastern pension obligations, which drove Continental itself into bankruptcy. Also, the U.S. Attorney in Brooklyn is investigating the prepetition transactions for possible criminal conduct. Whether charges ever arise from the investigation or not, the notoriety has hurt Continental substantially.

Frank Lorenzo, though he cashed out of Continental in the summer of 1990 with almost $40 million, has to be considered a loser in the Eastern debacle as well. His vision of creating a single low-cost airline empire was sidetracked by public relations battles and union skirmishes. In fact, it was Eastern's bankruptcy that led to the ultimate breakup of his control over the Texas Air empire. Although Lorenzo admitted afterward that he probably would have been better off not buying Eastern, but for a few public relations miscues he would have succeeded with his grand plan.

The unions ended up losing over forty thousand jobs at Eastern. The individuals who lost those jobs also lost a way of life, perhaps needlessly. Charlie Bryan, Eastern's IAM leader, more than anyone else involved in the Eastern case, lost credibility. His positions with Borman on wages in the early 1980s; his intransigence, which led to the sale to Texas Air in 1986; his determination to strike at any cost, which led to the bankruptcy filing in 1989, all, when taken as a whole, caused more trouble at Eastern than any other single action or event.

Frank Borman cannot escape blame either. His ill-fated growth strategy in the early 1980s, which put Eastern on its kamikaze course, had a lot to do with the eventual Texas Air takeover. However, Borman does deserve credit for keeping the airline intact during the early 1980s when it could easily have come apart on several occasions.

Judge Lifland lost a measure of both credibility and respectability. So much so that creditors of bankruptcy cases filed in Manhattan now cringe when they find out that their case has been assigned to Lifland. Lifland's reputation as a "pro-debtor" bankruptcy judge was, in the Eastern case, proven beyond a doubt.

Nonetheless, there were some winners. To a large extent Shugrue emerged from the debacle relatively unscathed. After all, he surprised everyone in the industry just by keeping Eastern afloat as long as he did. Also, his ability to convince Lifland to front a final $150 million for the airline's last eight weeks of operations will certainly go down in aviation history as one of the best sales jobs ever.

Unfortunately, the only people who really came out of this economically bettered are the professionals. Over $100 million has been paid out in professional fees to lawyers, accountants, consultants and investment bankers in the Eastern case. Even after Eastern stopped flying in January 1991, the professionals continued to feed, like vultures, off Eastern's rotting carcass. A former Eastern IAM official in Miami lamented, "It's a travesty when employees can't get their last paychecks from the week before the strike, but attorneys get millions." The professionals' feeding frenzy at Eastern should send a message to Congress that a more rational and fair claims-settlement process in bankruptcy must be found.

So, what killed Eastern? The partisan responses could fill volumes. Captain J. Randolph Babbitt, national president of ALPA, gives an example of such partisanship: "First, Frank Lorenzo killed Eastern. Eastern also died at the hands of cynical politicians. Judge Burton Lifland's handling of the Eastern bankruptcy allowed the company to waste millions of dollars in half-baked attempts to revive a company that it had already sucked dry through questionable transfers of vital assets."

In a more objective vein, what really killed Eastern were vanity and the personal animosity between and among many of the key players in the drama. Somehow, the welfare of the airline, its employees, the communities it served and the bankruptcy process were subsumed by a singular and vicious battle of ego and personal power. In an interview that Charlie Bryan gave which appeared on March 8, 1989 in the *Boston Globe,* just one day before the bankruptcy, he said, "Anybody who buys a ticket on Continental is contributing to something very evil. What we've had in Lorenzo is a corporate raider and a robber baron, typical of the robber barons of old, who's come along and stolen Eastern away from the employees after they've made those sacrifices."

With comments like this, in conjunction with a series of unfortunate events that could have been avoided, it's no surprise that Eastern eventually ended up in the trash heap of aviation history.

Notwithstanding the demise of airlines such as Eastern, Midway and Pan Am, airline deregulation has worked to the benefit of the American consumer by doing what it was designed to do: give consumers more flights, more convenient schedules and substantially lower fares. In fact, fares are now 20 percent below what the CAB would have set under its old formula. And that puts about $6 billion in travelers' pockets each year. Deregulation has forced the inefficient players out of the marketplace. Although it is painful to bid farewell to airlines like Eastern and Pan Am, in retrospect, they did not deserve to survive.

POSTSCRIPT

The Bar Harbor transaction, first described in chapter 5, provides an example of the kind of difficulty, caused by egotistical and self-serving individuals, that engulfed the entire Eastern affair. As a primary player in that transaction, I have added here a further description of the unfortunate events that occurred with Bar Harbor after the bankruptcy court approved Eastern's purchase of it.

From the date of the court hearing approving the Bar Harbor transaction on July 31, 1990, until the closing of the transaction with Continental, which was scheduled for August 15, our Bar Harbor implementation team worked twenty-four hours a day in order to be ready to take over the company's operations on the closing date. The team's flight operations experts, Richard T. Behrle and Jack J. ("Jeff") Miller, pulled off the impossible by getting the FAA to recertify Bar Harbor within two weeks under the new management structure. The

FAA later told us that they had never seen it done earlier than three months. Also, we were able miraculously to hire and train a sufficient number, over three hundred, of qualified people in an extremely short period of time. This was largely due to the efforts of Karen T. Averill, formerly with Eastern's human resources department, whom I appointed Bar Harbor's director of employee and customer service.

On the scheduled day for closing, Roland Moore, the Eastern in-house lawyer, and I flew to Houston where we met with Continental and Texas Air officials at Liddell Sapp's offices. After the signing of the documents, which went off without a hitch, Continental needed to wire-transfer to Eastern's account at Citibank the first $1 million of the total $3 million that was to be paid to Eastern. Shugrue, not wanting to take any chances with payment, instructed us to verify that the money had been received by Eastern's treasury department before we left the closing room. Unfortunately, by the time Continental got around to transferring the money, it was after 4:00 P.M. on the East Coast, which meant that we could not receive a Fed wire-transfer number to validate that the funds had in fact been received. I called Eastern's treasurer, Jim McGuinness and said, "Jim, I want you to have somebody in your office verify that the money was received, even if they have to stay there all night." The last thing I wanted was to wake up in Miami the next morning and find out that, for whatever reason, we hadn't received the money.

In the end, everything worked out just fine. The Bar Harbor deal was consummated. It was the only time in the history of American commercial aviation that an airline, while in bankruptcy, had acquired another airline, and had been paid to do so.

About the time that the Bar Harbor deal was closed, I became president and CEO of Bar Harbor Airways, Inc. d/b/a Eastern Express, a "substantially owned" subsidiary of Eastern. However, Shugrue also wanted me to continue to assist him with Eastern's reorganization efforts, and so I also assumed the title of vice president of corporate development at Eastern. "Two jobs, but only one paycheck," I lamented to my parents one day when I told them of my new duties.

Within just a matter of weeks, it became apparent that Bar Harbor would not be long for this world if we were forced to stick to the ridiculous parameters of the business plan devised by the creditors' advisers. American, which had earlier purchased Eastern's Latin American routes, was quickly establishing a large hub in Miami together with a commuter feeder network called American Eagle. Pan Am, though financially weary, was still the dominant carrier at Miami with an even larger hub than American, and it was also establishing a commuter airline called Pan Am Express. Bar Harbor, operating as Eastern Express, thus found itself at a tremendous disadvantage against American and Pan Am in Miami. While American and Pan Am's commuters had their respective jet hubs behind them to provide sufficient traffic, Bar Harbor didn't have such traffic support from Eastern because Eastern had by this time dismantled its Miami hub.

Thus, we had to pursue the only two options available to us. First, through aggressive marketing, we had to, in essence, create new traffic into and out of Miami, consisting of the intrastate business traveler who was driving because of a lack of convenient air service. Second, we had to diversify our revenue base by going into markets, such as Tampa, where there was little competition and better profit opportunity.

However, the creditors' business plan for Bar Harbor did not call for a Tampa expansion due to the perceived additional risk in expanding to markets where Bar Harbor was not presently flying. What the authors of that plan didn't realize was that Tampa provided the opportunity for substantially better performance, while a continued focus on Miami, given the competitive situation there, spelled certain death. Faced with such clear-cut choices, I was not about to kill the airline just to stay true to a business plan, frozen in time, which failed to take into account the rapidly changing nature of the airline business as well as that of the local competitive landscape.

After notifying Shugrue of our plan to diversify Bar Harbor's operations to Tampa, and receiving his approval on the strategy, I notified Adam Harris, the creditors' lawyer, and Bruce Holcomb, one of Shapiro's associates, that "prudent exercise of reasonable business judgment necessitates a change in the earlier-agreed-to business plan for Bar Harbor's operations." When told that we would be expanding Bar Harbor's operations to Tampa, Harris exploded. "You promised to follow our business plan, that was a condition of the committee's agreement not to oppose the transaction."

I reminded Harris that the trustee explicitly reserved the right to alter Bar Harbor's strategy if marketplace conditions so warranted. I then spent over forty-five minutes trying to explain to him that in the business world decisions have to be made, very often, in reaction to sudden and very fluid events, that, particularly in the airline industry, business plans devised even thirty days ago can be rendered completely irrelevant by such changes in the marketplace as the unpredictable invasion of Kuwait and the resulting spike in fuel prices.

All of this was to no avail. Harris was adamant that the business plan that he and the creditors' advisers had drawn up for Bar Harbor had to be followed to the letter. He then added, "If you go ahead with the Tampa diversification, I will recommend to the committee that Eastern not advance any more funds to Bar Harbor."

By this time, in mid-September, Bar Harbor was still in the process of ramping up its operations. Eastern was advancing funds to sustain the commuter's operations through the start-up period. If Eastern had cut off such funding, Bar Harbor would have been forced to cease all operations and would have been immediately liquidated. Thus, Harris's threat to cut off funding was a threat to force Bar Harbor into liquidation.

If Bar Harbor was forced to liquidate, who did Harris think would be harmed? Certainly it would have been disappointing, after having gone to all of that work to get the deal approved, to see the airline liquidated only one month after it was acquired. But the real losers in such a scenario would have been Harris's clients, the creditors. Bar Harbor's liquidation value was negative, meaning that the value of its liabilities far exceeded its assets. If Bar Harbor had been liquidated, according to an analysis done at the time, Eastern's creditors would have had to assume over $15 million in additional liabilities, not to mention losing whatever money Eastern had already advanced to Bar Harbor for operations. Even the additional $2 million that Eastern was to receive from Continental over the next four months would not have covered the shortfall. In essence, in the event of a Bar Harbor liquidation, Eastern's creditors would have taken at least a $15 million bath on the deal.

Harris's threat posed an even greater potential loss to the Eastern creditors. From the very beginning, Shugrue had planned that once Bar Harbor was up and running as an operating entity, it would immediately be sold to a third party so as to generate even more money for the Eastern estate. If Harris succeeded in cutting off funding to Bar Harbor, and therefore putting it into liquidation, obviously there would be nothing to sell. I had already received several inquiries from third parties interested in buying Bar Harbor, and the plan was, after Bar Harbor expanded its operations in early October, to put it on the block immediately. Harris's threats placed our asset-maximization strategy in jeopardy.

I suggested a meeting with Harris to explain our plans in more detail and why they were in the best interests of the Eastern estate. In late September, we met at the New York offices of Weil Gotshal. On Eastern's behalf were Roland Moore, who was now Bar Harbor's general counsel, Maurice Morissette, whom I had recently hired as Bar Harbor's chief financial officer, and myself. Also present on our behalf were Doug Little of Liddell Sapp and Deryck Palmer of Weil Gotshal. For the creditors, Adam Harris was there along with an associate of his from O'Melveny and Myers, Wendy Hill. On behalf of Shapiro, Bruce Holcomb and Harry Kimbriel, Shapiro's airline consultant, attended.

By this time, both Kimbriel and Holcomb had come around to being at least neutral on Bar Harbor. Harris, however, was definitely out for blood. After describing the reasons for Bar Harbor's expansion, we told Harris that we would try to sell the airline as soon as possible. However, Harris wanted a commitment that Bar Harbor would receive no further cash advances from Eastern without the prior consent of the committee. Such a demand was really a veiled request for complete management control over Bar Harbor. We had to blatantly refuse because, even if we had wanted to give Harris control over funding decisions, we were legally prevented from doing so. Only the trustee had the authority to make such decisions, and Shugrue had already agreed that Eastern would make whatever cash advances to Bar Harbor were necessary to support its operations until it could be sold.

We left the meeting with nothing really accomplished other than our promise to put the airline up immediately for sale. Issues as to funding were left unresolved.

By early October, the creditors had begun to get vocal regarding their unhappiness with Eastern's overall financial performance and business plan. Although their public outcry for the liquidation of the airline did not begin until early November, one could definitely hear the rumblings on the horizon back in October. It was in this very difficult environment that I began to shop Bar Harbor.

By the fall of 1990, fuel prices were at their highest level in ten years due to the invasion of Kuwait, the recession was in full swing, airline traffic had all but evaporated, Eastern was losing more than $2 million per day and the creditors were starting to call for Eastern's complete liquidation. This wasn't exactly the best environment in which to sell a commuter airline owned by Eastern. Nonetheless, after contacting just about everybody in the industry and financial community whom we thought had a strategic or financial interest in acquiring a Florida commuter airline, we were able to drum up several potential purchasers.

By mid-October, after conducting our seller's due diligence, it became clear to us that the parties who we had found were seriously interested in acquiring Bar Harbor most likely did not have the financial capability to consummate a transaction. I mounted one last-ditch effort to identify other buyers but with no success. The market for airlines was just in such terrible shape that there were no serious bidders at the time.

Seeing that a transaction with the existing bidders would, in all likelihood, fall apart, and realizing that Harris would attempt to maneuver to cut off all funding to Bar Harbor if a buyer wasn't found soon, I seriously began to consider mounting a bid for the airline myself.

To explore a bid, I contacted a friend of mine, Daniel E. Carpenter of Carpenter Financial Group in New York. Carpenter, who also runs Benefit Concepts New York, is the nation's leading expert on employee stock-ownership plans (ESOPs). He suggested that we could structure a transaction in which we would use an ESOP to fund the acquisition of Bar Harbor. Miraculously, given the environment we faced at the time, within a matter of just several days Carpenter and I had secured over $5 million in financing to acquire Bar Harbor.

With our financing firmly in place, I decided that I would submit a formal offer. A bidder's conference was scheduled for late October at the New York offices of Wertheim Schroeder, Eastern's financial advisers. The night before the conference, I had to decide what course of action I would pursue since my position, at that moment, was on the verge of becoming untenable.

As an officer of Bar Harbor, I owed a fiduciary duty to Bar Harbor and its shareholders. Bar Harbor's only shareholder (except for the three "hermits" in Maine who couldn't be found) was Eastern.

Thus, I owed a duty to Eastern to maximize the value it would receive from any bid to acquire Bar Harbor. However, I was also an officer of Eastern in my capacity as vice president of corporate development, which meant that I owed a duty to the creditors of the Eastern estate to maximize their value in any bid to acquire Bar Harbor. Therefore, if I submitted a bid to acquire Bar Harbor myself, I would be seriously conflicted in that as a bidder I would try to minimize the price I would have to pay yet I also had a fiduciary responsibility to maximize the amount received by Eastern. This obvious potential conflict of interest required that either I refrain from bidding on Bar Harbor or I resign from both Bar Harbor and Eastern.

The night before, I decided that I would reserve judgment on which course of action I would take until I saw who appeared at the bidder's conference at Wertheim Schroeder. If the only bidders were the several parties whom we had brought to the table in the first place, then I would mount a bid because I knew that they likely would be unable, in the end, to come up with the financing. I was not at all concerned with someone, like Harris, later alleging that I had purposefully brought weak bidders to the table so as to maximize my own chances because neither Wertheim Schroeder nor the creditors' advisers had found even one bidder interested in Bar Harbor. All of the potential bidders for Bar Harbor were there because of my efforts.

When I arrived at Wertheim Schroeder's offices, located at the Equitable Center on Seventh Avenue in midtown Manhattan, things occurred as expected. Only the weak bidders showed up. Since I knew that Carpenter and I were the only bidders firmly and fully financed on the deal, I immediately announced my intention to bid. For some reason, Harris suddenly became extremely upset. I couldn't understand why. After all, why should he care who was bidding so long as the accepted bid was the best available for the creditors? In fact, he should have been ecstatic that the only party interested in the deal who was firmly and fully financed even mounted a bid.

Nonetheless, Harris was so upset that he suddenly called off the bidder's conference altogether. The sale of Bar Harbor was off to a bad start. However, this was just the beginning of the bungling.

I felt invigorated that, all of a sudden, I was out on my own mounting a bid to acquire an airline. Luckily, both Carpenter and I had all of our financing and, in addition, we knew that the other bidders most likely did not. Further, nobody knew the operation or the financial structure of the company better than I did. The combination of these factors, in my view, gave us an unbeatable edge.

It took Wertheim Schroeder about two weeks to put together their own bid package for Bar Harbor and, in essence, to reopen the bidding. In fact, just about all of Wertheim's bid package consisted of the descriptive memorandum on Bar Harbor for potential purchasers that I had written myself in early October.

Upon my resignation from Bar Harbor and Eastern, Shugrue installed a former pilot friend of his from Pan Am, Terrence D. Hickman, as interim Bar Harbor CEO. Hickman had some familiarity with Bar Harbor because I had included him as part of the implementation team handling flight operations. Regrettably, almost from the moment that I left Bar Harbor, the airline began to disintegrate.

From late October until mid-December, Wertheim Schroeder, Adam Harris, Hickman and Jeffrey J. Weinberg, a Weil Gotshal attorney who had been brought in to handle the Bar Harbor sale, had negotiated with the other parties whom we had earlier brought into the Bar Harbor deal. After several weeks of negotiating with the other parties, and discovering their financial inability to consummate a transaction, Hickman and his advisers finally decided to negotiate with the only serious bidders who were interested, Carpenter and myself.

However, by that time they had delayed so long, and Bar Harbor was disintegrating so quickly, along with Eastern, that the amount of money Carpenter and I were willing to offer had been substantially reduced. If a deal had been done with us at the very beginning of the process, in late October, Eastern and its creditors would have received over $4 million in cash in addition to the assumption of over $15 million in liabilities. By late December, Bar Harbor had diminished in value so much that we offered only $2.1 million. And that was in the form of a note plus assumption of liabilities. Seeing that we were the only real bidders at that point, even Harris had to agree that our deal was better than liquidating Bar Harbor and having Eastern's creditors end up with absolutely nothing.

We executed a definitive purchase agreement with Eastern on December 22, 1990, and a court hearing to consider the matter was scheduled for January 22, 1991. By December, Eastern had barely escaped liquidation itself in a highly emotional and public battle with the creditors to keep the carrier alive at least through the first quarter of 1991. Carpenter and I felt that our best shot was to get Bar Harbor out of the Eastern mess as quickly as possible before the entire structure came crashing down upon the commuter, leaving it in ashes as well. Although January 22 was the scheduled hearing date, we tried, albeit unsuccessfully, to get an earlier hearing date because we were concerned that Eastern would go down the tubes before we had a chance to rescue Bar Harbor.

Unfortunately, our fears were realized. On January 19, Eastern ceased operations. Although Eastern, and Bar Harbor, stopped flying on January 19, Carpenter and I were still interested in going forward with the transaction scheduled for three days later on January 22. We felt that we still had a shot at resurrecting the airline, and saving over four hundred jobs. However, late on Sunday, January 20, for some reason Eastern put Bar Harbor into bankruptcy as well. The fact that Eastern put Bar Harbor into bankruptcy, late on a Sunday evening and just two days before a sale to us was scheduled to occur, was highly unusual. I later learned that Weinberg, the Weil Gotshal attorney, had argued for such a course of action, allegedly to "protect Bar Harbor's assets from repossession."

After Bar Harbor was placed in bankruptcy, and still was not flying, we continued to attempt to structure a deal to acquire the airline. In retrospect, we probably should have just let the airline die under the weight of Eastern's ongoing liquidation. However, we firmly believed that there was an opportunity for us in Florida that we could use to construct a viable entity.

After another couple of months of on-and-off negotiations, we agreed in early March 1991 to acquire Bar Harbor for $400,000 in cash plus assumption of $17 million in liabilities. Back in October we were offering over $4 million in cash, but the advisers handling the transaction had delayed and bungled the deal so badly that now their only offer was $400,000, and a rich offer it was at that.

In the end, even our deal for $400,000 was torpedoed in bankruptcy court because Judge Lifland decided that Eastern and its creditors would be better off liquidating Bar Harbor rather than selling it. And to add insult to injury, Lifland allowed the $32,000 that we placed in escrow with the bankruptcy court for the purchase to be retained by Eastern.

The most shameful part of the entire ordeal was that Carpenter and I were the only ones interested in saving the jobs of four hundred employees by trying to resurrect Bar Harbor from Eastern's ashes. In the end, even Lifland didn't really care about that. It seemed that all he could focus on was figuring out a way to defend the unjustifiable retention of our escrow deposit. We learned a $32,000 lesson: never place money into bankruptcy escrow!

The end of this tragic story is that Bar Harbor has been liquidated just like Eastern. Eastern's creditors ended up losing over $17 million on the deal, including roughly $6 million in cash that Eastern advanced to Bar Harbor that was never repaid. If Eastern had sold Bar Harbor to us back in October, when the commuter was still a viable entity, Eastern would have freed itself of $15 million in liabilities as well as received over $4 million in hard cash. Instead, the creditors ended up taking a bath on the whole deal. In addition, over four hundred jobs were lost.

I wonder if the creditors, had they been more attentive to what was transpiring throughout the entire Bar Harbor ordeal, would have taken matters into their own hands and overruled their advisers? In retrospect, I seriously doubt it. Just about every member of the creditors' committee relied completely, almost blindly, on the advice of their advisers. Sometimes it seemed as if the creditors had no minds of their own. One member of the committee later told me, "It was like something out of 'The Twilight Zone.' Except for myself and a couple of others, nobody on the committee even raised their voice when told that the only deal to sell Bar Harbor had fallen through and we would end up eating all of those liabilities."

Index

INDEX

INDEX

INDEX

INDEX

INDEX

INDEX

INDEX

About the Author

Jack E. Robinson is presently an airline industry consultant and bankruptcy attorney in New York, where he makes his home. He is also president of Florida Air. While at Eastern Air Lines he was vice president of corporate development as well as president of Eastern Express. He has also worked at Texas Air Corporation, Continental Airlines and MasterCard International in a variety of marketing, finance and strategic planning positions. Robinson received his B.S. degree in applied mathematics and economics from Brown University and his J.D. and M.B.A. degrees from Harvard University.